20th Century Aesthetics

Philosophy, Aesthetics and Cultural Theory

Series Editor: Hugh J. Silverman, Stony Brook University, USA

The *Philosophy, Aesthetics and Cultural Theory* series examines the encounter between contemporary Continental Philosophy and aesthetic and cultural theory. Each book in the series explores an exciting new direction in philosophical aesthetics or cultural theory, identifying the most important and pressing issues in Continental Philosophy today.

Derrida, Literature and War, Sean Gaston

Derrida, Myth and the Impossibility of Philosophy, Anais N. Spitzer

Foucault's Philosophy of Art, Joseph J. Tanke

The Literary Agamben, William Watkin

Merleau-Ponty and the Paradoxes of Expression, Donald A. Landes

Philosophy and the Book, Daniel Selcer

The Re-Enchantment of the World, Bernard Stiegler, translated by Trevor Arthur

20th Century Aesthetics

Towards a Theory of Feeling

Mario Perniola

Translated by Massimo Verdicchio

B L O O M S B U R Y
LONDON • NEW DELHI • NEW YORK • SYDNEY

Bloomsbury Academic
An imprint of Bloomsbury Publishing Plc

50 Bedford Square
London
WC1B 3DP
UK

175 Fifth Avenue
New York
NY 10010
USA

www.bloomsbury.com

Originally published in Italian as *L'estetica contemporanea. Un panorama globale*

British Library Cataloguing-in-Publication Data
A catalogue record for this book is available from the British Library.

ISBN: HB: 978-1-4411-9881-5
PB: 978-1-4411-1850-9

Library of Congress Cataloging-in-Publication Data
A catalog record for this book is available from the Library of Congress.

Typeset by Newgen Imaging Systems Pvt Ltd, Chennai, India
Printed and bound in Great Britain

Contents

Introduction

It is not customary to consider the contemporary age as the century of aesthetics *par excellence*, and yet no other historical period in the West has seen such an abundance of important works in aesthetics. Perhaps this is true of any philosophical discipline. Since the beginnings of the twentieth century, all the branches of philosophy have been organized around journals, associations, international conferences and specialized libraries. Are we running the risk of trading all this activity for a truly speculative wealth? As contemporaries, is our impartiality veiled and are we led to make unwarranted overestimations? Nevertheless, in the first half of the twentieth century, aesthetics has claimed to be more than just the philosophical theory of the beautiful and good taste. On the one hand, it has established a relation of complicity with literature, the figurative arts and music without letting itself be scared by the most daring innovations and the riskiest experimentations; on the other hand, it has been involved in the management of institutions, exhibitions, the organization and the communication of artistic and cultural products. It has confronted the great problems of the single and collective life, it has questioned itself on the sense of existence, it has promoted daring social utopias, it has been involved in the issues of everyday life and has singled out subtle cognitive distinctions. Furthermore, it has examined religious and theological issues of historical importance. It has investigated its own affinities and divergences with ethics and economics. It has established relations with all other philosophical disciplines, the human sciences and even the natural, physical and mathematical ones. Furthermore, it has gone beyond the frontiers of the West, creating original thinkers who, following its methods, have invented new theories and new concepts that have modernized the way of thinking of their traditions without breaking completely from them. In so doing, they have escaped both Euro-American colonialism and their burdensome historical inheritance. Finally, globalization has made aesthetics more similar to a philosophy of cultures than to a reflection on the essence of the beautiful and art.

This vast and many-sided activity has established its roots in four conceptual fields identifiable in the notions of (1) life, (2) form, (3) knowledge and (4) action. A chapter of this volume is devoted to each of them. Aesthetics as a whole (namely, when defined as such) can be categorized within these four problematic areas: the first two constitute essentially a development of Kant's *Critique of Judgment* (1790), the last two a development of Hegel's *Aesthetics* (1835–8). The fact that this vast edifice of aesthetics can be reduced, in its fundamental premises, to only two works reveals both the simplicity and the coherence of this discipline.

To these structural considerations we must add a further historical observation. All these problematic areas came to fruition in the first half of the past century. Around the 1960s, a turning point takes place within each of these notions. New contexts and conditions of previously elaborated conceptual apparatuses arise: (1) the aesthetic of life acquires a political significance; (2) the aesthetics of form a media one; (3) the aesthetic of knowledge a sceptical one; and (4) pragmatic aesthetics a communicative one. Whoever wants to place himself today within one of these areas in order to make an original contribution must come to terms respectively with politics, media, scepticism and communication. Is the opposite equally true? To be sure: aesthetics is also secretly present and active in bio-politics, mass media, epistemology and the theory of communication.

Two areas remain outside of this schema: (5) feeling and (6) culture. Aesthetics takes its name from the former, namely, from the sphere of sensitivity, affectivity and emotionality. Those who have made important contributions to this sector were not practitioners of aesthetics but psychologists, psychoanalysts, theorists of language and literature, philosophers of religion or sexuality, thinkers and writers! Why? What emerges as new in this field is irreducible to a feeling sooner or later reconciled and pacified with the aesthetic. In other words, the feeling of the contemporary age cannot be brought back to Kant or Hegel, but is deeply influenced by Nietzsche. After the 1960s, this field also underwent a shift that called itself deconstructive. Chapter 5 deals with this problematic.

Chapter 6 deals, by contrast, with the relationship between aesthetics and culture that has its distant origins in the work of the German writer Friedrich Schiller and, above all, in the work of Swiss historian Carl Jacob Burckhardt who grasped, well in advance, the warning signs of the decline of Western aesthetic culture. Hence, the focus of this chapter is on those non-European thinkers who tried to counter Western colonization opposing it with a modernization of aesthetic experiences and customs of their own countries. In other words, they tried to invent, by opening conceptual perspectives often very refined, other forms of modernity independent of Western ones. The West still does not have a clear idea of these changes because it has continued to believe that it has a monopoly on modernity. However, even worse is the self-destructive turn in one's own culture that has become apparent in the absolute and exclusive supremacy assigned to economic interests, constituting precisely the opposite of any aesthetic experience.

Finally, I must add a note on the composition and methodology of this work. Each chapter is divided into ten paragraphs: the first one introduces the main problematic, while the others deal with its development, the last one with the 'turning point' that occurred in the last years of the past century. I have always found misleading the methodological criterion that groups writers on aesthetics in philosophical schools, and even more inadequate and extrinsic the criterion that judges texts on the basis of their popularity. As far as my choices are concerned, considerations of space have obliged me to consider a limited number of authors: naturally, many important thinkers had to be left out. Some of them, for the breadth of their thought, should have been mentioned in more than one chapter. Also in this case I had to take drastic decisions. I assume full responsibility for all of it.

An even more delicate and complex question is the intersection of the theoretical dimension with the historical one, and the distinction between major and minor authors. On these two questions I have tried to maintain a balanced position. Within the theoretical framework outlined in the six chapters I have preferred to give a voice to a multiplicity of perspectives, rather than privilege one theory in absolute. In a work with an historical approach, one-sidedness and sectarianism of information constitute the greatest flaw. Furthermore, a theoretical focus with a wide array of solutions has led me to attribute a relative value to the distinction between 'major' and 'minor' authors and works of philosophy. The case of Walter Benjamin demonstrates how some authors who were deemed marginal can gradually acquire major importance 20 years after their death. The same notion of 'minor' seems to be at times an expression of dogmatism and conformism, especially when it is applied to the contemporary age in which everything is still at stake and there are no relatively stable canons. On the one hand, nothing is more deceitful, fragile and tendentious than the influence of the media, on the other hand, some aspects of present-day cultural life (the overabundance of publications, the plurality of languages and contexts, general inattention) contribute to the disregard, even by specialists, of many works and authors worthy of being read and discussed.

Mario Perniola, 2011

1

Aesthetics of Life

The 'meaning of life' and aesthetics

The idea that aesthetic experience entails a facilitation and intensification of life, an increase and a development of vital energies, is so widespread in contemporary culture that one finds it difficult to attribute to it a specific philosophical meaning. The very notion of *life* seems to be too vague and generic at first sight to have a distinctive conceptual importance. Furthermore, the expression 'philosophy of life' has been employed too often polemically to criticize those philosophical orientations that claim to reduce or subordinate philosophical activity to experience, to the empirical dimension of existence, to the mere psychic fact, thus negating the originality and the autonomy of philosophical performance. Finally, it is hard to understand why aesthetic experience ought to be essentially related to life. After all, if what matters is the inexhaustible richness and fertility of life, it seems inevitable that aesthetic experience be something secondary and incidental, if not even parasitical, with respect to the very powerful explosion and spontaneous assertion of vital forces. In short, both the critics of 'vitalism' and the apologists of life do not grasp the reasons for the relation that unites life with aesthetics.

And yet this connection exists! If the word 'life' points to something that goes beyond the mere fact of biology is because it implies the assertion of a purpose that makes it possible to think of particular events in relation to something more general and universal. In other words, the philosophical discourse of twentieth-century thought about 'life' coincides for the most part with questions concerning the 'meaning of life'. When I ask if the story of an historical subject (whether a single human being, a people or humanity as a whole) has meaning, it is precisely because I reflect on the possibility of relating its occurrence to a finality whose results are significant. This essentially teleological question confers on the notion of 'life' a lively and provocative character. In fact, to reopen the teleological question in the twentieth century means opposing the mechanistic and physicalistic orientation of modern science which, beginning with Descartes and Galileo, excluded finalism from the knowledge of nature. According to this view, the question of the meaning of life is nonsensical because it claims to bring to total unity or to final principles a series of events that are entirely explainable by the laws of physics and chemistry.

But what does the question of the purpose of life have to do with the aesthetic experience? Does the teleological question not belong rather to metaphysics or ethics? Why should it be regarded as an aesthetic question? To say that the aesthetic question consists in reflecting on the meaning of individual and collective life seems provocative. And yet the aesthetic reflection on life is connected with this challenge. That is why it tends to identify not only with teleology but also with the philosophy of history and with metaphysics. Whether we assert that life has meaning or we deny that it has one, the horizon within which this question is formulated in the twentieth century is strictly connected with aesthetics, which has dared to formulate the fundamental problem of existence.

The theoretical premise of this appropriation can be found in Immanuel Kant's (1724–1804) *Critique of Judgement* (1790), where he brings both aesthetics and teleology under the single faculty of 'judgement'. This faculty which consists in thinking the particular as the content of the universal makes it possible to have a coherent idea of the whole in its totality, as that provided precisely by a beautiful object or by a natural organism. In both cases, according to Kant, a human being rejoices and is pleased because he considers, from a cognitive and moral point of view, empirical entities in terms of unity and purpose that could never be brought back to a single principle. Thus Kant denies that finality can actually constitute the explanation of an event in the world. The unifying principle to which judgement brings back a plurality of phenomena cannot derive from experience, which is entirely subject to a mechanistic explanation (and not a finalistic one). Judgement does not proceed according to concepts but by means of the sentiment of pleasure, which derives precisely from discovering that disparate elements can be brought back to a unity. It is impossible to provide a cognitive answer to the question whether life has meaning or not. The 'meaning of life' cannot be the object of a scientific demonstration! It cannot even be a purpose to be realized, or a categorical imperative that can be imposed on the will. Kant excludes finality as a moral question because it is connected to pleasure and displeasure, and not to the faculty of desire. Even though, in the last instance, he places moral man as the 'definitive purpose' of creation, this statement has no moral validity in any strict sense. I am supposed to obey the command of reason independently of the fact that my life, nature or world have 'meaning'.

Lived experience

Foremost among those who have asserted the relation between aesthetic experience and the meaning of life is Wilhelm Dilthey (1833–1911). For Dilthey, the thinking of the purpose of humanity takes shape as a theory of historical knowledge, in opposition to the knowledge of the natural sciences both in method and object. In the essay 'The Three Epochs of Modern Aesthetics and its Present Task',[1] Dilthey claims that eighteenth- and nineteenth-century aesthetics has exhausted its historical task. Simply explaining and understanding the new philosophico-cultural situation, as well as the historico-social frame (as constituted after 1848) is completely inadequate.

Writing in 1892, Dilthey claims to be at the centre of a movement that began 50 years earlier and that marked the end not only of Classicism and Romanticism, but even the conception of life and art that began in the fifteenth century. He identifies this movement with the poetics of Naturalism and demonstrates its destructive aspects when seizing reality in an immediate way without even stopping before the physiological and the bestial, and thus reducing reality to a mere fact devoid of meaning. Among the exponents of this movement, Dilthey mentions Wagner in music, Zola in literature, Semper in architecture and Otto Ludwig in theatre.

With respect to Naturalism, which aims at a global aesthetization of life in terms of a total work of art, the three aesthetic methods (rational, experimental and historical) are revealed to be painfully inadequate. The living artistic aspirations, which tumultuously are asserted in the culture of his times, do not let themselves be dominated by the notion of an harmonious order of the universe, or can they be reduced to a totality of sensations, or, finally, can they find an adequate comprehension in an aesthetics like Hegel's which is too exclusively interested in the spiritual aspects of the work of art. The aesthetic dimension of Naturalism cannot be found in abridged versions or in voluminous textbooks. The crisis opened by Naturalism has also exploded that living, vital circulation of aesthetic opinions among philosophers, art critics, artists and the public that characterized both the neo-Classical era and the Romantic one.

In the years after 1848, Dilthey seized upon the beginning of a process of dissolution of Western philosophical and artistic legacy that, in his view, is far from being concluded. What preoccupies him, in particular, is the yielding to mere empirical duality inherent in the poetics of the reproduction of reality. Art is never a copy of reality, but a guide, a direction towards a deeper comprehension of reality. He suggests, therefore, a renewal of the science of aesthetics which must be able to answer to the challenge of Naturalism and guarantee the continuity between the great Renaissance tradition and the new artistic manifestations. After all, he writes, naturalists are motivated by the same need that moved the great artists of the Renaissance, namely, to see reality with different eyes, to compel men to make their experience of life, their vitality, more intense.

But perhaps this need can no longer be satisfied neither by art nor by aesthetics as traditionally understood. Kant distinguished aesthetic judgement (immediately perceiving the finality of an object by means of the subjective feeling of pleasure or displeasure) from teleological judgement (thinking nature as an objective system of ends). For Dilthey, the search for 'meaning' was either oriented towards the perception of natural and artistic beauty or towards the understanding of nature as an organic whole. Even though he considered the hypothesis that even human culture in its guise as civil and cosmopolitan society could constitute an ultimate end,[2] he excluded history from his consideration of finalism. Only with Hegel is the ultimate end of humanity located in the historical process, for which the ideal is not to be realized in the future but rather is something already realized, objectified and completed in the three forms of Absolute Spirit (art, religion and philosophy). The task of philosophy in the fullness of its development and articulations (one of which is in fact the aesthetic) is to capture the 'meaning' of life, but, like the owl of Minerva that flies only at dusk, everything will have already occurred. Hegel attributes to philosophy as a whole a function that Kant had limited to aesthetic and teleological judgement, namely, to identify the ultimate purpose of humanity. Hence the characteristic of 'great novel' that confers an 'aesthetic' colouring to the entire Hegelian philosophy: reason makes use of the passions and the interests of individuals to realize its ends. To the highest form of social organization, namely the State, Hegel attributes the same characteristics that Kant attributed to Nature, namely, that of 'an organic whole' in which every single moment is at the same time a means and an end.[3]

Dilthey also locates the sense of human existence in history but, unlike Hegel, he believes that it cannot be founded metaphysically in universal reason, but rather discovered critically in the historico-social reality. The protagonist of this operation is the writer of history who, on the basis of his lived experience, connects the testimony of the past in an organic narrative from which the meaning of life emerges. The faculty of connecting disparate elements together and bringing the particular back to the universal, which is the function of judgement, is exercised not on nature but on the remnants of what has been. The real protagonist of aesthetic experience, therefore, is the historian who, through the characterization of dynamic connections, grasps a continuity from which the meaning of the past emerges. The historian, therefore, more than anyone else, is in direct relation with lived experience. In his essays on Lessing, Goethe, Novalis and Hölderlin (now collected in *Poetry and Experience*[4]), Dilthey demonstrates this activity with the greatest subtlety. In his analysis of poetic imagination, which transforms empirical facts into meaningful events and makes possible the access to a wider, richer and more profound dimension of life, Dilthey is able to reflect upon his own historiographical research. After all, the poet and the historian, the artist and the philosopher proceed in the same manner. Through the elaboration of dynamic connections, they discover the meaning of life. Hence, Dilthey's tendency to identify aesthetic experience with the work of the narrator.

By contrast with Naturalism, Dilthey believes that the meaning of life cannot be grasped immediately. For Dilthey, what has primacy is not natural and empirical life but rather *Erlebnis*, lived experience or, better, *relived experience*.[5] The highest form of understanding is reliving. Only by reliving can we prevent the present from disappearing by transforming it in an always available presence. Therefore, the task of the poet and the historian is extremely important. They alone can snatch the human world from caducity, oblivion and death by conferring on it a sense, forever. By identifying aesthetic experience with a participating narrative that reconstructs the past on the basis of structural connections unknown to those who have lived them, Dilthey transforms the search for the purpose of life in an infinite labour of emotional re-elaboration and rethinking of what has been. The emphatic treatment that the notion of life finds in his theoretical work is functional with respect to an intellectual strategy that views the impermanence and fleetingness of natural existence as the enemy to be overcome. Aesthetic experience acquires, therefore, the aspect of a continuous and endless struggle against death. Poets and historians revive their ancestors. In fact, they make them live again since their natural life was only a continuous disappearance!

Living is evaluating

Unlike Dilthey, who accounts for life in its temporal dimension, George Santayana believes that aesthetic experience is essentially objectification. For Santayana, what is relevant is not the opposition between life and death, but between life and objects, between the animate and inanimate, the organic and inorganic.

Santayana's aesthetics also has its roots in Kant, but, his thought is not mediated by idealism but rather through Herbart's realism, proud opponent and sharp critic of Hegel. Herbart separated distinctly the discourse on being, proper of theoretical sciences, from judgements of value, in which he also included moral evaluations. Aesthetic experience, therefore, consisted for him in the exercise of evaluation, in approving or disapproving, in appreciating or depreciating something. Kant's faculty of judgement was understood in the literal sense of critical activity. Santayana's first work *The Sense of Beauty*[6] considers aesthetics a theory of evaluation, without even referring specifically to Herbart. Aesthetic experience, however, is something more than just an intellectual judgement. It is an appreciative perception and implies a sensible gratification that goes beyond a simple thinking exercise. It is a vital act that pours forth from our deepest and most hidden dimensions of our existence. For Santayana what is important is the emotional participation of those who assert value. This cannot be considered to be something objective and independent of individual appreciation. However, in contrast to Herbart, Santayana distinguishes aesthetics from ethics. Aesthetic judgements are positive: they consist in asserting value. Aesthetic experience is saying 'yes' to life with energy and enthusiasm, with purity and immediacy. Moral judgements, instead, are negative: they stem from the perception of an evil and aim at preventing it. While aesthetics is linked to a vital pleasure, ethics is oriented towards the prevention of suffering. The first entails praise, celebration, an exaltation of existence, the latter censure, blame, a detraction of some aspect of life. Moralists forget that morality is a means to avoid pain, and not an end in itself, the latter can only be grasped by aesthetics. Santayana goes so far as to assert that all values are to a certain extent aesthetic because the aesthetic is the positive appreciation as such. In actual fact, the ugly understood as a negative aesthetic value does not exist. When it produces an actual displeasure it falls within the area of the ethical, which, in fact, is not concerned with pleasure or joy, but with preventing evil. After all everything is beautiful because everything is in some measure capable of raising attention and interest. But this does not mean that everything is equally beautiful. Things differ greatly in their capacity to please us and, therefore, in their aesthetic value. Santayana refuses to define his theory of aesthetic experience as 'hedonistic'. Hedonism, precisely because it posits pleasure as a purpose to be realized, precludes access to that affirmative immediacy that characterizes aesthetic evaluation.

If experience coincides with an admired, moving and satisfied appreciation of reality, what does its specificity consist of? In other words, is the contemplation of a view the same as eating a pizza? Is admiring a painting the same as indulging in the pleasures of the flesh? In what does aesthetic pleasure differ from other types of pleasure? Kant had defined the peculiarity of aesthetic pleasure in its disinterestedness (i.e. devoid of interest with respect to the real existence of the object), and in its universality (i.e. capable of soliciting everyone's consent). Santayana denies these two properties. As far as the first is concerned, any pleasure is interested, that is, sought after for itself. Aesthetics, for Santayana, coincides with the empirical dimension of living. Finalism, the search for 'meaning' permeates every vital activity. Whoever has aesthetic experiences has interests enormously greater than he who is concerned only with his house, but for both of them the care of oneself coincides with the care of the things they love. As far as universality is concerned, Santayana believes that appealing to the agreement of others betrays an insecurity with respect to sensation and evaluation. What is important is not how many people like a work of art, but how much it is liked by those who appreciate it more![7] The specificity of aesthetic experience, according to Santayana, must be sought in the phenomenon of objectification, in the fact that, differently from physical pleasures, which are connected with the organs that feel them and remain their prisoner, aesthetic pleasures direct our attention immediately towards an external object. While physical perception remains closed within a subjective feeling, in aesthetic experience the senses become transparent and make possible the direct access to something that presents itself as external and objective. In fact, beauty consists precisely in not having an autonomous and independent existence, apart from being the object of a personal evaluation. Therefore, beauty as a pleasure, considered as the quality of a thing, is an ultimate end that opens us to the external world and frees us from ourselves. In this way, Santayana finds an original solution to a problem that has been much debated in his time, that of *Einfühlung*, empathy.

With this term we understand the transposition of our sentient self in the form of an artistic object. The theorists of *Einfühlung*, among whom the most important is Theodor Lipps (1851–1914), claimed that aesthetic experience consists in projecting the life of the self on a person or on an external object. For Lipps, aesthetic pleasure derives from the fact that I take delight in myself in a sensible object distinct from me, that is, I find myself in the outside world, I experience myself, I feel myself in it. The key notion of empathy is life, but it is separated from the finalistic problematic, the questioning of 'meaning' and the value of experience. The claim to scientificity that the theorists of empathy lay claim to for their theories undermines the distinction between the sciences of nature and human sciences, between intellectual consideration and aesthetic evaluation, denying the specificity and the difference of aesthetic judgement. In the empathic process there is no challenge, no hazard, no risk and not even knowledge of the outside, because one does not leave the self which, through its own psychic activity, gives life to the external world. There is something narrow and lifeless in these theories that in their time raised so much discussion. We find their echo also in Santayana when he questions the strangeness of the phenomenon of aesthetic objectification and compares it to animism, namely, to the belief that natural things are endowed with life. However, Santayana emphasizes the exceptional character of the phenomenon of objectification with respect to the scientific way of relating to the world.

The amalgamation of feeling in the thing is different from empathy. It is not a question of extending the subjective feeling to things, but, on the contrary, of confronting the singularity of an experience that removes us from our subjectivity and persuades us to admire the beauty of things, as if it were an intrinsic characteristic of theirs and not the result of our evaluation. In short, in aesthetic appreciation there is an impulse which is completely lacking in the empathic emotional perception, a force that leads towards something that we do not believe we have in ourselves and that therefore generates wonder and admiration. That is why aesthetic experience is similar to love, but not to sexual pleasure. While the latter encloses us in an intimate and private feeling, love crystallizes the evaluations around an external object that seems perfect and worthy of our greatest consideration. But it is distinct from love in that it turns its attention not to an individual alone, but to the world as a whole.

For Santayana the enemy to combat is scepticism that plunges us in an emotional indifference worse than fanaticism. While the latter is an illicit and harmful extension of a positive, and essentially aesthetic evaluation to a moral and religious sphere, scepticism seems to compromise in the most radical way the vital character of experience. In *Reason in Art*,[8] which is part of the work *The Life of Reason,* Santayana defines art as the most splendid and complete incarnation of reason, within the general framework of a reflection whereby thinking constitutes the vital act *par excellence.*

Living is duration

Starting from an analysis of aesthetic feeling, Henri Bergson (1859–1941) arrives at a metaphysics of life, exciting and full of glamour, which has exercised an enormous influence on the literary and philosophical culture of the first half of the twentieth century. From his perspective, aesthetic experience tends to be resolved in a 'total experience', quite stimulating, which can be considered as a very original development of Kant's aesthetic judgement.

In his first work, *Time and Free Will: An Essay on the Immediate Data of Consciousness*,[9] Bergson distinguishes two orders of reality: an homogenous one characterized by the supremacy of spatial dimension, quantity and multiplicity; the other, heterogeneous, characterized by an experience of time as duration, by the perception of qualities and by numerical indetermination. The first is connected with extension and exteriority, the second with intensity and interiority. We move in the first order when we are involved in everyday needs and interests, or in perspectives and predictions of techno-scientific inquiry. The second order, instead, is that of deep feelings which are sufficient unto themselves and involve the deep layers of consciousness. Among these Bergson places aesthetic feeling which entails the promise of a manifold and always different future, together with the tendency to be transmitted to others according to a movement of spontaneous sympathy. However, aesthetic feeling is not a particular feeling among others but an aspect that permeates every deep experience. It constitutes for Bergson a kind of paradigm, which he constantly refers to when he needs to provide an example of what he considers to be opposite and an alternative to the physico-mathematical mechanism.

In order to explain his own notion of 'free act' Bergson refers to the relation that exists between the artist and his work. We certainly do not find freedom in the causal determinism of the physical world and its laws, but we should not place it either, as Kant does, within the sphere of morality, the thing in itself, the noumenon of which we know nothing and of which we don't even have any awareness. Although the 'free act' is determined without any reason, and sometime against any reason, it answers to the totality of our feelings, our thoughts and our deepest aspirations. Bergson also criticizes the thesis of the supporters of 'free will' who understand freedom as auto-causality because they also represent the act of decision according to a spatial configuration, as oscillating between two points in space. In actuality, free action emanates from our entire personality and it is immersed in that continuous becoming that characterizes the way of being of living organisms. To relative 'scientific' knowledge, founded on symbols and oriented towards the study of inorganic matter, Bergson opposes an absolute, active metaphysical knowledge inseparable from the vital process. The latter resembles literary composition: in one as in the other it is necessary a propaedeutic work that for the writer consists in notes and documents, for the philosopher in observations and reflections. Both in literature and in philosophy, however, it is essential an impulse that propels us in a creative dynamism in which we identify with the life of the whole world.[10]

This process is investigated and described in *Creative Evolution*,[11] where Bergson takes up and develops the central notion of his philosophy, *duration*. What does it mean to think living as duration? First of all we have to free ourselves of the false idea that the experience of time is a succession of

autonomous instants almost as if the present were separated from the past and were in need to recreate it somehow through an a posteriori revision. To live is not to relive the past (as for Dilthey). Between past and present there is no caesura. In the experience of time as *duration*, nothing is lost of the past. The present is only the extension of the past which like a wave moves on unceasingly towards the future. Everything changes constantly but this change must not be thought of as the passage from one state to the other, but as a continuous transition, a flowing without end, precisely, as *duration*. As a continuity that always moves forward, *duration* excludes repetition. At every moment, something new is added, in fact, something original and unforeseen. Life is therefore a kind of continuous creation that ceaselessly remodels the forms of experience. Despite the etymological proximity, Bergson's *durée* has nothing to do with the adjective 'hard' (*dur*). On the contrary, it refers to the idea of permanence which is passed on thanks entirely to its flexibility and its infinite ability to always generate and incorporate the new. Therefore, it is not the most appropriate crafted model to exemplify duration. In fact, the works produced through artistic doing no longer have any importance. The creative feeling of which Bergson speaks does not need works of art. The essential is experience which is affirmed autonomously by any external work, any artistic doing. It creates itself. It is 'autopoetic', to employ a word which has been used recently to indicate the vital phenomenon. Therefore, in Bergson is implicit a theory of aesthetic experience and not a theory of artistic doing!

But has this 'duration' a 'meaning'? Or better what is the 'meaning' of life? What differentiates it essentially from the world of inanimate bodies? The teleological question emerges as the central problem of Bergson's reflection. He rejects both the mechanism of modern science, which is sympathetic with a conception of the world that excludes the possibility of the new, and radical finalism, according to which the world is the realization of a programme drawn once and for all. The first considers every act under the aspect of necessity and repetition and therefore precludes a priori the possibility of understanding life, which is precisely the emergence of the new. The second only apparently recognizes the freedom and difference of the living because in actual fact it obliges it on a plan already given once. Both mechanism and teleology are, after all, theories of the inorganic, which eschew the very essence of life. Bergson also criticizes the finalism limited to the individual who attributes to each being an internal finality separate and independent of the surrounding world. Finality, he claims, it is either global or it does not exist at all. In fact, any individuality is made up in turn of infinite elements each one claiming its own autonomous vital principle.

The experience of living as *duration* takes us in a completely different direction. It grasps reality as a ceaseless flow of unforeseeable novelties. It is useless to assign a purpose to life. Life exceeds any pre-existing model and goes beyond any prediction. The rational interpretation of events is always something that occurs a posteriori. It has a merely retroactive value. Bergson's theoretical strategy is greatly more ambitious than Dilthey's. The 'meaning' of life does not emerge from reliving with intelligence and sensibility particular moments of the life of individuals and the collectivity, but from evolution understood in its totality. It is permeated by a vital impulse, an explosive force that creates many lines of development. Some of them prosper and grow, others, instead, are interrupted, deviated, come back. We should not imagine evolution as a harmonious development: chaos, the unforeseen, chance, play a very important role. Despite everything, life has 'meaning'. What does it consist of?

The answer to this question was already in Kant, in the first part of the *Critique of Judgment,* where in order to define beauty he introduces the notion of 'a purposiveness without any representation of a purpose'.[12] If I connect any entity with an objective purpose I will find utility or perfection but not beauty which cannot be enclosed in a concept and implies freedom with respect to a determined purpose. Beauty is also equally independent of a subjective purpose which is always tied and conditioned by attractions and personal emotions. Now the way Bergson elaborates the notion of life can be considered, precisely, as an extension of the entire evolutionary process of this 'purposiveness without any representation of a purpose' which Kant limits to a feeling experienced with respect to a beautiful object, whether natural or artistic.[13] For Bergson, finalism is the essential aspect of life. It is what differentiates it from the mechanical, static and spatial world which is entirely subordinated to the laws of causality. But this finality cannot be formulated in terms of a planning intention or a pre-established plan because it is essentially action and freedom, but not chance or whim. The vital impulse, in short, is an exigency of creation. The idea of genius, limited by Kant to the creative activity of the artist, is extended by Bergson to the entire nature which contains an infinity of virtual dimensions that exceeds any number and measure. In short, the human being ceases to be the centre of the 'meaning' of life as in Dilthey's lived experience and in Santayana's enthusiastic evaluating. Life is similar to an immense wave that starting from a single centre develops in an infinity of directions that have different and divergent events and destinies. Although man is the highest point of the evolution of life and the greatest manifestation of freedom, nonetheless it would be wrong to think that the whole world was produced in function of man.

Does, then, aesthetic experience lose every specificity for Bergson? In his *Creative Evolution,* he links it to a special tendency different from intelligence and instinct, *intuition.* While intelligence is directed towards inert matter and, for this reason, is the organ of science, and instinct is turned towards life in its subconscious dimension, intuition is something between the two, that is, an instinct which has become disinterested, conscious of itself and capable of reflecting on its object. Aesthetic experience, therefore, is something different from everyday perception connected to utility and need, but shares with it the attention towards the individuality of things. When intuition rises above the individual and takes life in general for its object, it becomes philosophy, that is, metaphysics. By establishing a sympathetic communication between us and humanity, metaphysical intuition introduces itself in the dominion of life and continues its run. The 'meaning' of life, therefore, is not something that can be grasped from outside, making it the object of a detached reflection. By means of the aesthetic and metaphysical experience we place ourselves in the heart of things and their becoming. They are life itself experienced and lived directly.[14]

Laughter and naked life

Not everyone can be a philosopher and lose himself in the metaphysical experience of duration, but everyone can laugh. Bergson is also the author of a small book, *Laughter: An Essay on the Meaning of the Comic*,[15] where he outlines the characteristics of a minor aesthetic experience connected with the comic, and which are essentially three: vitality, insensibility and sociability. Laughter seems to Bergson to be strictly connected with life, that is, with human life, because neither an inanimate object nor an animal can make you laugh, unless it is compared to a human being. Kant had already observed that laughter fosters a feeling of health by rebalancing the vital forces and defined it as 'an affection arising from the sudden transformation of a strained expectation into nothing'.[16] For Bergson, the relationship between laughter and life is much more substantial. The comic is a return of life on itself. In fact, sometimes life forgets itself, slips into habit, repetition, routine, thus losing its mobility and plasticity. Laughter is the corrective and the remedy to this oblivion. What makes us laugh is the discovery of rigidity and automatic functioning where we would expect flexibility and finalistic tension. The example of the puppet is the most simple and obvious but Bergson groups under this same device the totality of comic situations and events. The phenomenon of reification, that is, the reduction of the person to a thing constitutes the essence of the comic. In short, for Bergson what is opposite to the *élan vital,* namely, exteriority, repetition, reification, are comical, they make us laugh! Seriousness of life is strictly connected with freedom and action. When these are lacking, human existence becomes ridiculous. As for

Kant, then, for Bergson the comic derives from a lack of tension: the tone of life, its varied, progressive and undivided continuity, should never fail. And yet, perhaps, health itself is in need of some distraction, just as we need to sleep and to dream! Bergson would like that life could never stop or rest. His theory of the comic is for this reason opposite to Kant's who, by attributing to laughter a less solemn and more pragmatic meaning, renders it greater justice.

We find similar echoes of Kant's aesthetics in the other two characteristics of laughter: insensibility and sociability. The comic, writes Bergson, requires a momentary anesthesia of the heart and turns to pure intelligence. It implies a certain detachment, an absence of participation, a distancing with respect to the needs and necessities of life. Therefore, it is like art which subtracts objects to the dimension of functional utility, to desires and to the interests that are connected with them. In laughter, therefore, there is at work something similar to aesthetic taste, which was defined by Kant as the faculty of evaluating an object by means of a pleasure without any interest. However, it remains problematic if this same aesthetic disinterestedness has to be understood as a departure from action and, therefore, as a tendency contrary to life. In the end, Bergson seems to locate laughter half way between art and life. A more precise determination would have required a more systematic treatment of aesthetic problems, which Bergson announced but never carried out.

Even the other characteristic of laughter, sociability, is derived from Kant according to whom aesthetic judgement requires everybody's consensus. The universality of aesthetic judgement in Bergson is transformed in the essential sociability of the comic. In his view, social life requires tension and elasticity. Therefore it clashes with the formalistic and ceremonial tendency that transforms collective experience in a masquerade, in a ridiculous and superficial spectacle, in an exhibition of vanities and hypocrisies. Slavish imitation, disguise, hypocrisy appear grotesque and ridiculous to Bergson, just as everything that shifts the attention from interiority to exteriority, from the spiritual to the material, from the soul to the body. His criticism is not limited to the Baroque aspects of social productions, but it extends to bureaucratic formalism that submerges with suffocating regulations the creative and progressive life drive of humanity. In his last work, *The Two Sources of Morality and Religion*,[17] Bergson finally opposes the 'closed society', founded on habit and obedience, to the 'open society' that perpetuates the creative life drive.

In the first years of the twentieth century, there was another thinker for whom laughter and life were strictly connected, the great Italian writer Luigi Pirandello (1867–1936), who is the author of an essay on humour, *On Humor*,[18] where he outlines a conception of life different from Bergson. Humour, which Pirandello distinguishes decidedly from other forms of laughter, is not a minor experience but a feeling that makes possible the access to a deeper and more essential dimension than the ordinary one. Everyday life is based on a series of fictions, appearances and representations: our psychic, cultural and social identity is a mask that hides a continuously changing and contradictory reality. Humour is precisely linked to a perception of the latter: it is defined by Pirandello as 'the feeling of opposites'. In other words, the humourist, differently from the comic, is not only aware of the contrast between the way in which things present themselves and the way they should be, but he adheres emotionally, at the same time, to different types of feeling. He takes part in the process whereby everything turns into its opposite and, thus, enters in consonance with a reality more essential and covert than logic presented us with.

The experience of humour, which is neither cognitive nor moral, can only be aesthetic but in a sense that goes beyond art. Essentially, art is also an ideal and illusory construction, just as the other forms of social and cultural life. It assembles and creates coherent works, while life disassembles and introduces dissonant and discordant elements. Art tries to give a sense to life but this is just as illusory as that provided by social conventions, religion or philosophy. Just as judgement, humour is non-conceptual but being 'without concept' is closer to the intellect than to the faculty of which Kant speaks. While judgement is the faculty that brings the particular to the universal, the intellect disrupts and distorts what is ordered and established and, as the English philosopher Francis Bacon used to say, makes marriages and divorces illegal among things. It introduces flux and disorder where the task of concepts is precisely to fix and arrange the chaotic and magmatic world of experience.

Humour demonstrates the inconsistency of the aims that are commonly pursued and introduces us to the experience of *naked life*, that is, a life deprived of illusions and masks, and brought back to its arid and mysterious naturalistic crudeness. Of the two words employed in ancient Greece to refer to life, *bíos* (human conduct of life in the ethical sense) and *zōḗ* (life understood in the naturalistic sense which is common to men, animals and the vegetable world), Pirandello's notion can be said to belong to the latter. *Naked life* is precisely *zōḗ* understood as the vertiginous force that man can capture only by means of laughter. Pirandello's idea of life is at the opposite end of Dilthey for whom 'lived life' is inseparable from its historico-cultural meaning. The opposite of Pirandello's naked life is not death, the past or immortality but the 'clothed' life of culture and history that assembles and hides the contradictions and violence of living.

Does 'naked life' have a sense? Could its meaning be understood by the Kantian formula of a 'purposiveness without any representation of a purpose'? What is certain is that to a conception of life as the self-preservation of identity Pirandello opposes a conception of life as continuous change and unresolved contradiction. However, this idea of life still seems 'aesthetic' to me not only because Pirandello's entire literary work bears witness to it, but because there are more specific philosophical reasons that can be found in the enormous influence exercised on the twentieth century by a philosopher which I have not yet discussed, Friedrich Nietzsche, whose work is marked by a search for an opposition that goes beyond Aristotelian and Hegelian logic. In the last years of his activity he had discerned in the notion of life the keystone of experience and reality but even more significantly, he advocated the cause of a comic, parodic art characterized by an ironic self-involvement that in some ways anticipates the work of Pirandello.

Living is destroying

Even more than in Nietzsche, Schopenhauer's influence is evident in the work of Georg Simmel (1858–1918) in whose thought the problem of the meaning of life found a very different solution from Kant's. In fact, Schopenhauer claims that finalism belongs to the world of phenomena, understood as representation, not to the noumenal, which is understood as a blind will to live, without motivation and goals. Thus, life acquires in Schopenhauer's philosophy a wild and irrational character, which man can only avoid by means of art and ascesis. Nonetheless, Schopenhauer defined aesthetic experience in two ways: with relation to the figurative arts, where it is determined as a contemplation of forms, and in relation to music which is the direct and immediate manifestation of the will.

Simmel's philosophy constitutes a radicalization of the aesthetic ideas of Schopenhauer: form and life become two antithetical principles in perennial conflict with one another, but not symmetrically. In fact, during its long career as essayist in which he dealt brilliantly with the most varied and unusual arguments (from fashion to money, sexuality to ruin, caricature to picture frames), Simmel tends to attribute to life a more essential and original role with respect to form. This supremacy is evident both in his aesthetic writings, which he devoted to Rembrandt, Michelangelo and Rodin, and in his writings on Kant, Schopenhauer and Nietzsche. But it is in the essays of his later period that we find the greatest in-depth analysis of the notion of life. In *The Conflict in Modern Culture and Other Essays*,[19] he attributes to the concept of life a historical and epochal meaning, similar to the concept of

God in the Middle Ages, Nature in the Renaissance, society in the nineteenth century. He regards it as the point of intersection between metaphysics and psychology, ethics and aesthetics. The subject of the essay, in fact, is on the conflict that, on the one hand, opposes the forms, whether works of art or political constitutions, organizational systems or social structures, and on the other, the life that produced them, but which soon took its distance from them and which regards them as something rigid and foreign because it does not recognize them as its own product. The tragedy of culture consists precisely in this lack of recognition: while for Dilthey the highest form of life consists precisely in the possibility of a different repetition that confers a meaning to what was lived once unconsciously, for Simmel life rebels against its own objectifications and pretends to free itself from the coercion of form. Thus life acquires a destructive and annihilating character. The aesthetic experience, *par excellence*, is that of the expressionist painter who looks at the canvas as the immediate outpouring of his inner life and considers it, therefore, as an additional and superfluous exterior. Therefore, it is not just a question of negating sclerotic and oppressive forms, but of rejecting form altogether which appears to block the inexorable becoming of life in something fixed and static. Living life, understood as autonomous force, immediate and without veils, turns all its action towards the annihilation of any form, and goes on flowing without feeling the need to be objectified in anything. In the last instance, it avoids even any conceptual determination because the ground of conceptualization is at one with the realm of form. But in so doing, doesn't it invite unreality, a pure interiority suspicious of any realization that recalls the eighteenth-century 'beautiful soul'? Doesn't Simmel present us with an overexcited and frenetic variation of that pessimism of which Schopenhauer constitutes the resigned and passive version? What is certain is that Simmel clearly distinguishes himself from the other founding fathers of the aesthetics of life – Dilthey, Santayana and Bergson – precisely because his conception of life lacks the positive and, at times, triumphal orientation, which these authors inherited from Hegel, Herbart and Darwin, respectively.

Simmel's distance with respect to Dilthey is evident in the different evaluation that he provides of naturalism which, in his view, does not represent at all a rejection of the creativity of the artist with respect to actual naked reality but, on the contrary, a triumph of artistic experience on the ideal forms that pretend to impose on them obligations and external constraints.[20] The fact that naturalism considers reality as a formless mass devoid of pre-established meanings must be understood as a manifestation of the full autonomy of aesthetic experience, which can finally leave out of consideration, completely, concepts and values in order to let itself go to the pure flux of life. The more the external world is without sense the more art for art's sake is triumphant: naturalism is not at all interested in nature, but in experience. By taking under examination theatrical naturalism, Simmel anticipates the theory of *performance*: the actor no longer plays a work but is the work!

For Simmel, the opposite of life is not death (as for Dilthey) but immortality! Death dwells in life from the start and belongs closely to it: the more life is full and strong, the closer is its connection to death.[21] In his view, it is important to overcome the inorganic conception of death that considers it an external threat to life and contrary to it: death is a constitutive element of the continuous process of life. Paradoxically we could say that for Simmel 'to live is to die'. What deprives life of meaning is precisely the absurd claim to an eternal life, which isolates and separates from life the forms and the contents of culture and art by bestowing upon them a static and burnt-out perpetuity.

In his last work, *The View of Life*,[22] Simmel pursues an even more ambitious project, that of overcoming the opposition between life and form in a wider and more comprehensive conception of life. The tendency of life to go beyond any limits is not understood here so much as destruction but as transcendence, as an act that constantly shifts forward the limits of experience. It is inherent in the essence of life to be at the same time *more life and more than life*. Under the first aspect, life self-transcends itself by being manifested now as life, which is preserved and exalted, now as life which is annihilated through aging and death. Under the second aspect, it extends towards an alterity which at times can also be determined in opposite and contrary ways to life itself, for instance, as an ideal objective form, an autonomous spiritual category. For Simmel this is art which constitutes an emancipation from the finalism that characterizes life in its more elementary and practical forms. Man is the least finalistic being there is: he is free, that is, he is not necessarily oriented towards the realization of a pre-established end. For Simmel only the life that frees itself from the representation of an end and is devoted entirely to an independent and separate objectivity has meaning and value. While ordinarily we see to live, the painter is the one who lives to see. Thus, is form the only one to succeed in really satisfying the destructive fury that moves life? In order to be faithful to itself to the end, must life self-destruct in the form?

Aesthetic life and religion

By introducing the notion of transcendence in his last book, Simmel associates aesthetic experience to religion. A real encounter between aesthetics and religion under the aegis of life occurs in different ways and modes of spirituality in the work of the French thinker Henry Bremond (1865–1933) and the Spaniard Miguel de Unamuno (1864–1936). The author of a vast literary history of religious thought in France, in *La poésie pur*[23] and *Prayer and Poetry*[24] Bremond claims the substantial affinity between mystic states and poetic inspiration. In his view, the protagonists of the modern poetic adventure (Baudelaire, Mallarmé and Valéry) continue the mystical tradition of the sixteenth and seventeenth centuries. What links the religious souls of devout Humanism and Quietism to the rebel souls of Romanticism and Symbolism is a particularly intense experience in which the subject is displaced from itself and thrown in a kind of exciting ecstasy of vital acts. The problematic point of this experience is, precisely, the relation between passivity and activity. Bremond does not consider prayer an act or a question but a state, a full adherence to the will of God: *pure* prayer is not a request of anything but total acquiescence that excludes any mediation. The idea of *pure* poetry is determined on the basis of this paradigm. Prayer and poetry mark the entrance to a deeper dimension of life, but also poorer and more naked. It is not by chance that the New Testament in order to indicate life makes use of the word *zōḗ*, the vitalistic-natural life, and not *bíos,* which is the ethico-social one. Bremond proposes a kind of aesthetic mysticism of the naturalistic type, hostile with respect to religious or literary institutions. The aesthetico-religious experience he describes has little to do with the contemplation of Schopenhauerean forms; *pure* love, disinterested and theocentric is not Nirvana. It maintains a subversive aspect with respect to any form and ritual, to any organized behaviour which appears in full evidence in the story of the conflict that opposes the contemplative mysticism of the quietists to religious institutions. That is why Bremond's historiographical work constitutes a very important contribution to the study of a topic on which there is very little research: that of the existing relation between quietist or pietistic religious sensibility and the aesthetic sensibility which is grafted onto it.

If Bremond's spirituality is driven by an experience of subversive serenity, that of Miguel de Unamuno is characterized by an anxiety that subsides only in literature. A writer of essays, a novelist, playwright and poet, one finds in Unamuno a restless and unconventional Christianity in which religion and aesthetics are intertwined and mingled. His point of departure is the opposite of Bremond: not the disappearance of subjectivity in a feeling of ardent expectation with respect to the transcendental, but a cry of rebellion against death perceived as an inadmissible scandal, as an unbearable and inacceptable reality. For Unamuno life is not a metaphysical force, anonymous and impersonal, but the existence of a single subject that wants to seize the entire universe without ceasing to be itself, that wants to become everything without losing its own singularity. For Unamuno experience has a unique and irreducible character to any generality or abstraction. Reason, unable to find in life a true finality, enters into conflict with the emotive and affective dimension of life, which, instead, aspires to immortality. This conflict generates a tragic sense of life that seems incapable to arrive at a reconciliation or a catharsis.[25] 'All or nothing' is Unamuno's slogan. Life does not accept compromise. The 'meaning of life' rests in the challenge that the individual directs at the world. Don Quixote is the symbol of this struggle and it is not by chance that we are dealing with a literary character. In fact, it seems that the last word belongs to literary experience which opens up a territory beyond truth and falsehood, reality and imagination, which in making man doubt his own existence suspends his suffering in an endless questioning. In *Mist* (1913), one of the most well-known Unamuno novels, the existence that he describes is, in the last instance, vague and always changing. In this novel, better than in his theoretical and critical essays, Unamuno expresses his own conception of life and literature. They are intertwined to one another in a play of references and metaliterary duplications that dissolve any planning and any fixed form: 'To write as one lives, without knowing what comes after.' This is how Unamuno reformulates the purposeless purpose of aesthetic experience.

Life between aesthetics and ethics

The close link between the 'meaning of life' and aesthetic experience, which constitutes the common ground of all the authors considered so far, is loosened and even runs the risk to break in the thought of the German philosopher Karl Jaspers (1883–1969) and the Spaniard José Ortega y Gasset (1883–1955). In fact, for both thinkers life is the bearer of expectations and demands that art is sometimes unable to satisfy. In both authors the question of the 'meaning of life' acquires an eminently ethical dimension that acquires a religious tonality in Jaspers, and a socio-political connotation oriented in a secular sense in Ortega. In Jaspers the influence of the Danish philosopher Søren Kierkegaard is determining, according to whom the aesthetic and ethical forms of life are opposed and alternative to one another. While the first, symbolized by the figure of the seducer, is characterized by a search for novelty and intensity of experiences, the latter, symbolized by the figure of the husband, is characterized by choice and repetition. Ortega y Gasset, instead, is influenced by the teaching of Hermann Cohen (1842–1918) who transforms Kantian ethics in a science of pure will. However much Jaspers and Ortega continue to show great interest in aesthetic experience, nonetheless they diminish and reduce the role it occupies in the general economy of life. In their view, a real answer to the problems of the 'meaning of life' is not provided by aesthetics but by ethics.

In Jaspers and in Ortega what defines life is no longer an aesthetic determination as in the founding fathers of the aesthetics of life (relived experience in Dilthey, positive evaluation in Santayana, creation in Bergson, destruction in Simmel). For Jaspers the notions of *existence* and *situation* play a fundamental role in the definition of life. The first one, in fact, clearly distinguishes human life, characterized by self-reflection and the relation to the transcendental, from the other forms of life. The second one defines the relationship between man and world by conditioning and founding their possibility. Likewise, in Ortega the notions of *circumstance* and *enforceability* qualify life as an ought to be, a task to be carried out, something to do which is determined with reference to a particular context. Life is only an ensemble of relations.[26]

This squashing of life on beings tends to relegate aesthetic experience to a different dimension from real life, one ruled by the ethical problematic of decision and planning. Therefore, for Jaspers art is a *cipher of transcendence*, that is, not an objective but a symbolic presence of transcendence in existence. Jaspers distinguishes clearly thinking *on* art from thinking *in* art. While the former establishes the science of art, only in the latter can thinking, through artistic intuition, turn its gaze towards transcendence.[27] Even for Ortega art is on a different plane from life. It is essentially *unattainable*.[28] It appears to make evident the intimacy of life when in actual fact it places itself in a territory which is at the limits of the real world. Art de-realizes reality by replacing it with its sentimental transposition.

Both Jaspers and Ortega are aware that in the twentieth century the status of art has changed profoundly. Jaspers, therefore, speaks of a process of *degeneration* of art, through which it loses its seriousness and authenticity, by being transformed from number into mere play. Ortega devotes to this decadence a brilliant pamphlet, *The dehumanization of Art*.[29] Art (and especially poetry and music) was at the beginning of the twentieth century of great importance both for its content, which covered the great problems of existence, and for the solemnity and dignity that were conferred by its practice. In a few decades this high function was lost. It was invested by a process of de-vitalization that pushed it to the perimeter of vital experience. Art has become closer to play or even to sports, while the entire West seems to have entered the stage of puerility.

For the purpose of a further determination of the relations between ethics and aesthetics, Ortega's writings on Goethe, Jaspers and Leonardo are particularly interesting. In taking into account the life of Goethe,

Ortega emphasizes the underlying conflict between the commitments in which it was squandered (writing, scientific studies, public duties) and his profound vocation that pushed him towards the search for an 'authentic life', which remained unfeasible and unattainable. From this conflict came his dissatisfaction, the impression of not being able to coincide with his own exclusive destiny. Here Ortega opposes to a conception of life as industriousness, entirely taken up with the occasional circumstances that from time to time present themselves, a conception of life as exclusive choice and univocal determination.[30] Which of the two presents the character of a purposiveness without any representation of a purpose? In other words, which of the two is aesthetics? Ortega would say the first one because he wants to maintain its availability without being subject to a determined figure. But isn't it paradoxical to identify aesthetic life with the practical life of someone who is always ready to answer positively to the work opportunities that the world offers him? And, what if this dispersion were to derive from an insatiable curiosity for knowledge which is unable to focus on one activity alone? This is precisely the case of Leonardo, universally celebrated as 'universal man'. His grandiose form of life, Jaspers remarks, entails necessarily a fragmentary nature and incompleteness.[31] Was his life aesthetic or ethical?

Aesthetic life between play and politics

A conspicuous part of the aesthetics of life in the twentieth century leads the aesthetic experience back to play. By referring more or less directly to Kant, who had remarked on the affinity between aesthetic judgement and the play of thoughts, and Schiller who had emphasized the educational function of the instinct of play, many people saw in the play dimension the best manifestation of that purposivenss without any representation of a purpose which constitutes the essence of aesthetic experience. But it is only in *Eros and Civilization*, a work by Herbert Marcuse (1898–1979)[32] that this juxtaposition is inserted in a rich web of notions that shift the axis of the aesthetics of life to politics.

Although the exaltation of life understood as the source of excellence for creativity and a desire of liberty was constantly present in the philosophy of anarchism,[33] Marcuse does not belong to this tradition, as his philosophy takes its inspiration from Marx and Freud. The influence of these two authors, in fact, has marked a decisive turning point in the philosophy of life, shifting it from metaphysics to politics. For Marx, it seems, the opposite of life is not death, the inanimate, the mechanical but *commodities*: this 'enigma', this 'social hieroglyph', 'this sensibly supersensible thing',[34] which constitutes a kind of double falsification, an opaque material casing of living labour, or better yet, this 'fetish' that sums up in itself the opposite characters of abstraction and corporeity. Analogously for Freud, it seems that the opposite of life is not death, the inanimate, the mechanical, but *reality*. In fact, he has shed light on the antithesis between the vital impulses grounded in the unconscious and essentially oriented towards the satisfaction of pleasure, and the restrictions imposed on them by civilization which oppresses when it is not in agreement with the outside world.[35] On these bases it is possible to see in life the revolutionary force which fights against the reality of capitalism and against the oppression of sexual impulses. By combining the fight to the middle classes with the fight against sexual repression we have arrived at a kind of vitalism that looks at the liberation of biopsychic energy as the condition of good health and happiness.[36]

With respect to these simplifications in which the relation between life and aesthetic experience is completely lost, Marcuse's theoretical strategy is more refined and complex. First of all, he undoes the relation between reality and capitalism. The claim of the middle class to appear as the sole reality by confining to dreams, the imagination and utopia, any manifestation more direct and more immediate of the vital impulses, is arbitrary and illegitimate. This claim is based on an 'additional repression', that is, on a *surplus* of repression which does not derive from the necessity of fighting for existence, but from the social organization of capitalism. Marcuse rejects the identity between civilization and repression and affirms the possibility of a 'new libidinal order' based on harmony between vital impulses and reason, liberty and civil morality.

This new order is essentially *aesthetic*, because it is characterized by a 'purposiveness without any representation of a purpose' and by a 'legality without law'. The first determination defines beauty, the second liberty. They are the qualifying traits of a life which is worth living because it is entirely governed by a unified harmonizing and gratifying principle. Thus, Marcuse demolishes the limits within which Kant contained aesthetic experience and attributes to it a leading role also with respect to knowledge and morality. In fact, on the one hand, all the conditions are present by now so that the scientifico-technological progress and the development of the productive forces lose their coercive character and are placed at the service of individual aspirations, on the other hand, the utility of those psychic mechanisms has failed, which by arising a sense of guilt in the individual constituted the primary cause of his malaise and neurosis.

In Marcuse, the question of the 'meaning of life' is enriched by new meanings. The aesthetic experience not only guarantees a life rich in intrinsic values because it has its own end and its own law in itself, that is, it is auto-teleological and autonomous, but also allows a new approach to sensory activity and sensuality. Thus, Marcuse discovers the original meaning of the word 'aesthetics' understood as sensible knowledge and considers an essential part of aesthetic experience also the pleasure that accompanies the exercise of the senses. However, he distinguishes between 'sensuality' and 'sexuality', and advocates the transformation of the latter in Eros, that is, in a non-repressive process of sublimation through which sexual impulse, redirected towards a non-sexual destination, makes possible the constitution of lasting social activities and relations, capable of intensifying and amplifying individual satisfaction.

The strength of Marcuse's theory is in having demonstrated the real possibility of an alternative life with respect to the world of commerce and a repressive society. Therefore his theory is not utopian at all, on the contrary, it marks 'the end of utopia'.[37] In *The Aesthetic Dimension*,[38] Marcuse reiterates the political significance of aesthetic experience, which consists precisely in the fact that it introduces us in a world of feeling and thinking alternatively with respect to everyday life, burdened by money and the power of bureaucracy. Its revolutionary character does not depend on its contents but on its intrinsic characteristics. Under this aspect art can be considered a manifestation of life, free and autonomous life, already present and operating, here and now.

Coming from a cultural tradition completely different from Marcuse, the anthropologist Gregory Bateson (1904–1980) outlines an aesthetic of social life directed towards the search for integration and harmony.[39] The basis of his dynamic vision of reality is essentially biological. His attention and creative experiences, such as art and religion, in which conscious purpose has only a small part, are inserted in the study of factors that hold together the echo system that guarantees the coherence of the whole, which is thought as something living. With Bateson the aesthetic of life regains a cosmic afflatus that reminds us of Bergson.

Aesthetics of power and biopolitics

The relation between aesthetics and life is present in the work of Michel Foucault (1926–84) in a completely different way from the thinkers so far examined. In *The Order of Things*[40] Foucault contrasts the Classic Age (seventeenth and eighteenth centuries) to the Modern Age (nineteenth and twentieth centuries). The former is characterized by the continuity, horizontality, synchronicity of its culture which, in close relation to the transparency of its knowledge, undoes, analyses and reconstructs its own objects of study according to a movement that develops on the surface of representation, as in a painting. The epistemology of the Classical Age is ordered and positive, transparent and fluid. There are no dichotomies or radical dualisms in it. The world is thought as a cosmos in which man does not occupy a privileged place. The end of the eighteenth century marks the decline of the Classical Era and a profound change occurs both at the level of practice as well as in theories of language, classification and exchange. Language takes the place of discourse, life succeeds natural history and production replaces exchange: hence philology, biology and political economy are born. Philosophical thought begins with Kant and refers to the unthought, to a submerged continent from which fragments, substitutive formations, traces emerge here and there. It matters little that the unthought is called the in-itself, will, life, *etnos* or being. The essential is that everywhere there is a teeming of forces and unrepresentable entities that hurl experience down in a constitutive and essential turbidity.

Where can we place the aesthetic in this scenario? The answer is not an easy one because Foucault does not account for it explicitly. At first sight, we are tempted to place it in the Classical Era which is an epoch of harmony and representation. But a more careful and overall consideration of his production suggests another answer. Where is the purposiveness without purpose that characterizes aesthetic experience according to Kant? In actual fact, only in modernity the infinite search for a meaning, which constantly escapes and avoids any definite determination, originates and develops. Nietzsche is the one who inspired Foucault. Where Nietzsche speaks of 'life' and 'will to power', Foucault speaks of 'power'. While Marcuse's thought rests on the opposition between life and power, in Foucault life is identified with power. Its positive, productive and dynamic function is more important than its negative, repressive and static one. Power is not the institution but it is like life: impersonal, anonymous, ubiquitous and all-embracing. In the first volume of his *History of Sexuality*, which bears the title of *The Will to Knowledge*,[41] Foucault criticizes the repressive hypothesis proposed by Marcuse and lingers on the study of the devices productive of sexuality. What characterizes modernity is not the erasure of sexuality but precisely the opposite, the abundance of discourses on sex, the systematic stimulus to the imagination, the persistence in presenting it as what is pre-eminently desirable. As already in Bergson, it appears impossible to locate and separate what in his discourse is specifically 'aesthetic' because the fundamental inspiration of his thought is basically aesthetic in the vitalistic sense. It is a type of vitalism that goes well beyond sexuality as is clear from the second and third volumes of the *History of Sexuality*: *The Use of Pleasure*,[42] and *The Care of the Self*.[43] In these works Foucault's attention shifts towards the ancient world, Greece of the fourth century BC and the Greek-Roman world of the first century AD. What interests Foucault is to find in classical Greece already a practice oriented towards the mastery of oneself, which is expressed in the elaboration of a series of prescriptions relative to the discipline of the sexual act. This parenetic is inspired not so much by an ethical model of life as by an aesthetic exigency felt, it is true, only by a few men but precisely for this reason it is so much more meaningful in a social situation characterized by widespread sexual promiscuity. Subsequently, during the first century, this orientation is clarified and consolidated within the framework of the influence exercised by Hellenic philosophies which confer a fundamental importance to the supremacy of the passions.

The aesthetics of life of the twentieth century seems to conclude, then, on a renewed interest with respect to life understood as *bíos*, as a behaviour rich in value and meaning. In this direction moves an American scholar of ancient philosophy Martha C. Nussbaum (b. 1947), author of *The Therapy of Desire*,[44] where she emphasizes the modernity of Hellenic thought in general and the Stoics in particular. By taking her distance from Foucault's philosophy, which she criticizes for the excessive importance given to the notion of power, she becomes the bearer of a cosmopolitan humanism engaged in the defense of liberty and equality, rich in cultural and spiritual values.

Giorgio Agamben (b. 1942), too, takes his inspiration from the ancient world in his *Homo sacer*,[45] where he develops Foucault's ideas on biopolitics, namely, on the claim of contemporary powers to extend their control on human life reduced to its purely animal dimension. Not the *bíos*, but the *zōḗ*, naked life, is at the centre of this Italian scholar's thought. In his view, in fact, the figure of 'homo sacer', the man who according to archaic Roman law could be killed with impunity, constitutes a kind of paradigm of the present human situation. The new political subject is the 'life that is not worth living', the prisoner in the concentration camp or the human guinea pig of transplants and experiments of genetic engineering.

The grandiose aesthetic project of keeping together the *bíos* and the *zōḗ*, man's cultural and natural aspects, undertaken by Kant and followed up by Bergson and Marcuse seems to have failed. Perhaps it is the very notion of life that turns out to be inadequate to explain a situation such as the present one in which the boundaries between life and death, organic and inorganic, animate and inanimate, spirit and thing, culture and commodity, pleasure and reality become more than ever uncertain and ephemeral. If the fundamental aspiration of aesthetic judgement is that of establishing connections and of considering particular events with reference to something more general and universal, the idea of life appears too one-sided to constitute the pivot on which experience rotates. With the decline of the idea of life, however, the question on the 'meaning of life' does not disappear. It shifts towards other spheres and other theoretical narratives.

2

Aesthetics of Form

Form and transcendence

The term 'form' is just as widespread in the aesthetic culture of the twentieth century as the term 'life'. Both these notions constitute a polarity within which a very conspicuous part of the sensibility, taste and artistic projects of our century takes place. The 'friends of life' and 'the friends of form' represent two opposite tendencies within which it is possible to locate a great number of intermediary positions that in various ways attempt to reconcile the aspirations to a fuller and more intense existence with the experience of an entity which transcends the ceaseless flow of life. In fact, in the concept of form, the reference to anything objective and stable is implicit. With respect to the continuous and unstoppable flow of time, the appeal to form represents the impulse to overcome the ephemeral, transitory and fleeting character of life.

However, those who thought that the aesthetic experience of the twentieth century was motivated solely by the admiration for the infinite stability of nature or the permanence of a 'more lasting monument than bronze' would be wrong. What livens up the fascinating occurrence of twentieth-century formalism does not derive simply from a desire to defeat death in the contemplation or in the production of imperishable entities. The compulsion towards transcendence, which is at the basis of the aesthetics of form, stops neither before the beauty of nature, which by renewing itself cyclically remains always the same, nor before the beauty of the artistic object whose stability seems to defy the centuries. This compulsion is not satisfied with so little! In the history of the West, it has often presumed to transcend form itself by giving way to aniconic and iconoclastic tendencies, if not downright vandalistic, that appeal to an idea of the transcendental and the eternal understood as form-less. According to these movements, to attribute form to the transcendental entails remaining victim of an anthropomorphic, if not actually idolatrous, conception that disregards its absolute difference to the world and man. In this case, it is clear that there is no place for an aesthetics which goes beyond to religion where the compulsion towards transcendence and the eternal finds its fullest satisfaction.

The aesthetics of contemporary form seems to occupy, instead, an intermediary space between deification and demonization, exaltation of the beautiful appearance and its denigration, idolatry and iconoclasm. In actuality, the difficulty of a univocal formulation of the problem derives from the fact that the Western concept of form is not at all unified. It contains within itself a deep conflict that derives from the merging of two notions into a single term which for the ancient Greeks were semantically very distinct. The *eidos*, in Latin *species*, intelligible form, was thought to be somewhat different from *morphé* (in Latin *form*), sensible form. Within the same concept of form, therefore, there is an opposition. Contemporary aesthetic theories can be understood as the different solutions to this problem.

It is as if form, after having transcended life, cannot be placated in an outcome but is forced into a movement of self-transcendence which in its turn must remain formal somehow, with the risk of passing into pure religious spirituality. As in the case of the aesthetics of life, the theoretical premise of the contemporary aesthetics of form lies in Kant's *Critique of Judgment* where he distinguishes the sublime from the beautiful. While the beautiful implies a sensible form which is adequate to human faculties, so that it appears predisposed to our capacity to judge, the true sublime cannot be contained in any sensible form, so that it is pleasing not for its consonance but for its opposition to the interest of the senses. In the sublime is inherent a type of transcendence which is moral and not aesthetic. It attests to a faculty of the spirit which is superior to any measure of the senses. And yet this inadequacy can only be made manifest through sensible form!

Kant derives his examples of the sublime directly from nature. The problem of the aesthetics of form concerns instead the existence of 'sublime' artistic forms, that is, forms that contain in themselves the factors of self-transcendence, which somehow aspire to be more than forms. This problem is grafted on the antagonism between intelligible form and sensible form giving way to a plurality of different solutions which, on the one hand, attests to the richness of the contemporary reflection on this issue, on the other, to the complexity of articulations on which different traditions of thought and various religious and artistic sensibilities intertwine. In fact, beside the two notions of form to which we have referred, there are at least four that interfere with this problematic: the Greek idea of form as *schema* (in Latin *habitus*), which refers to an order that applies also to actions, the Anglo-Saxon idea of form as *shape*, which derives from the same Germanic root that gave way to the German word *Schöpfung* (creation), the idea of form as *Gestalt*, a German word which has a specific meaning in the 'psychology of form' and, last but not least, the Kantian notion of *Form*, understood as an priori condition of knowledge. However, to find one's way in this tangle where related questions of a practical and cognitive character have been linked to aesthetics, it is important to focus on the fundamental question from which the contemporary aesthetic of form originates and develops: which artistic forms allow aesthetic experience to transcend form?

The Baroque beyond the form

The historical search for an artistic form that contains a tendency to its own overcoming begins with the Swiss art historian Heinrich Wölfflin (1864–1945) whose *Renaissance and Baroque*[1] marks the start of a reflection on the limits of form destined to involve many other scholars. According to Wölfflin, Renaissance and Baroque are opposite categories characterized by formal, cultural and conceptual orientations absolutely in contrast to one another. While the former is tied to a respect for norms and symmetry, the latter is driven by a search for the exceptional and the unusual. The philosophically relevant aspect of this opposition does not consist simply in the contrast between two different styles but in the fact that the Baroque constitutes the attempt to go beyond form. It marks the dissolution of form performed with full awareness. Motivated by an instinctive repulsion for any precise limitation, for any external figure, for any individual existence, the Baroque attempts to reproduce through artistic means the effects of the sublime: it tends towards the infinite, the formless, the inexhaustible. The Baroque aesthetic experience is an excitement that overcomes the single identity and throws whoever attempts it in an abyss where any particular life is suppressed.

However, this tendency towards the infinite continues to rely on art and, therefore, it produces a form of representation opposite to the classical one that Wölfflin defines with the term 'picturesque'. Its character is, above all, the search for the representation of the movement obtained through nuance, the contrast between light and shadow, the dissolution of the outline, the rejection of symmetry. One can add to this the call to the indeterminate, the elusive, the boundless which is manifested formally in covering up, concealing and hiding some essential parts of what one wants to represent. What lies underneath the surface of forms, or even what lies outside of them, excites the imagination and introduces it to wonderful worlds, boundless and unfathomable.

The experience of the Baroque form, however, is not a spiritual liberation. On the contrary, according to Wölfflin we feel entangled in a vast, heavy and chaotic mass that precludes individual action: the grandiose, the massive, the colossal imply the impossibility of grasping the object sensibly through a single perception. The single form is assimilated and absorbed in a wider context. For example, in architecture in the place of the column we find the pylon which is compressed in a single wall. The mass lacks articulation and pretends to spread out without possibility of continuity to everything which is next to it. Where the single element cannot be chained to the mass it is replicated in identical copies, in multiples that dissolve its identity. For Wölfflin the Baroque form recalls an idea of matter seen as something pasty, juicy and soft. The formless mass breaks out everywhere. It seems that here Wölfflin opposes to classical form not so much another conception of form but formless matter which, endowed with an inexorable movement, resists individual action. Thus the exaggerated and emphatic character of Baroque performance, for instance in the theatre, would be the result of an impetuous but indispensable effort for those who don't want to succumb to complete dejection and degradation.

These ideas find a more precise and rigorous expression in Wölfflin's *Principles of Art History*[2] where the classical and the baroque are thought to be the two fundamental forms of representation. Wölfflin does not privilege either one or the other but makes an effort to identify their characteristics in the most objective possible way. The conflict between form and matter seems to have left room for a conflict between two different types of form, each one correlated to a particular conception of the world. What matters to Wölfflin is to emphasize the inseparability of form and content. The forms of visual representation are not something external but become almost the conditions for the possibility of aesthetic experience. It seems that Wölfflin wants to extend to aesthetics a use of the term 'form' that Kant had limited to knowledge. In fact, for Kant we can speak of a priori conditions of experience only in the case of space and time (which are, in fact, forms of sensibility) and categories (which are the forms of the intellect). The 'aesthetic ideas' cannot play a function analogous to forms of sensibility and of the intellect because they do not guarantee anything that may concern objective reality,[3] but they refer exclusively to subjectivity, to the sentiment of pleasure and displeasure, whose universality does not depend on sensibility. For Wölfflin, instead, the Classical and the Baroque almost constitute a historical a priori: 'not everything is possible in every age'. The way of seeing has its own history. The forms of visual representation are independent of the expressive choices of the individual. They impose themselves on the single artist because they condition his way of perceiving reality. 'Seeing by lines' is essentially different from 'seeing by spots'. The 'linear' and the 'pictorial' constitute two opposite orientations of sensibility similar to two different languages. The first is linear and tactile, because it sees the limits of the objects, feels their shape and confers on those who look the impression of touching the margins. The second, instead, is pictorial and optical, and because it has a fluctuating and faded perception of form, dissolves the continuity of the outlines, confers autonomy on the composition, the light and the colours. The former places emphasis on the 'reality' of the world, the latter on its 'appearance'. Wölfflin exemplifies this opposition in a very broad and detailed way by means of pairs of antithetical concepts. The linear way of seeing is characterized by the sequence of surfaces, the pictorial way of seeing is characterized by depth and the juxtaposition of space. The first privileges a closed form and absolute clarity, the second an open form and relative clarity. Finally the Classical aims at a harmony of independent parts and, therefore, it is connected with an experience of multiplicity, while the Baroque dissolves all formal identities and re-establishes the continuity of the world.

This last consideration brings us back to Wölfflin's fundamental aesthetic intuition, the idea that the Baroque is not a form to be placed beside the Classical form of art, rather, it is the transcendence of every form. For Wölfflin the closed form refers to itself in every part; vice versa, the open form tends to overcome itself in every part, and wants to appear unlimited. It surprises us constantly because it undoes the form in itself. For instance, the representation of ruins, crowds, the ragged mantle of a beggar, the rugged face of an old man, lead us into the realm of the elusive and uncovers the beauty of the incorporeal. In Wölfflin's thinking, therefore, is present a great challenge, not only with respect to the habitual idea of beauty but, actually, with respect to every form.

The will to art before the form

An analogous compulsion towards the transcendence of the notion of form can be found in the work of the Austrian art historian Alois Riegl (1858–1905) who in *Problems of Style*[4] launches the bases for a new evaluation of the ornament which constitutes a more recent and more refined artistic manifestation of the plastic reproduction of the form of objects. Riegl's attention aims, first of all, at those ornamental styles which, like the geometric or arabesque styles, move in a direction opposite to that of Greek classical art. While the latter is characterized by a 'beautiful liveliness', Riegl's object of study is, first of all, the phenomenon of abstraction and the tendency towards the inorganic.

The theoretical assumptions of his great appreciation of ornamental art results evident from his lecture course entitled *Historical Grammar of the Figurative Arts*,[5] published 60 years after his death. In his view, the fundamental thrust towards art is not generated from an impulse to imitate nature, but in competition with it. From nature man becomes aware of transience, causality, imperfection and, therefore, he is led to replace it with something eternal, perfect, unchangeable. The first aesthetic experience, therefore, is connected with the creation of art and is characterized as the perfecting of Nature. The art of ancient Egypt constitutes the most evident manifestation of this tendency that entails the primacy of the inorganic over the organic.[6] The next step implies a rejection not only of living nature but of the inorganic as well. All sensible forms appear imperfect and transitory with respect to the spiritual perfection of God who transcends every determination. This radical negation is connected to Jewish monotheism and its influence. The Jews, writes Riegl, are important in the history of art, not for the works they created, but for those they did not. At the origins of civilization, they introduced not only an aniconic component but one that was absolutely antiformal which has been even more productive and prolific than the exaltation of organic form. Greece and the Renaissance, that is, the two culminating points of organic and vitalistic aesthetics, seem to Riegl two brief parentheses of a history in which the struggle against form has constituted the underlying theme. Byzantine art, which suppressed organic themes, late-Roman art which considered form as a necessary evil, the Islamic one that tried to suppress it, constitute for Riegl as many examples of a conflicting relation between art and form that constitutes an essential aspect of aesthetic sensibility. Not even modern art can avoid this conflict. For Riegl it starts around 1520 with the Reformation when in Northern Europe the most virulent iconoclastic movement of the West became rampant. The various tendencies and national schools constitute as many forms of compromise between persistent organic-naturalistic orientations and tendencies towards the overcoming of form.

These general considerations on the history of art constitute the background against which Riegl's most famous work revolves, *Late Roman Art Industry*.[7] In polemics with the theory that the work of art is the mechanical product of the use to which it is destined, the material of which it is made and the technique which it employs, he formulates the theory of *artistic will* (*Kunstwollen*), which he asserts in opposition to these three elements. The artistic will is something positive and determined that comes before the forms and, in a certain sense, its condition. Under this aspect, the notion of artistic will seems to have affinity to Kant's notion of 'form' understood, precisely, as a priori, as a function that conditions the creation of works of art. While Wölfflin considered the Baroque as the 'beyond of form', Riegl's thinking is directed rather towards locating the before of form. Artistic will responds to the attempt to determine an essentially artistic element before its actual result. Riegl takes into consideration a very concrete historical problem, that of late-Roman art. To someone used to Classical art it appears ugly, awkward and lacking in liveliness. Riegl does not deny the correctness of this judgement but claims that these characteristics must be placed in relation to an artistic will positively oriented towards ugliness, inertia and lack of liveliness. In other words, behind late-Roman art there is something that transcends the beautiful formal appearance and the vital pleasure. One would be tempted to define it in strictly religious terms, with reference to Christianity and its exaltation of humility. But Riegl has no intention of leaving the sphere of aesthetics. On the contrary, he wants to expand its boundaries by introducing experiences and sensibilities that, as in late-Roman art, are extraneous to the Classical world.

According to Riegl, the evolution of figurative art in antiquity has followed three distinct phases, the most interesting of them are the first, which is typical of the Egyptian world, and the last which is typical of the late-Roman world. The Egyptians confer great importance to the outline, the line, the continuity of the surface. They create an art that can be defined 'tactile' because it conforms to the indications provided by the sense of tact. The late Romans, instead, place emphasis on the importance of light, they exalt the autonomy of the figure, they are preoccupied above all by the effect that works have on those who look at them from a distance. Their art can be defined as 'optical' because what counts is precisely the impression of depth. Greek art, compressed between the tactile artistic will of the pre-Classical world and the optical one of the post-Classical, is a kind of compromise between the two. It identifies, prosaically, with a 'normal point of view' which is kept away from extremes. In actual fact, for Riegl, what is important occurs only toward the extremes, where a certain and precise artistic will is revealed. Therefore, those wills that seem to have made a mark on Western art are essentially two: the inorganic tactile and optical illusion.

Inorganic style beyond the image

If Riegl at times seems to waver between the rejection of form and that of the image, a much more precise thesis is advanced by the German art historian Wilhelm Worringer (1881–1965), the author of the most important and fortunate work on the aesthetics of form of the early twentieth century, *Abstraction and Empathy*.[8] Worringer not only separates but he even opposes the organic image to the more pure and radical experience of form, which he defines with the term *style*. Thus he avoids the danger run by Riegl of abandoning the field of art and passing into religion, according to the dynamic that was described by Hegel with explicit reference to the Protestant reform.[9] Obviously, the originality of the contemporary aesthetics of form does not consist in its pure and simple negation, but in identifying a *sublime* form, that is, a type of art that contains elements that refer to the limitations of form without however abandoning the aesthetic field.

In Worringer, the opposition between aesthetics of life and aesthetic of form is introduced with extreme radicalism. On the one hand there is a tendency to facilitate and intensify life, which can be defined as *empathy* (i.e. the attribution of one's own feelings to an external object), or as *naturalism* (i.e. art drawing closer to the organic, the probable, the beautiful natural appearance). On the other hand, there is the tendency to avoid the arbitrariness, the causality and the violence of the vital process and to go beyond appearances, which can be defined as *abstraction* (i.e. reasons of self-alienation, emancipation from the apprehension of subjectivity and time), or simply as style (i.e. as art that finds its own point of reference in the inorganic and more generally in any law or external necessity).

Although Worringer recognizes to both tendencies the status of art, his orientation, more than Wölfflin and Riegl, is anti-Classical and anti-Renaissance. The examples of inorganic style that he provides are in themselves very significant. There is above all the ornamental style. Here Worringer takes up and develops Riegl's considerations underlining the opposition between ornament and imitation. To the latter, Worringer does not even recognize an artistic quality. In ornamental abstraction the will to transcend nature is manifested in a pure and absolute way. The vegetal and animal motifs of ornamental art must not deceive. They are also subordinated to a stylization that looks for the essence of reality. Then, it is the turn of Byzantine art that for Worringer also aims at entirely avoiding the organic and tri-dimensionality, opting for abstraction and plane representation.

Worringer's most original contribution is in his reflections on Gothic art and represents a decisive step forward in the experience of the inorganic because it is not limited to providing a static, geometrico-crystalline representation of form. The Gothic is pervaded by a mysterious pathos that confers dynamism to the inorganic creating a kind of 'artificial life', a 'living' mechanism endowed with an intensity greatly superior to natural life. With the Gothic, abstraction celebrates its own triumph because it also appropriates its opposite, the empathic dimension. But this appropriation does not imply at all an harmonic synthesis, on the contrary, it is a disturbing mixture of materiality and sensibility that appears to the vital feeling, organically tempered, as an 'excess of dissoluteness'.[10] The perversion of the Gothic consists in transgressing the limits of organic mobility. In fact, as soon as the energy is reversed in the dead lines of the stone, it acquires an infinite power that demolishes any obstacle. Therefore, the Gothic leads us to an experience of form that dissolves the very notion of form understood as determined configuration endowed with a precise identity. We could ask what 'formal' element is still present in such experience. In my view, it is best to emphasize not only the character of 'transcendence' which is common to the founding fathers of aesthetics of form, to Wölfflin, Riegl and not the least to Worringer, but more essentially the character of 'exteriority' opposed to any type of organico-vitalistic subjectivity. The energy which the Gothic cathedrals seem to possess is entirely autonomous and independent of us, in fact, it challenges us. The excitement with which it throws us has nothing to do with pleasure or play. On the contrary, it is something of which we would willingly do without, if we could! In short, the will of art does not belong to the subject, the artist, but it is imposed on him as extraneous and despotic. The feeling that goes beyond the senses of Gothic experience must not be understood as the longing towards a dematerialized spirituality, but as the strangeness, the enigma of a stone that vibrates. Once again aesthetic experience is something different from religious experience because it is indissolubly tied to the *res*, the thing, the mass. Gothic art is asymmetrical and a-centric, while Classical art tends towards symmetry and the determination of a centre. Gothic art insists on the infinite repetition of a single motif, on an unlimited development that never subsides. It is affected by a kind of 'sublime hysteria' that forces it to find only in stupor and in intoxication a spasmodic and unnatural satisfaction.

A consequence of the inorganic aesthetic experience described by Worringer is a different perception of the body which loses its dimension as a living autonomous organism so celebrated in the nudes of classical Greece. In Gothic art the dress is more important than the body which takes on an existence and an importance independent of what it covers. The victory of the inorganic over the natural finds its culmination in the treatment of drapes when they appear to be invested by a movement not attributable to life. Once again, it is the mixture of abstraction and materiality to arise the strongest and most disquieting emotion.

Wölfflin's formless, Riegl's artistic will and Worringer's inorganic style emerge as a struggle against the discriminations of Classicism which had excluded from its idea of beauty the production of subjects thought to be inferior, such as mental patients, primitives, children or those considered to be different, such as extra-European cultures. The theory of form of these three historians of art opens the way to a 'widened' aesthetics to which many others in the course of the twentieth century have made important contributions. For instance, as far as psychopathological art is concerned, of great importance is the work of the German psychiatrist Hans Prinzhorn (1886–1933) to whom we are indebted for the notion of 'schizophrenic formation (*Gestaltung*),'[11] which is characterized by a formal law that does not look for any meaningful unity and that, therefore, presents close affinity to problems raised by the ornament.

Finally, on the relation between artistic will and formative activity we should recall the reflection of the Japanese philosopher Nishida Kitarō (1870–1945) who is the author of a vast work based on a contrast between Western thought and Japanese tradition. Particularly interesting is his idea of aesthetic experience understood as seeing the form of what is without form and hearing the voice of what is without voice. This would be, according to Nishida, the essence of Japanese culture which has neither been a culture of *eidos* nor a culture of ritual, but one of pure feeling. It utilizes form to express the *without form*, however, not in the sense of being its symbol. The *without form* is determined in time which, in its turn, is the self-determination of nothing.[12]

A notion of form still very different from previous ones but possessing a certain affinity with them for its subversive character with respect to the normal, the regular, the habitual, the customary is the Korean notion of *meot*. It applies not only to works of art but also to all sorts of objects and phenomena and in Korea it is the term *par excellence* of aesthetic appreciation. An essential contribution to its conceptualization was made by the Korean philosopher Park Ynhui, also known as Park Yeemun (b. 1930), who in various books and essays has outlined the differences between Korean aesthetics and Chinese and Japanese aesthetics.[13] The fundamental characteristics of Korean sensibility are simplicity, refinement and, above all, an artificial deviation from the norms that create defamiliarization and estrangement.

The work of art as living form

The three main theories of form that have been examined so far share one point in common in their search for a form beyond Renaissance Classicism whether Baroque, late-Roman, Gothic or, at least, eccentric with respect to the Western canon. The same aim is shared by the Russian scholar Pavel Florenskij (1882–1937) who subjects the Renaissance conception of art to a close questioning that aims at a philosophical re-evaluation of the icon of orthodox religion. Differently from the previous three Western scholars, however, Florenskij has, paradoxically, a more immanentistic and realistic conception of aesthetic experience. For him, in fact, the two ancient notions of form, the *eîdos* (supersensible form) and the *morphé* (sensible form), coincide completely in the icon which has no need to refer to anything transcendental because it is already the point of contact between the invisible and the visible, the point at which the two worlds touch each other and their union becomes possible. The icon is not the imitation of the original but the very same original.[14] The sources of this conception, therefore, are not in Plato who thought that sensible form is ontologically inferior to the supersensible but in Plotinus and in Byzantine aesthetics for whom being and beauty are inseparable.[15] The image must be considered not as a simple representation of the original but as an evocation, a 'door' through which God enters the sensible world. For Florenskij to negate the image is equivalent to negating the incarnation of the spirit, that is, to abandoning the entire physical world to the shadows of evil and corruption. The original, the Platonic idea, is for this type of aesthetic sensibility capable of sensible evidence. Florenskij's is a concrete metaphysics, a visual theology that sees in the icon the point of union between the visible and the invisible world.

According to Florenskij, the Church alone has been able to preserve the spirit of this tradition, which goes back to the paintings of mummies of ancient Egypt, was passed on by Hellenic culture and has found its highest flowering in the work of painters of icons like Andrej Rublëv in the fourteenth and in the fifteenth centuries. The Roman church, instead, was deformed in the very same structure of its spiritual life by the Renaissance experience, whose worldliness it has never been able to overcome. The images of the West, the oil paintings, have little relation, if any, to the supersensible. They remain on the surface and never succeed in being true 'forms' limited as they are to providing the most garish testimony possible of themselves.

The destruction of form in the West depends on the establishment of the linear perspective in the Renaissance. In fact, the latter is based on a qualitatively homogeneous, infinite, unlimited and, therefore, undifferentiated and informal conception of space, which is that of Euclidean geometry, transformed by Kant in the a priori condition of experience. Florenskij reconstructs the history of perspective by locating its origins in theatre stage designs of late antiquity and in its illusionism that claim to escape reality and substitute it with a phantasmagorical appearance. In this fashion, all forms lose their concreteness and become interchangeable. Florenskij invests great theoretical commitment to show that perspective is not at all a simple and natural vision of the world.[16] Neither children nor primitive people, and not even the ancients (although it was not at all unknown to the Greeks and the Romans), draw according to the rules of perspective. In fact, linear perspective requires a forced psycho-physiological reeducation which is functional with respect to the abstract exigencies of the new conception of the world. It destroys the form of what it represents because it considers all the points of space on equal terms and devoid of quality, conferring an absolute value only to the skilful eye of the painter, placed in a state of immobility (precisely as the theatre spectator). Seeing is reduced to a mechanical process that eliminates the psychic and even the physiological aspects of vision. Perspective painting unifies all the representations of the world in a unified, indissoluble and impenetrable weft of Kantian–Euclidean relations focused on the 'I' of who observes the inert and specular world.

To perspective painting, Florenskij opposes an aesthetic experience that embraces in an unique complex representation an entire series of consecutive experiences and constitutes a synthesis of sensations and thoughts. Only this complex and articulated unity can be considered *form*. It matters little that it also represents what cannot be seen. After all, even many great Western painters have transgressed the rules of perspective introducing in the same painting many points of view and many horizons. An aesthetic experience of space must capture its essential discontinuity. The light, the force, the intensity are disseminated in an uneven way according to dynamic lines that confer on the work of art a kind of autonomous and independent life from the subjectivity of the author and the spectator. Thus, Florenskij eventually considers art as a living form, a thing that acts (*érgon*). Therefore, the museum which condenses in itself the philological and spectacular approach constitutes a betrayal of the work of art. It places it in a state of anabiosis, lethargy, from which it is very difficult to remove it.

It is interesting to observe how in the Western tradition the notion of *living form* takes on a meaning opposite the one in the Eastern tradition. *Idea*, the very erudite work by the German scholar Erwin Panofsky (1892–1968), demonstrates how intelligible form is understood as the mental representation of the artist.[17] This is precisely the conception of form elaborated by Mannerism that on the one hand depreciates sensible form claiming that nature can never be perfect, and, on the other hand, views the work of art entirely dependent on the pre-existent presence of the idea in the spirit of the artist. Michelangelo considers even the 'concept' as synonymous of the 'idea' and believes that the free mental representation created by the artist constitutes the model of the work of art. Similarly, Dürer claims that a good painter is internally full of figures (i.e. supersensible forms) and attributes to him a faculty that the Middle Ages attributed to God. Panofsky traces the history of this subjective metaphysics, whose premises can be found already in Cicero and in the comparison between supersensible form and the *cogitata species* (the living representation in the intellect of those who practice the art). By means of a journey that goes from Plotinus and Augustine to Meister Eckhart and Marsilio Ficino, the idea loses completely both its independent existence with respect to the inner spirit, and its relation to the sensible world. The material realization of the work of art is always inadequate with respect to the ideal representation because matter opposes a continuous resistance to form that wants to shape it, and conserves an essentially negative, hostile and impenetrable character.

Thus, Panofsky outlines with great effectiveness an aesthetic sensibility radically different from the one described by Florenskij. The idealistic spiritualism of the West, which finds its highest manifestation in Mannerism, is precisely the opposite of the immanent philokalia of the West, whose highest realization is represented by the painting of icons. Here, form is 'living' in the soul of the artist, there, in sensible matter. Here, it shines in the mind of the subject, there in the extraneousness of the thing. To be sure, the entire formal experience of the West cannot be forced into subjective spiritualism. For example, fifteenth-century Renaissance and sixteenth-century Classicism make a different use of the notion of 'idea'. For the former the idea is the ideal understood as perfection of nature, for the latter the idea is a vision of nature purified by our spirit. However, in Panofsky's perspective, Renaissance and Classical form are either parentheses or preparations of the pure inner idea which exists only in the spirit of the artist.

Panofsky's analysis adds and integrates the theories of form that have preceded it. It also takes up the fundamental question from which the contemporary aesthetic of form takes its origin: Which artistic forms allow aesthetic experience to transcend form? After the Baroque (Wölfflin), late-Roman illusionism (Riegl), the Gothic (Worringer), even Mannerism is co-opted in the category of forms that transcend form. The way described by Panofsky, however, is even more significant than the others. It shows that the connection between form and transcendence is maintained in the West even when the *eidos* is no longer understood as a metaphysical entity independent of man (according to Plato) but as a representation that lies in the mind of man (according to the subjective turn accomplished by Cicero).

However, a question remains open. The thrust that powers Mannerism towards transcendence and the overcoming of sensible data, does it halt before mannerist art? Is it satisfied with the 'serpentine' figures, with distorting the proportions between the various parts of the human body, with the non-finite, the grotesque and similar morphological aberrations? Or it ends by devaluating not only nature but also the work of art considered inessential just as natural forms are with respect to the living *eidos* in the inner soul of the artist? Is the point of arrival of this process an aesthetic experience without a work of art, not far from the irony of the Romantic poet who refuses to take his own productions seriously? Or does the distinction hold firm between vitalistic subjectivism, hostile to form by definition (to which Romanticism could be assimilated) on the one hand, and ideal formalism of Mannerism, on the other? What is certain is that in the aesthetic experience of mannerism is inherent an iconoclastic tendency, which only recently has received the attention of scholars.[18] It is in this direction that the aesthetic reflection opened by Panofsky deserves to be pursued and developed.[19]

Form as schema and historical sequence

The aesthetics of form is not exhausted in the reflection on the notions of *eidos* (supersensible form) and *morphé* (sensible form). On the contrary, its vitality is manifested precisely in the effort of thinking form in ways that transcend or overcome the opposition between spirit and matter, the intellectual and the sensible. Of these, deserves attention the work of the French art historian Henry Focillon (1881–1943), author of *Vie des forms*,[20] who formulates a notion of form independent of the Platonic or Aristotelian metaphysical tradition. For him, the essential characteristic of form is exteriority. But how can one think the exterior without remaining prisoner of a dialectic that opposes it to the interior? Classical antiquity provides us with a third alternative that opens a semantico-conceptual horizon completely different from what we have seen so far. The schema (in Latin *habitus* but also *figura*) refers us precisely to the idea of an external form that can also be abstract and intellectual. In the *schema*, the metaphysical problem of the separation between the sensible and the supersensible does not even come into play. The Romans used to translate *schemata* with '*habitus, cultus, vestitus, gestus, sermones et actiones*'. The common denominator of these expressions is precisely exteriority attributed to attitudes, clothing, modes of behaviour, dance forms, government, lifestyle, rhetorical figures, and to grammatical, geometrical, astronomical forms, etc., and, last but not least, works of art. Focillon refers explicitly to this plurality of meanings when he understands it as a construction of space and matter, and when he is careful not to separate the activity from the results: intention, imagination, intellectual intuition are not yet forms because they don't have 'body'. Extension, matter and technique constitute essential aspects of form, since there are no artists without hands or forms without external recognizability.

Focillon, a scholar of Romanesque art, confers a general philosophical meaning to an aesthetic sensibility that has its roots in the ancient Roman tradition. In fact, the ancient Romans were the ones who elaborated the notion of form on the model of religious rituals and the legal system. It is form, namely, the external execution of convenient and pre-established acts which confers actuality to religious ceremonies and to legal practice. What counts is not so much the subjective content of actions as much as their form which has no need of an added 'sense' by those who realize it, because it has already a 'sense' inherent in it. Focillon sheds light on the difference between 'sign' and 'form'. The first refers to something other than itself, form, instead, 'signifies itself'. As the rituals of the ancient Romans, it is exceedingly flexible and elastic. It presents itself as a 'kind of empty mould' where man from time to time pours very different materials. After all, the Greek word *schema* comes from the verb *écho* which means 'to hold'.

But form must not be thought as a mere shell capable of containing anything indifferently. In the last instance, the most important thing is not what it contains but how it transforms itself. In fact, it has the 'genius of impropriety' which, like Proteus, changes constantly. It is born from a change and it prepares another. The movement of form is no longer transcendence but transit, namely, the continuous, ceaseless, transformation of form. This is how Focillon overcomes the opposition between the Classical and the Baroque, decoration and figuration, primitive and civilized, in which contemporary theorists remain caught. In fact, in his view, any style (i.e. any formal sequence that unfolds on the assimilation of anterior experiences) passes through various phases or states (experimental, Classical, Baroque, academic). Even here Focillon shows an aesthetic sensibility typical of the Roman tradition, namely, the idea that we can arrive at the new through a different repetition, through the variation of a formal order to which one must necessarily refer. The more a style has limits, the more numerous are the variations which it generates. The lack of formal relations generates imitation, not originality!

According to Focillon, forms have their own autonomous 'life' independent of the organic life of man. Between organic and inorganic, Focillon sees an exchange, a transit that, on the one hand, extends biology to 'things', on the other hand, by means of ornamentation and fashion, it creates an 'artificial humanity'. Forms also have their own history which is autonomous and independent of social, political and economic history. It is possible, therefore, to establish relationships and filiations between artists who belong to different eras and cultures, who never had any knowledge of one another and who are still solidly held together by the objective and impersonal development of forms. The nation, the environment, the contingencies of the moment are not only insufficient but they are even misleading and mystifying for the purposes of an essential and historical knowledge of aesthetic and artistic experiences. To subjective and organic feeling, Focillon opposes a 'feeling by forms' independent of the images and individual memories, where the sensible dimension (touch) and the supersensible one (inspiration) cannot be distinguished from one another.

An interesting development of Focillon's aesthetics of form can be found in the work of the American art historian George Kubler (1912–96) with whom the aesthetic reflection on form finally acquires a planetary dimension. Kubler takes into account both Western and Eastern art and the material production of peoples without a written tradition and elaborates a general theory of a 'history of things' in which the same conceptual instruments count for both the knowledge of works of art and utilitarian objects. A specialist in Amerindian art, where the artifacts exhibit a very repetitive character, the names of the artists are not known to us, and the productions do not have a conscious artistic statute, Kubler is the author of *The Shape of Time*,[21] which is a fundamental contribution not only to the philosophical study of the history of art but also of any other cultural aspect. He introduces criteria of intelligibility of temporal processes that do without vague notions such as 'style' as well as metaphors derived from biology like birth, flowering and sunset, proper of a certain form of art. In his view, every work finds its place more or less consciously within a chain of similar works or, as he puts it, within a 'formal sequence' that goes through centuries if not millennia. In other words, there is no such a thing as a regular historical cycle as those outlined by the founding fathers of the aesthetics of form (such as Renaissance, Baroque, Romantic, etc.). The formal sequence, even if inactive for centuries, can always be reactivated on the stimulus of new techniques or new events. The becoming of formal sequences has little to do with that confused and ruffled mass of events which is history understood in a chronological sense. Kubler inserts in historical reflection an exquisitely philosophical preoccupation: the dynamic towards transcendence which, as we have seen, constitutes the typical trait of every aesthetics of form, is present here both as the organization of the single thing in an invisible series that keeps it tied to similar things that precede it and follow it, and as emancipation from empirical chronology.

In fact, things have a 'systematic age' that has nothing to do with chronological age. What matters is their position within the development of formal sequence, not the fact that they are simultaneous with respect to this or that event that belongs to another sequence! Thus Kubler develops a philosophy of history which is not merely retrospective as that of Dilthey. Works of art, but more generally human works, are like stars whose light starts a lot before it appears to the observer. Even the activity of the historian does not escape this condition. The signals that he retransmits towards the future, after having deformed them, can never be complete or definitive. For Kubler history is always open. There is nothing that cannot become actual again. For instance, who could ever have imagined that the paintings of the Australian aboriginals would become after millennia the beginning of a formal sequence followed by some painters in the twentieth century? Who could have seen in Hero's aeolipile the prototype of the steam engine?

The formal sequence, the *schema*, makes it possible to consider the historical process according to a multiplicity of axises each one with its own well-determined dynamic rationality. It inserts in the chaos and in the flux of becoming the presence of problems and continuous scales of interconnected solutions that follow one another in a recognizable order. This does not mean that every point of the sequence corresponds to a thing that really existed. Many things have gone lost, others have never really existed, the important thing is the existence of historical networks of repetitions of the same section, gradually modified. The formal sequences are of a limited number. Their duration can be very long (as that of tools), or very short (as fashion). Their speed is also very varied. There are series that see tight formations of many operators contemporaneously active to the solution of the same problem. Others are characterized by a discontinuity of interventions. However, no work of art exists outside the continuous sequences that connect all the objects made by men ever since the most remote antiquity. Each thing has its own determined position in this system. No operator is ever alone in the *mare magnum* of history. All active men are connected with one another. Their existence is tied dynamically between them forever. In fact, things are as Thomas Aquinas' angels, in an intermediary dimension between eternity and time. They dwell in the *aevum*, that is, in a duration that has a beginning but not an end!

To be sure, the fact that the essence of art for Kubler is based on classification and the propagation of things could perplex someone who believes in aesthetic experience as a 'feeling the form' that lingers and appreciates the single work of art. It appears that the preoccupation to guarantee the social relation with the mediation of things is more important for Kubler than aesthetic experience. From a different perspective, his theory can be interpreted as the prevailing of the collector's professional perspective over that of the amateur connoisseur. In actual fact, he introduces in the problematic of form a special attention to the phenomenon of repetition and the sensibility connected to it. *Schêma* is rendered in Latin as *habitus* from which we derive 'habit'. In the theory of formal sequence the attention is placed not on the original but on the copy. It is the repetition that gives it meaning. If nothing were ever repeated nothing would be recognizable. Kubler sees the essence of aesthetic experience not in the originality that creates from nothing but in the small variation. In his view, there is no such a thing as a completely new operation but at the same time it is not possible to perform an operation absolutely identical to another. It follows that human behaviour, in all its manifestations, is essentially *ritualistic*, entirely shaped by the logic of different repetition. Human existence is structured by the invisible multi-level net of habits. Originality is disruptive, repetition is protection. In actuality for Kubler the great changes are more apparent than real. An accurate analysis reveals small variations of repetitions. At any moment, originality is limited to narrow confines. No invention goes beyond the potential of its era. Every instant is almost the exact copy of the one that preceded it. Nothing new happens immediately!

But if everything happens through a different repetition how is it possible to explain the beginning and the end of things? Can an object exist before it inaugurates a new formal sequence? How can one discard a thing definitively without substituting it with one of its slightly different copies? How does the shift occur from the last copy of an old series to the first element of a new series? For Kubler the event of a first object remains an exceptional phenomenon, evasive, enigmatic, certainly dangerous. Very often it is the result of a flaw in transmission, a casual interference. In any case it makes necessary a revision of the entire past, which cannot be instantaneous but gradual. It must be combined with all previous data which, for this reason, must be rethought and reorganized. Even in this case, therefore, the tearing, the fracture, the discontinuity is an illusion. The recognition of originality requires a long labour of re-elaboration that proceeds along well-known and proven rules. The end of a formal sequence is not any less paradoxical. To be sure, sometimes there are external traumatic events such as the Spanish conquest of Mexico that force entire populations to learn techniques and imitate models that are foreign to them. But Kubler, slyly, suggests that while the aboriginal products belonged to a formal sequence begun recently, the Spaniards brought to America 'old things', that is, manufacturing and building techniques that in Europe go back to the Middle Ages. Discarding something entails a difficult decision. To reduce to waste or garbage anything seems to go against the main ritual of human society: the preservation of 'old things'. Some scholars explain the phenomenon of discarding by recourse to the notion of 'aesthetic fatigue' (i.e. an ensemble of boredom and contempt that comes from habit). In actual fact, for Kubler the world of things never truly ends. There is only an interruption that can last thousands of years! The indefinite persistence of formal sequences has only one enemy: iconoclasm! The history of the West is studded with iconoclastic excesses from Savonarola's Florence to the Sack of Rome of 1527, to modern functionalism. . . . It seems that even iconoclasm is a recurrent ritual which is why, perhaps, it cannot avoid the logic of different repetition!

Form as etiquette

The aesthetic of form is concerned not only with the object but also with the subject: the individual. The process of forming, in the sense of shaping something on the basis of a pre-existing model concerns also behaviour, ways of acting, styles of life. After all, the first meaning of *habitus* refers to conduct.

Already in the Middle Ages, the Byzantine and Papal courts prescribed very ritualized behaviour. It is only in the Renaissance, and above all in the sixteenth century, that the process of civilization is manifested as the elaboration of rules of etiquette, 'good manners' and 'worldly wisdom'. This is the birth of an 'artificial humanity' which attributes an essential value to self-control and stylization of action. The great scholar of this aesthetics of ceremonial forms is the German sociologist Norbert Elias (1897–1990) whose work can be considered an application of the notion of *schêma* to the historical world of social relations. In *The Society of the Court*[22] he demonstrates how in the France of the *ancient régime* formal attitudes are not at all a mere decorative superstructure but constitute the fundamental axis of a very real 'logic of prestige'. In other words, aesthetics and politics are inseparable. Court society is an extremely solid and coherent structure in which it is impossible to preserve an elevated social status without providing a sumptuous public representation. Luxury has an eminently public and official dimension which on the one hand establishes and on the other testifies to the rank and power of everyone. Behaviour must be functional with respect to a dynamic system where through relentless competition and permanent social pressure, individuals are constantly the object of evaluation. It is as if there were an invisible 'stock market' in which neither commodities nor companies but people are being continuously appraised. Their 'ascent' or 'descent' are not at all casual or arbitrary but depend on a rationale not any less restrictive than the economic or scientific one which measures, above all, the power potential of each. The work done by Elias in studying the aesthetics of behaviour shows a deep affinity with the study of ornament conducted by Riegl and Worringer. In both cases one discovers in dimensions believed to be merely exterior and superficial, if not altogether frivolous, intrinsic meanings that invest the substance of spiritual occurrences and social relations.

In the two volume work, *Über den Prozess der Zivilisation*,[23] Elias deals, instead, with those changes of habits, civil structures and sensibilities that in the modern age have made possible the birth of a society based on self-control. A civilization of 'good manners' requires, in fact, a complex and subtle process of internal growth that has to do with the most intimate part of personality. In order to access and play an important role in the 'world', it is necessary to cover a long and difficult journey of mental refinement and improvement founded on the control of emotions and mastery of formal and symbolic codes. However, between an aristocratic and a middle class family there is a difference. While in the former the imperatives of 'good manners' are justified by a recourse to considerations of practical prudence (good name, reputation, reliability), in the latter they assume the character of absolute moral laws that are imposed on the individual starting from his inner side (conscience, inner voice, purity of will). This distinction could lead one to contrast aristocratic society as essentially 'aesthetic', and the middle class as essentially 'ethical', but this does not seem to be Elias' conclusion who is interested above all in proving the continuity of the Western process of civilization.

In this regard, it is useful to introduce two considerations. The first one concerns the profoundly alienating and reifying character of the mechanisms and dynamics of aristocratic society, whose members are not producers of commodities or managers of capitals, but a species of 'living money' condemned to a labour of ceaseless self-valorization. In my view, this condition anticipates the society of media and explains the fascination wielded by Elias' analysis and the materials he studies.[24] In fact present-day society is more similar to court society than to nineteenth-century capitalism.

The second consideration concerns the notion of individual. Just as for Kubler any object must comply with a formal sequence of similar objects, so for Elias the individual exists within a chain of interdependences that condition his behaviour. For Elias, the conceptual model that places the autonomous subject at the centre of a series of circles is entirely illusory. In reality, each one is an element of wider formations that transcend it and function by imitating pre-existent models of behaviour.[25] Even under this aspect Elias reveals himself to be a great thinker of the *schêma*, of ritual form. He integrates and completes Focillon's and Kubler's analyses through extremely acute and circumstantial analyses of the formal interweaving that connects individuals to one another.

Form as *Gestalt*

Among the attempts made by contemporary aesthetics to overcome the opposition between *eîdos* and *morphé*, between supersensible and sensible form, an important place goes to the art psychologist of German origin Rudolf Arnheim (1904–2007) who applied the notion of *Gestalt* to aesthetics, developed from the psychology of form. In *Art and Visual Perception*, he develops the notion of *shape* by which he means the primary and simplest aspect of perception.[26] This is not at all something merely perceptible that only following a process of generalization becomes conceptual, but from the beginning it is present already as a generalizing conceptual formation. For instance, if I see a dog it is present to me immediately under the aspect of 'dogness'. This way Arnheim moves in the opposite direction to Panofsky and the three fathers of the aesthetics of form. He does not go searching for a 'sublime' form beyond the sensible form but finds already in this one aspects of more abstract and elevated mental and spiritual activities of which it partakes. Perception consists in the formation of 'perceptive concepts'. Any external vision is already an internal vision. It conceives the object as a tri-dimensional totality with constant shape and not limited to any particular projective aspect. Shape never gives information on a single object but on the category to which it belongs. It is not the form of a particular thing but of a type of things. It is closer to the notion of *schema* differing from it by a greater emphasis on the active aspect of experience. In Arnheim the emphasis is not placed so much on repetition, on *pattern*,[27] as on the exploration of the world, on simplification, on globality and on the essentiality of experience.

However, shape is only the immediate moment of seeing: beside it and together with it the image is present as the *form* of a particular content. Only with form we enter into the sphere of true art, into the transformation of an object into image. In this regard, Arnheim is very critical of naturalism in art that sees in the image the naïve imitation of reality. For instance, death masks and plaster casts are in his view without form because they are not the result of an invention. The naturalistic tendency that became popular in Western art beginning with the Renaissance with the advent of perspective, forgets the difference between reality and image and considers the work of art simply as the replica of what is perceived by the eye of the artist. The specificity of art, to be precise, is not the invention of a subject and not even of a shape but of a form. Its faculty is precisely the imagination that Arnheim defines as the activity that makes possible to translate things in images. In this regard, he introduces a notion of fundamental importance for the later development of the aesthetics of form: *medium*. Any form must be inferred from the particular *medium* in which the image is fashioned. The intrinsic formal relation is not the one between the image and the thing reproduced, as naïve naturalism believes, but the one that intervenes between the images that belong to the same *medium*. For example a view of the Grand Canyon will have to be compared with pictures of other landscapes if we want to grasp its form. However, this does not mean that every *medium* is closed into itself. For Arnheim, there exists the possibility of translation from one medium to another, but in order for this to occur it is necessary to know both *media*. Leonardo's scientific designs constitute a great example of translation from scientific knowledge to artistic representation. Thus, any abstract reasoning can be translated into visual form and as such become an authentic part of a visual conception. In *Visual Thinking*,[28] he radicalizes this connection and claims that all thinking, fundamentally, has a visual form. Thus, he places himself at the opposite pole of the advocates of the aesthetics of the sublime. It is entirely meaningless to look for forms that go beyond the senses because the spiritual activities themselves are essentially sensible and formal!

A philosophically rigorous approach to these problems can be found in the work of the American Monroe Beardsley (1915–85) who focused his research on the specific traits of aesthetic experience that distinguishes itself from other types of experience because it is endowed with coherence, completeness, intensity and complexity. He defends energetically the legitimacy of *the aesthetic point of view* connecting it strictly with *gratification* which can be obtained from paying attention to the formal unity of something perceived as a whole and appreciated for itself.[29]

Aesthetic form and theology

We have seen how the problems of the contemporary aesthetics of form are deeply rooted in many aspects of religious sensibility of the various faiths. Aniconism and iconoclasm are attitudes that find their inspiration in Judaism, Islam and in the radical tendencies of Protestantism. Vice versa iconophilia has close relations to the orthodox Byzantine tradition. But the panorama of the relations between aesthetics and religion does not end here.[30] From the point of view of the aesthetics of form two authors are particularly important: the Swiss Hans Urs von Balthasar (1905–88), author of a Catholic theological aesthetics and the Anglo-Indian thinker Ananda K. Coomaraswamy (1877–1947) who studies the aesthetic premises of Asian religions in their connection with European culture. They both strive towards a theophany that is based on the notion of form.

The starting point of Balthasar's monumental work, *The Glory of the Lord: A Theological Aesthetics*[31] is precisely the word *Gestalt* which gives the title to the first volume, *The Perception of Form*. Not differently from Arnheim, the notion of *Gestalt* is useful to Balthasar to overcome right away the inherent difficulties in the metaphysical conception of form. In fact, on the one hand, he unifies the two aspects of supersensible and sensible form (*species=form*), on the other, he includes in the new notion of *Gestalt* also those elements that transcend form because they refer to an experience of the beautiful as event, incident, irruption of light (*lumen=splendour*) . These opposite characteristics of aesthetic experience, in fact, are united among them in the notion of *glory* (in Hebrew *kabôd*, in Greek *dóxa*) that both the Old and the New Testaments attribute to God. It sums up both the beautiful and the sublime, the form understood as mediation of sacred texts and ecclesiastic institutions, as well as the beyond of form understood as ecstasy, rapture, transport towards the invisible. Catholicism, thus, is the bearer of a religious sensibility that goes beyond the one-sidedness of both orthodox theology (too ritualistic and ceremonial), and Protestantism (too actualistic and energetic).[32] Nonetheless this does not imply a shift towards a type of religious-aesthetic syncretism. For Balthasar only Christianity is the aesthetic religion *par excellence* because only in it God resurrects as *form*, only in it historical form is not opposed to infinite light. In short, Catholic theological aesthetics implies a radical objectivism that both differs and is opposed to pure Protestant interiority, alien from any exteriority, and to any other meta-historical mysticism.

According to Coomaraswamy, in the Indian aesthetic-religious sensibility the whole world is considered as a form of God. The Sanskrit expression *nama-rupa*, in fact, considers in their unity *nama* (name, form, quiddity, *eîdos*) and *rupa* (phenomenon, aspect, appearance, body).[33] Aesthetic experience is realized as a real and proper identification between artist and model, contemplator and contemplated, spectator and work. Thus, Coomaraswamy opposes the Oriental mode of feeling to the Western one. While in the West life and form, the organic and the inorganic, are viewed as contrary and irreconcilable, in the East the experience of reality takes place in an act of non-differentiation between the poles of the sentient and non-sentient. On the one hand, the West produces a perverse idealism (which is manifested, for instance, in the iconoclastic refusal of sensible form[34]), on the other, it generates an astonishing insensibility (of which is proof the blind and deaf functionalism with respect to any beauty). In the East, instead, the aesthetic and the useful are harmonically joined together. While modern Western art, born in the Renaissance, privileges human form and it is conditioned by a concern with naturalistic imitation, Oriental works of art, in general, do not look for resemblance with something external; they tend to find God in a rock and in colours rather than in the flesh and they do not care at all for biological verisimilitude.

Form between media and the sublime

If Marcuse's work marks the passage of the aesthetics of life from metaphysics to politics, that of the Canadian scholar Marshall McLuhan (1911–80) marks the passage of the aesthetics of form from the philosophy of art to the philosophy of media. In his work, *Understanding Media*, McLuhan takes a turn of the greatest importance in which the problems of aesthetic form are reformulated in relation to the media.[35]

His starting point is a brilliant generalization and extension of Wölfflin's theories of forms of representation (Classical and Baroque). Even for McLuhan, there are two fundamental modes of perception. One homogeneous, simple, linear, visual, hierarchical, explosive (strictly connected with writing, print, photography, radio, cinema and automobiles), the other multicentre, participating, tactile, instantaneous and implosive (corresponding to electricity, telegraph, telephone, television and computer). The first form is typical of the 'hot' medium. It extends the single sense of sight up to a high definition that limits enormously the possibility of participation of the consumer. It is full of data that imply an even and mechanical consumption. The second form, instead, belongs to the 'cold' medium which, being at a low definition, requires the active intervention of the consumer.[36] It is representative, 'gestaltic', totalizing, related to orality and multi-sensorial. 'Hot' media have conditioned the modern age (from the Renaissance on) which, however, is only a parenthesis comprised between two 'cold' ages, between the oral, tribal and primitive age and the electric age of our day, of which McLuhan is the enthusiastic interpreter. The various aesthetics of form, with which we have dealt so far, located the alternative to the Classical in some past formal dimension (Baroque, Gothic, Byzantine, etc.). With McLuhan, instead, the high road of Western technological development provides the antidote to the uniform and homogeneous linearity of the mechanical era through a radical shift that opens the way to an essentially new and highly creative aesthetic era! But what is really a *medium*? At first glance we could define it as a kind of historical a priori in the Kantian sense, namely, a form that conditions the experience of an era. Under this aspect the content, the message that it transmits, is entirely secondary and subordinate. For McLuhan, the formative power of the medium is in itself, as he states with a particularly happy formula: 'The medium is the message.' Beside this definition there is another that underlines the relation between form and exteriority: the medium, he writes, is an extension of ourselves, our senses and our perceptive faculties. It reproduces, technologically, processes that belong to man, yet rendering them unrecognizable to him. Every extension is numbness, anesthesia, amputation. It is no longer the 'I' who feels something but the technological extension of my faculty that feels in my place. Technology, therefore, opposes me who do not recognize it as one of my extensions, as something that belongs to me. It is the idol that has taken my place. With the advent of electronic media we have placed our central nervous system outside ourselves. How to get out from this technological shock? Here emerges the third aspect of media that differentiates it from the 'a priori' form: their tendency to hybridize. They do not remain closed in themselves but they interact, running into each other and generating unforeseen effects. In short, the media have an enormously more rapid and surprising dynamic than traditional aesthetic forms.

In his last work, *Laws of the Media*,[37] McLuhan offers a very interesting view of this dynamic that unfolds in four stages. The first one, *enhancement*, consists in intensifying some aspect of a situation in which a meaning is extended. In the second one, *obsolescence*, the past situation is made impotent through its removal. In the third one, *retrieval*, something which for some time was obsolete is put back into service. Finally, in the fourth one, *reversal*, creates a new shape that has characteristics both similar and opposite to the starting point. By means of this tetrad McLuhan interprets many phenomena of contemporary life. From the point of view of the aesthetics of form, the significance of this theory consists in the fact that it underscores once again the connection between form and transcendence. The forms do not stay close in themselves but are constantly moved by a movement that goes beyond them. One of McLuhan's strengths is to have pointed out that this movement is not unidirectional but takes on an infinite variety of shapes.

However, there are only a few thinkers who share McLuhan's enthusiasm for the new *media*. Towards him we find repeated the iconoclastic attitude that views sensible forms with suspicion,[38] which brings about a renewed interest in the notion of sublime. The French philosopher Jean-François Lyotard (1924–98) sees in avant-garde art the manifestation *par excellence* of the sublime. In fact, it nourishes a radical suspicion with respect to the beautiful appearance of the forms and sets itself the task of asserting the presence of what escapes representation.[39] However, Lyotard rejects the spiritualistic conclusions to which iconoclasm leads (as we have seen, for instance, with respect to the notion of form as idea in Panofsky's analysis). Although he recognizes that the destination of the sublime is what makes possible an experience of the absolute through the deficiency of form, he does not want to abandon the sphere of immanence. Therefore, Lyotard ends by attributing to avant-garde art the paradoxical task of manifesting the immateriality of the sublime through matter. This materiality can only be 'minimal'. The mystery of the sublime, of which Kant was the greatest interpreter, consists, precisely, in perceiving through the sensible something that the sensible cannot represent under the aspect of form. Aesthetic experience exceeds sensibility but refuses to get lost in the fog of the transcendent. It is entirely concentrated in asserting the presence of something unnamable that escapes sensation. Lyotard describes it as 'neuter', 'grey', blank' that dwells in the shades of a sound, a chromatism, a voice.[40]

From the immaterial to the virtual the step is short. It does not appear that the aesthetic reflections so far devoted to the virtual bring about a new conception of form. It is difficult to avoid the impression that just as the aesthetics of life the aesthetics of form has also ended up in a blind alley. We get this impression from a closer examination of the respective theses of McLuhan and Lyotard. They represent two opposite ways of understanding the relation between media and art. Whereas the former sees exchange and interaction, the latter sees opposition and incompatibility. Both, however, are engaged in the basic problem of any aesthetics of form: 'how to think form without being dragged by its movement toward transcendence?' And if this is inevitable, 'how to think the movement of "going beyond" in an immanent way?' And yet, while they try to provide an answer to these questions, the entire problematic field, within which they move, is changing. McLuhan identifies as the point of arrival of his research a 'unified sensorium' which goes beyond the limits of a formal, divided experience. The interaction of all the senses ought to create an involvement that unifies experience. Lyotard sees in 'enthusiasm' the extreme mode of the sublime. In it the failure of the attempt at representation reverses in a strongly energetic experience of the limitless.[41] Nonetheless, the aesthetics of form finds here its conclusion and another chapter opens on the aesthetic of feeling. An interpretation of the notion of sublime in this sense was attempted by the Slovenian philosopher Slavoj Žižek (b. 1949) who combines the Kantian notion of sublime with a problematic that derives from the French psychoanalyst Jacques Lacan, and defines the sublime as the awareness of the nullity of what is beyond phenomena.[42]

3

Aesthetics and Knowledge

Aesthetic truth and self-referentiality

The aesthetics of life and the aesthetics of form, with which we have dealt so far, claim both their origins in Kant. The same is not the case for the aesthetics of knowledge, that is, that aspect of contemporary aesthetics that considers art as the bearer of truth and attributes to it an essentially gnoseological value and function. Kant had expressly excluded this possibility. In his view, aesthetic judgement provides no knowledge of its object whatsoever, not even a confused one. Neither the judgement of the beautiful nor that of the sublime can make any cognitive claims.[1] Other eighteenth- and nineteenth-century philosophers have had different opinions. The founder of aesthetics as an autonomous discipline, the German Alexander Gottlieb Baumgarten (1714–62), considers it as that aspect of gnoseology that focuses on sensible knowledge distinct from logic which is concerned with intellectual knowledge.[2] The German philosopher and theologian Friedrich Daniel Ernst Schleiermacher (1768–1834) views aesthetics as part of the cognitive function and emphasizes the role of art in the knowledge of the individual.[3] Finally for the great German philosopher Georg Wilhelm Friedrich Hegel (1770–1831), art together with religion and philosophy is a moment of absolute spirit and constitutes, therefore, one of the highest historical manifestations of truth.[4]

This tendency finds a significant development in the twentieth century. The extraordinary success of the physical and natural sciences take importance and credit away from philosophy with the result that many philosophers take a stand against them. They question whether they hold the monopoly of knowledge as Kant thought. Even more dangerous for philosophy is the application of scientific methods to traditionally humanistic areas. The growth of psychology, anthropology and semiotics seem to remove entire fields of knowedge from philosophy in general and from aesthetics in particular. Instead of examining the actual philosophical novelties that the human sciences can bring, various strategies are developed to counteract their infiltration mostly by negating the legitimacy of their knowledge. Entire philosophical currents such as neo-Hegelianism, phenomenology and hermeneutics, are constituted on this reactive base with respect to the human sciences aiming to reassert the gnoseological primacy of philosophy. These currents reserve a different treatment for aesthetics: sometimes they attribute to it a role of the greatest importance that aims at routing the competition of the human sciences; in other cases, they overcome it in new philosophical approaches to art that are thought to be more suitable than aesthetic tradition to capture the essence of the artistic phenomenon. From the 'hard liners' of neo-Hegelianism, phenomenology and hermeneutics, we pass to the 'soft' strategy of thinkers like Cassirer who place the human sciences into the background by emphasizing the direct affinities between the physico-natural sciences and art.

Cognitive aesthetics, therefore, offers a very wide and complex panorama. What brings together so many different philosophers and scholars is the claim of attributing a truth value to art. The question posed by all of them can be put this way: 'What kind of knowledge brings artistic experience?' To be sure, this is a strange question. It is difficult for me to argue that it was particularly present to the attention of contemporary artists and poets. To be sure, it is a reaction to the celebratory exigencies of contemporary art, but only in certain cases philosophy appears to be worried enough to meet these needs. The real motor of cognitive aesthetics resides in an exclusively philosophical preoccupation, not different from the one that led to the constitution of aesthetics in the eighteenth century. At the time, the problem was to elevate the sensible to the dignity of knowledge and to situate within the philosophical system the so-called inferior faculties.[5] Now it is a question of laying claim to the essentially theoretical character of art and to bring back under philosophical jurisdiction those territories that the human sciences had appropriated. This way, I do not mean to diminish at all the importance of the aesthetic solutions proposed by neo-Hegelianism, phenomenology and hermeneutics. In an era hostile to philosophy they brought back under the aegis of philosophical thinking entire fields of knowledge and they asserted, above all, the independence of artistic experience with respect to empirical approaches very often reductive and trivial. However, it is very difficult to avoid the impression that the price paid for these genial strategic operations was very high. The theoretical celebration of art responds to exigencies that are more philosophical than artistic. To assert the cognitive value of art means not only to grant to art something that after all it is not interested in, but also to deploy expectations and issues that are extraneous to it. Philosophy ends up by finding in art nothing but itself. In cognitive aesthetics philosophy does not make the effort to understand what is other from itself but looks for and finds itself. Self-reference, self-referentiality, circularity, seem to constitute their surreptitious assumptions. In speaking of others, in fact, they speak about themselves because, essentially, they maintain that true knowledge is self-knowledge. Hence the truth of the arts is not in themselves but in the philosophy that interprets them or, better yet, that philosophical thinking is the bearer of a truth that art could not arrive at by itself or, at least, which it cannot be fully aware of without the help of philosophy. Under the guise of a celebration we end up by placing in evidence a lack.

Aesthetics as intuitive knowledge

At the beginning of the twentieth century cognitive aesthetics finds in the work of Benedetto Croce (1866–1952) one of its most powerful and radical expressions. In *The Aesthetic as the Science of Expression and of the Linguistic in General* and in other works, Croce elaborates a complex and original theory that assigns to aesthetics a leading role.[6] Croce's starting point consists of asserting the identity of intuition and expression in which he joins together in an inseparable relation intuition, an essentially cognitive faculty (which the philosophical tradition considers a form of knowledge that has an immediate relation to its object) and expression (which philosophical tradition considers an external manifestation of something). In order to be able to establish this identity he is compelled to force somewhat the traditional meaning of these terms. Intuition, which for him is synonymous of art, loses its contemplative aspect and acquires an active one, while expression, identified with art, cannot be simply the manifestation of something internal that preserves its own independent being from external appearance. In other words, the intuited image does not exist before its expression and is not independent from it. The expression is not the physical translation because one does not exist without the other. For Croce an intuition without expression is not even conceivable. On the one hand, this excludes those who claim to have extraordinary inner experiences without having the ability, the time or the opportunity to express them. On the other, it confers an intrinsic ideal meaning to artistic forms, which can never be either the result of mere technical activity or mere natural things. Thus, any spiritualistic conception, which considers intuition as something sublime that cannot be represented, is excluded. Croce has only sarcasm for religious and mystic aesthetics 'which is hospital material when it is not political' (*A*, I, 8). There is no beauty so pure that can do without expression! At the same time any merely technical or naturalistic conception of art is put aside. Aesthetic experience has nothing to do with expression, reproduction or communication which are practical activities and not theoretical. Croce also excludes the possibility of the naturally beautiful. There is no such a thing as a beautiful thing because the beautiful is not a thing, does not belong to things but to the activity of man, to his spiritual energy. There is no such a thing as a so-called natural beauty which an artist would not modify somehow!

While Kant distinguished three faculties (theoretical, practical and aesthetic), Croce reduces the fundamental forms of the Spirit to two: the theoretical (which includes aesthetics and logic) and the practical (which includes economics and ethics). Aesthetics, therefore, has nothing to do with the practical which does not produce knowledge, but actions. With the theoretical form man understands things, with the practical form he changes them. Therefore, Croce also condemns all those theories that connect the aesthetic to anything practical. He defends with great energy the freedom of art from any moral claim. To discriminate moral works from immoral ones is equally absurd, like 'judging the square moral and the triangle immoral'![7] The image in itself is neither moral nor praiseworthy or blameworthy. It is more difficult, in case, to safeguard the independence of aesthetics with respect to intellectual knowledge, but also on this point Croce is categorical. While intellectual knowledge is always realistic, that is, it aims to establish the reality or unreality of its own object, intuitive knowledge does not care whether the image is real or not. It considers the image in its value as mere image. Just as moral judgement, the discrimination between true and false in art is equally out of place. Its realm is that of fancy. The problem created at this point can be put this way: 'What is the theoretical value of knowledge if it disregards completely questions of truth and falsehood?' Although art is knowledge of the individual, it also has a more or less legitimate claim to universality. On what is it based? Beside intuition and expression a third element intervenes: feeling. Differently from the immediate feeling, the feeling of which art is the expression has a universally valid character. It transcends and transfigures the specific particularities of the emotional and affective experience of the single. Croce attributes to feeling a total and cosmic dimension. In every work of art the entire universe is depicted.[8] Therefore, art implies acquiring a distancing with respect to the passions and the reaching of a state which is theoretical precisely because it disregards the empirical events of the artist. This is what the ancients meant by the term 'catharsis' and the moderns with the theory of 'impersonality' of art.[9] The three fundamental elements of aesthetic experience, intuition, expression and feeling are held together by a kind of 'synthesis a priori'. In fact, feeling must not be considered a particular emotional content but a way of looking at the world *sub specie intuitionis* (*BA*, II), that is, according to an optic which is free from pleasure and pain, desire and fear.

But there are other aspects of Croce's system that are worthy of attention because they illustrate how broad is the sphere of the aesthetic. In the first place, the assertion that the only possible knowledge is art and philosophy, may come as a surprise to the modern reader. In his youthful work, Croce regarded history to be closer to aesthetics than to logic. It is not subject to laws or concepts but posits intuitions and therefore it can be reduced under the general concept of art. The distinction that it makes between real and unreal depends on memory (and therefore on the contrast between different types of intuition), and not on a distinction between truth and falsehood. What has really happened, just as what has only been imagined, is the object of intuition and memory, not conceptual knowledge (*A*, III).[10] As far as the 'natural sciences' are concerned (psychology among them) they are not sciences at all. For what in them is true they partake of either history or philosophy. Linguistics is also said to be completely identical with aesthetics, which takes on the function of monopolizing the entire sphere of non-conceptual knowledge.

Differently from Hegel, to whom one often reproaches to have placed art under the aegis of conceptual knowledge, Croce asserts in the most energetic way the independence of art with respect to philosophy: the first can very well stay without the second but the relation is not reciprocal as the concept cannot stay without the expression. As for the practical forms, the economic which looks for the useful and ethics which is the will of the universal, they presuppose the theoretical forms. As a result, the aesthetic is the only form of the spirit which is independent of the others. If linguistic expression is itself immediately a theoretical act, language, as a result, is creation and languages have no reality outside the works of art in which they exist concretely. Rarely has aesthetics been assigned such a great historical and social role. Its importance is also manifested in the negation of the ugly. If the beautiful is identified with expression, there is no expression that does not contain a degree of beauty!

In Croce the coincidence between idealism and immanentism is striking. For instance, it derives from an interesting parallelism between aesthetics and economics, both considered to be 'mundane sciences', unknown in the Middle Ages, born in the modern era and inspired by a radical anti-ascetic and anti-transcendentalist attitude.[11] Croce grants to aesthetics complete autonomy with respect to logic, just as he totally emancipates the search for the useful, which is at the basis of economics (identified with politics) with respect to ethics, raising it to a fundamental category of the spirit. All the major concepts of modern philosophy, Croce remarks, derive from these two sciences without which we could not have arrived at the logic of dialectics, science of the concrete universal.

Finally, it is important to underscore the identity Croce establishes between genius and taste, between the productive activity of the artist and the reproductive one of the consumer of the work of art. In fact, Croce claims that both the creator and the beneficiary of art partake of the same lyrical intuition, which constitutes the essential. This way Croce confers the greatest importance on the experience of reading poetry, on the visualization of the figurative arts and on music listening. These activities are placed on the same level *tout court* with those of the poet, the painter and the musician! Thus, is there no substantial difference between writing the *Divine Comedy* and reading it? Is there only a simple 'diversity of circumstances' between the two activities? (*A*, I, 16). Very rarely in the history of aesthetics, the fruition of the work of art has been held in such high esteem. Equally rare is the full and total capacity of judgement assigned to the artist. On the one hand, Croce's aesthetics implies an intelligent public and a class of well-educated artists, on the other, he constitutes it. It is organic with respect to an artistic-literary civilization that assigns to philosophy the task of legitimizing its own foundation. Therefore, the assignation of aesthetics to the theoretical sphere of the Spirit is an almost obligatory strategic choice. It is Croce's merit to have asserted and reiterated with extreme energy the existence of a theoretical experience which is nevertheless completely independent of the distinction between truth and falsehood. Thus, Croce saves at one and the same time the solemnity and the freedom of art safeguarding it from any intrusion in its field of moral and conceptual preoccupations. He succeeded remarkably (and perhaps in an unparalleled way) to guarantee both the social relevance and the absolute autonomy of aesthetic experience, attributing to it at the same time a widespread and propaedeutic character with respect to all human activities.[12]

Aesthetics as intentional knowledge

According to Croce, there exists a cognitive experience that can disregard completely the distinction between truth and falsehood: it is aesthetic intuition! According to the German philosopher Edmund Husserl (1859–1938), a similar experience is not only possible but constitutes the essential characteristic of philosophical knowledge which is radically different from the knowledge of the natural sciences and psychology. For Husserl philosophy is constituted as a 'rigorous science' precisely through a 'phenomenological *epoché*' that leaves out of consideration the existence of the things of the world and even the existence of the world as a whole. For Husserl it is possible to gather the essence of things only by means of 'eidetic intuition' that places their existence in parenthesis just as it excludes any psychological aspect. The characteristic of philosophical knowledge is precisely its 'intentionality', that is, the reference to an object different from the knowing subject.

We cannot help but be struck by the existing affinities between Husserl's theory of knowledge and the traits that an entire philosophical tradition, from Kant onward, has attributed to aesthetic experience. The act that throws off course the reality of the world in the 'phenomenological epoché' is similar to the 'disinterestedness' that Kant attributed to aesthetic judgement or to Schopenhauer's aesthetic contemplation. Husserl himself was aware of these affinities. Even though the aesthetic question was essentially extraneous to his interests, he remarks in some writings between 1906 and 1918 on the deep concordance between the phenomenological method and aesthetic intuition.[13]

Both require an essentially divergent positioning from the 'natural' one. The work of art is poles apart from any existential claim, just as it is from any feeling or willing anything real. The activity of the artist differs from that of the psychologist and anthropologist, but is similar to that of the phenomenologist. For art as for philosophy, the reality of the world is indifferent. They don't accept any existence as 'pre-data'. For both what counts is the evidence, which is the manifesting and the presenting of the object in its essence to consciousness. Nonetheless between the philosopher and the artist persists a difference. While the former grasps the sense of the phenomenon through concepts, the latter tends to appropriate it intuitively.

The aesthetic problem, instead, is at the centre of the interests of the Polish scholar Roman Ingarden (1893–1970), the author of a monumental work, *The Literary Work of Art*.[14] In this phenomenology, the 'essences' become the 'metaphysical qualities' of experience that present themselves in minimal measure in ordinary life. Only art can give us a serene contemplation of them. In art metaphysical qualities are not realized but concretized and revealed. But what type of knowledge does it allow us? In what sense can we speak of a 'truth' of the work of art? After excluding the most common meanings in which this expression can be understood (factual truth, explanatory truth, objective coherence), Ingarden concludes by asserting that the truth of art consists in the 'essential concatenation brought to intuitive self-presentation' (*LWA*, #52). But in what way the emergence of a self-representative dimension is reconciled with intentionality, the strong point of the phenomenological method, which is the exact opposite of any self-reference? One must distinguish between 'metaphysical qualities' and works of art. The latter is not at all an ontologically autonomous entity which could vie for the crowning of autonomy which is self-reference. In fact, Ingarden's whole work aims at emphasizing the heteronomous and intentional character of the literary work which is a complex, polyphonic entity organized in four heterogeneous levels: vocal linguistic formations, unity of meaning, multiple schematized visions and represented objectivities.

The result is that the ontological status of art is, so to speak, intermediary between reality and ideality. The intellectual strategy pursued by Ingarden has a twofold orientation. On the one hand, it aims at distinctly separating art from naturalistic and psychological data. Aesthetic experience entails the existence of a distance with respect to factual data. For instance, the declarative propositions that appear in the literary work have only a *quasi* evaluative character. On the other hand, Ingarden does not mean to identify art at all with essence. He wants to keep the work anchored to an apparently external and extrinsic phenomenon, such as the vocal-linguistic layer. They are considered as necessary elements of the work and prevent its transposition in purely ideal and not intentional contexts.

These two aspects are reasserted with particular energy in the *Aesthetik* of the German philosopher Nicolai Hartman (1882–1953) which constitutes the most considerable product of phenomenological aesthetics.[15] Hartmann too asks the question of the cognitive character of aesthetics. His answer is a drastic one: this cognitive claim concerns exclusively the aesthetic as philosophical science of the beautiful, but does not concern at all either the producer or the consumer of works of art. Hartmann excludes categorically that artistic experience is in itself a mode of knowledge. Art has nothing to do with knowledge. It is simply the object of a science of which neither the artist nor the consumer have any need. This is what aesthetics is about. This way Hartmann preserves the intentional character of aesthetic knowledge which in no way can be identified with its object. Art is something too complex and enigmatic to be resolved in philosophy!

Hartmann's aesthetic approach echoes Husserl's invitation to turn directly to the 'things themselves'. In his view, one has to free oneself of the aesthetic idealism that blinds us with respect to the real given. The sensible, concrete, immediate aspect of the artistic object constitutes 'a vision of the highest order', not unlike the common, daily vision of things in the world. Hartman recalls us energetically to the real object of perception, just as it presents itself in a vision that it is not yet aesthetic and constitutes the 'foreground' (*Vordergrund*) of the work of art. Idealism claims to do without this immediate given. Plato, Plotinus, Marsilio Ficino consider the beautiful as something independent from perception and from the real object, something supersensible and intelligible. But the real given is something unavoidable for aesthetic experience, it is what establishes it as such, distinguishing it from philosophy. A theory that negates the sensible aspect of art regarding it as form of knowledge, disregards its essence.

On this 'vision of the first order', according to Hartmann, is grafted a 'vision of the second order' which has a supersensible character. It adds to the sensible given something new that separates it clearly from everyday perception, conferring upon it its particular aesthetic character. This is the background (*Hintergrund*) of the work of art which is equally objective as the first level but, differently from it, it is not real. One could define it by appealing to the 'imagination' but this term runs the risk of being understood in a too subjective manner. In reality, the beautiful, according to Hartmann, has an essential duplicity. It is both real (in its sensible and thing-like dimension) and unreal (in its extension and in its supersensible expansion). It has the character of 'enigma' because it is and it is not itself at the same time. The work of art is exuberant with respect to the materials of which it is composed. It is detached and 'suspended' with respect to actuality. Non-implementation (*Entwirklichung*) is one of its essential aspects. That is why naturalism, which claims to provide the illusion of the real, is absolutely extraneous to true art. The departure with no return from reality constitutes the essence of the beautiful which is 'shielded' with respect to the real.

The point of arrival of phenomenological aesthetics, therefore, seems to be a kind of ontology of the work of art that thinks aesthetic experience under the notion of 'apparition', a status half way between the real and the possible but not for this reason transcendental and other worldly. With respect to Croce and his genial 'political' strategy that connects the aesthetic to all the other human activities and succeeds in joining it to the life of culture and society while asserting its autonomy, the phenomenologist gives the impression of being a 'monastic' philosopher . The freedom and the isolation that he claims for art resembles the freedom and isolation that he asks of philosophy. The art that he theorizes is the bearer of a quasi-truth and resembles a quasi-philosophy. The fact is that his philosophy is already since its beginning a quasi-art.

Arts as hermeneutic knowledge

The most radical identification of art with philosophical knowledge is the work of the German philosopher Hans-Georg Gadamer (1900–2002) whose work *Truth and Method* contains a close critique of Kant's aesthetics and of neo-Kantianism, as well as the proposal of its dissolution in hermeneutics.[16]

According to Gadamer, Kant's notion of truth is too narrow and limited. He restricts the concept of knowledge to the theoretical and practical use of reason, that is to say, he has misunderstood the cognitive character of humanistic culture. Kant regards as rational only the method of the natural sciences and the moral categorical imperative, confining the experience of art and the exercise of critical taste to the sphere of subjectivity and feeling, genius and aesthetic consciousness. Like Croce, Gadamer rejects Kant's proposal to found aesthetics autonomously outside the tutelage of speculative thought. But while Croce preserves the autonomy of art with respect to the claims of the concept, Gadamer, with greater theoretical extremism, brings art back under the domain of speculation. From this viewpoint, his theoretical strategy is closer to Hegel than to Croce. Therefore, both the aesthetics of life and the aesthetics of form fall under Gadamer's axe, both considered unhappy products of Kantianism. As far as the first is concerned, it is the result of the exaggerated importance acquired in aesthetics by the subject and by the attendant emphatic exaltation of the living and the immediate, of which Bergson and Simmel are the leaders.[17] As far as the second is concerned, the object of Gadamer's critique is above all the persisting of organic metaphors. In fact, as long as the symbol is understood as a 'living form' which develops spontaneously (as opposed to allegory, considered as something cold and intellectualistic) we cannot escape aesthetic vitalism (*TM*, I, I, 2, c).

According to Gadamer, the aesthetic mode introduces a way of positioning with respect to art that is entirely inadequate. The experience of art cannot be reduced and confined within the ephemeral circle of 'aesthetic consciousness'. He criticizes, in particular, the phenomenon of 'aesthetic differentiation' through which art is placed in an ideal sphere completely severed from reality, which now is defined as 'pure', now as 'apparent'. Thus, the ontological significance of the work of art and its profound co-appurtenance to being and truth is being misunderstood. The theories of 'pure seeing' or 'pure hearing' are dogmatic abstractions: artistic perception always gathers some meaning.

Moving to the *pars construens* of his theory, Gadamer, surprisingly, introduces the notion of *play*. At first sight, therefore, his intellectualism seems mitigated by the role that he assigns to the experience of play. However, by 'play' he does not mean to refer at all to the subjective meaning of the term (employed in the eighteenth century by Kant and Schiller, and in the twentieth century by Marcuse).[18] 'Play' is an impersonal entity that sets its own rules on those that partake in it. It absorbs the player to itself and frees him from the obligation of a merely subjective initiative. However, even play is the object of a choice. One always plays at something and in the course of its unfolding various options are possible. Play, therefore, is the first ontological determination of the work of art. On it is grafted what is perhaps the most important aspect of art, representation, its transfiguration in a form that implies by definition the existence of a spectator, of a consumer. Performance arts, which entail an execution such as music and theatre, constitute for Gadamer the model starting from which any other form of art is thinkable. In his view, even figurative art is the reproduction of an original in the sense that 'it is in the place of' this. This law applies to architecture, which implies a double intrinsic relation as to the purpose and as to the place in which it rises, as well as to literature to which the moment of reading is intrinsic. The fundamental intention that drives Gadamer's reflection on art consists in emphasizing on any occasion the mediated aspect of artistic activity. The latter does not have at all the character of absolute spontaneity and creativity without assumptions that vitalism attributed to it. Gadamer places value on the importance and the constant presence of the humanistic and philological tradition, of its leading concepts (culture, common sense and good taste). Therefore, he rehabilitates, against the method of the Enlightenment, the notions of historical transmission, authority and even prejudice!

Only by proceeding so radically, can Gadamer, in fact, reduce artistic experience to a particular case of textual interpretation, dissolving it entirely in what he considers the cognitive activity par excellence, namely, hermeneutics. Therefore he claims that aesthetics has to give its place to hermeneutics. In fact, not only every fruition of art is a textual interpretation but even any art is already an interpretation, a positioning with respect to something given, a reproducing it and representing it. This way the theoretical dimension is not something that depends on a philosophical approach to art but belongs essentially already to art which has therefore an intrinsic relation to truth. In other words, it is not the philosopher who establishes a posteriori relation between art and knowledge but it is the artist who already in his actions behaves as a hermeneut. This excludes any eccentricity and subjective arbitrariness because hermeneutic understanding is not a private action of the single but the intervention in the heart of a process of historical transmission where past and present merge.

Therefore, it seems more legitimate to ask what is the difference between what an artist does and an interpreter does, between philosophy and poetry. On this point, Gadamer's position is considerably far from Hegel's. Poetizing seems to have a closer relationship with interpreting than with philosophizing. Or, better, the inexhaustible ambiguity of poetic language seems capable of constituting a real determination of being better than what the interpreting reflection can.[19] Interpretation can never be resolved in complete self-transparency. While science claims to objectify experience to such an extent that it forgets its own historicity, hermeneutics is always aware of itself as historically other with respect to its object. However, this self-awareness can never be resolved in a knowledge completely open and spread out because the clarification of the situation in which we live is a task which is never resolved (*TM*, II, II, 1, d). The dissolution of the aesthetic in hermeneutics does not imply the identity *tout court* of the hermeneut with the philosopher. In Gadamer there is a transfer of knowledge beyond philosophy, not in the direction of science but towards poetry and art. This brings about a paradoxical outcome. While science, in fact, claims by definition its own statute as holder of knowledge, poetry and the arts do not make a similar claim. It would seem that with Gadamer philosophy reasserts its primacy, indirectly, through the ontological celebration of art without that the latter requests or supports such action.

In the last instance, what characterizes Gadamer's thought is the tension between hermeneutics and the ontology of art. On the one hand, what arrives at expression is not the activity of the subject but the universal ontological structure towards which the subject is passive. However, on the other hand, the being of the work of art does not have an 'in itself' that can be distinguished from its execution or from the occasional circumstances in which it presents itself. On the ruins of aesthetic and historic conscience, philosophy, having refused the road of self-consciousness and spiritualism, abandons itself completely to appearances in the certainty, nonetheless, of always finding itself. It is precisely with this recurrence that philosophy asserts it own diversity from art.[20]

Art as symbolic knowledge

To re-establish the legitimacy of the philosophical approach to art, language, myth and religion, without breaking the relation between philosophy and the sciences of nature, this was the fundamental intention of the German philosopher Ernst Cassirer (1874–1945) who, without devoting an entire work to aesthetics, occupies an important place within the panorama of cognitive aesthetics. In fact, differently from Croce, Husserl and Gadamer, he claims that attributing a theoretical value to art is not at all in contradiction with recognizing a cognitive value to science. Therefore, he arrives at asserting the primacy of philosophy, as others have done, but in ways less tortuous and fortuitous. Cassirer agrees with the three other fathers of twentieth century cognitive aesthetics on one point: the rejection of vitalism. In fact, he deplores the turn to subjectivism carried out by Bergson who placed the concept of life at the centre of every problem,[21] which looks for the essential element of the spirit in pure intuition, in an origin that precedes all mediated formations. But this metaphysical paradise is mere illusion. Human knowledge cannot do without mediations and externalizations. Even in art, which constitutes the privileged ground of the philosophy of life, the shift to creative spontaneity brings at best a hypnotism that has nothing to do with real aesthetic experience.[22]

Art and science, just as language, myth and religion, can be brought back to a common notion, that of *symbolic form*. They constitute, despite their internal diversity, the elements of a unique, great problematic connection and converge in reaching a single purpose: the transformation of a world of pure passive impressions in a universe of pure spiritual expressions. The same concept of 'symbolic form', which constitutes the pivot around which Cassirer's entire thinking turns, is the convergence point between the aesthetic use of the term, borrowed by nineteenth-century aesthetic[23] and its scientific use derived from the epistemology of his own time.[24] Knowledge is never the reflection of an external reality but an incessant edification of symbolic constructions that are placed as something external with respect to human subjectivity. Cassirer is interested in emphasizing the fact that cultural productions so diverse as art and science can be brought back to a common cognitive function, which becomes the task of philosophy to discover and illustrate.

In polemics with Husserl's phenomenology, whose theory of experience makes reference to the most original primary and sensible data of every meaning, Cassirer claims that in perception the order of signification in which it is inscribed is already present from the start.[25] There is no mere perceptual given of whatever content (such as Hartmann's 'vision of the first order') on which a symbolic meaning can be grafted. The phenomena are already situated in a symbolic horizon. Their pure way of manifesting cannot disregard the order of relations within which they are placed. They have a 'symbolic pregnancy', that is, they are inseparable from the dense gamut of intellectual connections that make possible and condition their appearance. Every sensorial data does not exist in an autonomous nakedness and purity, but it is always already at the service of a 'meaning'. For instance, the simple stroke of a line is viewed differently according to the symbolic horizon to which it belongs. What in a scientific work is recognized as an illustration of a geometric law, in an aesthetic context is recognized as an artistic ornament.

Only man possesses symbolic intelligence. Only man lives in a world of 'things'. Animals are unable to externalize their own experiences. They live in a sphere of wide ranging qualities that are not determined in definite and distinct objects, stable and permanent. Their world is for them fluid and unrecognizable. Now, among the symbolic activities the artistic one moves towards the greatest objectification. It does not create a world of vague sensations but of precise figures, melodies and rhythms.[26] And, in fact, art is above all form, knowledge of forms. Without art the most profound aspects of reality would be inaccessible to us. While the scientific symbol shortens and impoverishes reality by providing an abstract representation, art entails a process of intensification and concretization of reality. But this does not imply an exacerbation of conflicts. In fact, the essence of aesthetic experience consists precisely in the harmonization and the reconciliation between different trends.[27] That is why tradition has justly reserved to artists alone the attribute of 'genius'. With respect to art, science is a unilateral activity.

This notwithstanding, even for Cassirer, as for neo-idealism, phenomenology and hermeneutics, the last word rests with philosophy. It is the only activity capable to grasp the unity of the human world whose fundamental characteristic is that of being strictly interwoven with cultural mediations. These envelop it on every side and do not allow any space that would make it possible to grasp its substance in an immediate and intuitive way. Anyone, as Kleist wrote, 'who travels around the world to see if by chance it has an opening in the back at some point', will observe that this point does not exist.[28] The work of philosophy, however, is not done out of love for itself but to ground knowledge on foundations that are certain but not absolute. This work cannot be conducted by the human sciences (psychology, ethnology, anthropology, history) because although their analyses are thorough and penetrating, they do not succeed in controlling and organizing the empirical data in which they are imprisoned. Nonetheless, one cannot avoid the impression that the last word of Cassirer's philosophy is meta-philosophical in nature. Once again the search for the conditions of knowledge is resolved in a discourse on the activities that develop this research. As long as self-referentiality remains the ideal model of every rigorous knowledge, aesthetics will speak more of itself than of art.

Aesthetics and the knowledge of alterity

The four tendencies that we have examined so far – Croce's neo-idealism, phenomenology, hermeneutics and the philosophy of symbolic forms – present two common characteristics: a rejection of subjective vitalism and the attribution to aesthetics or art of a cognitive dimension. These two premises are also shared by the father of analytical psychology the Swiss Carl Gustav Jung (1875–1961) and, at least the first one, by the French thinker Gaston Bachelard (1884–1962). They, however, do not recognize a cognitive value to philosophy and claim, rather, that it is science to hold the key to knowledge.

By drawing on Schiller's distinction between 'sentimental poetry' and 'naïve poetry', Jung identifies two different types of works of art: those that are characterized by the author's claims, his intentions and conscious aims, and those whose creative process seems to have, instead, its own autonomous dynamic, independent of the subject.[29] In the former, the driving force is represented by the subjective will of the author. Over all these works do not contain more than what he has put in himself. In the latter, instead, the creative force is present as an extraneous force, 'other', which asserts itself on the author in a despotic manner. He is not fully aware of what he does because he is ruled by an aspiration that goes beyond the subject. It is to this second type of works of art that Jung turns his attention and appreciation. In fact, these express dimensions that are characterized by a radical alterity with respect to the conscious life of the individual and are endowed with a symbolic value capable of exercising a vast and lasting influence. In fact, their most profound relation is not with the personal subconscious of the author but with that patrimony of primordial images, archetypes, mythical symbols that constitute the 'collective unconscious' of humanity. Analytic therapy cannot reach it because it is neither repressed nor forgotten but constitutes an innate possibility which is actualized only by the creative imagination when it is freely exercised. Thus, it is capable of releasing a voice a thousand times more powerful than that of the individual. Symbolic and visionary art, differently from the merely subjective and psychological one, is the only door through which the unfamiliar, numinous and primeval world of archetypes becomes knowable.[30]

The great importance attributed to the cognitive function of art is not, however, the only reason that makes Jung appear more tied to the aesthetic tradition than either Freud or other exponents of psychoanalysis. Notwithstanding the quantitative scantiness of the specific contributions and the lack of understanding of contemporary art, Jung's thought has an 'aesthetic colouring' that stems from his tendency to provide reconciling and harmonizing solutions to psychic conflicts. Even the most traumatic human experience, the *enantiodromia*, that is, the reversal of a psychic characteristic into its opposite, represents a source of energy *par excellence* because it gives to the existential events of the individual the possibility of a 'new beginning'. Furthermore, it lays the premises for the constitution of a dynamic image of the Self, more synthetic and total, which dissolves tensions and harshness, and constitutes an effective synthesis of opposites.[31]

Bachelard, instead, at first sight, seems to be a thinker internally divided and dualistic. He is the author of two different types of work, one dedicated to epistemology and the other to the study of the imaginary. Bachelard's point of departure is closer to Husserl and Gadamer in the rejection of naturalistic vitalism. The struggle against vitalism, however, is not led in the name of philosophy but in the name of science.[32] The scientific spirit is born from the struggle against nature and from the refusal of animistic metaphors that claim to see manifestations of life everywhere. Reason can only be actualized starting from the moment when it breaks all ties with lived experience and creates a world other than the natural one. While the latter is chaotic and impure, the world created by techno-scientific civilization is an ordered cosmos, artificial, made of pure objects, which represents for man the only source of happiness and intimate satisfaction. It is not at all the reflection of the existent but a construction interwoven with thought and reason. Bachelard examines the long struggle conducted by scientific knowledge against the obstacles interposed on its way not only by naïve and primitive experience but also from philosophy which is a type of reason corrupted by the imagination and subordinated to the obscure vital impulses of nourishment and sexuality. Through its ties to the pre-scientific spirit of alchemy and natural history, philosophical thinking has placed itself at the service of life, it is the accomplice of natural chaos, the needs of the body and subjectivity. Therefore, Bachelard proposes a psychoanalysis of science that would free it and purify it of all the subterranean conditioning stemming from the biologico-natural components of human beings. The one thing certain is that in his apologia of the anonymous, impersonal and inorganic character of scientific knowledge, Bachelard places such great emphasis that it appears more a rhetoric of science than a work of epistemology. Besides, he himself considers science to be an 'aesthetics of intelligence'.[33] In fact, in his analysis, he seems animated by an aesthetic ideal of purity that finds its object in science.

If science becomes the object of aesthetic experience *par excellence,* what about literature and art? Bachelard poses the problem in *The Psychoanalysis of Fire*[34] and *Lautréamont*[35] that represent a moment of transition in his speculative journey. These two works mark the transition from a negative evaluation of the imagination, understood as the expression of naturalistic vitalism and a source of error, to a positive evaluation of the same, considered as *rêverie* endowed with its own autonomous purity and integrity.[36] Fire lends itself very well to establish the starting point of a research on the imaginary, precisely by virtue of the vitalistic symbolism that it implies: it is the ultra-living, the most secret intimacy, it shines in paradise and burns in Hell! In short, in its image merge multiple impulses that sink to the depths of our biopsychic constitution: from the tendency to seize the knowledge of our fathers (Prometheus complex), to the desire for a cosmic death (Empedocles complex), to the need for sexual warmth (Novalis complex), to seeking to transcend oneself through self-combustion where alcohol is the mean *par excellence* (Hoffman's complex). However, fire is also the symbol of purity. This last idealization opens the way to the detection of another realm emancipated as science with respect to nature and the world of life: precisely that of *rêverie*, that is, daydreams. It occupies an intermediary space between the dream and contemplation. One becomes acquainted with it, above all but not exclusively, through the work of poets. In fact, individual experience is the first door to which one gains access to it.

However, imagination is fully redeemed from vitalism only in the book on Lautréamont. Here Bachelard comes to terms with one of the most violent works in the history of literature, the famous *Songs of Maldoror* in which find expression the most aggressive and wild, inhuman and brutal aspects of animal life. Lautréamont, poet of the muscle and the scream, rebellion and cruelty, reverses itself in its opposite, in the virtual and in the abstract, through a device that recalls Jung's *enantiodromia*. Thus, Bachelard discovers a new world as pure as that of science. Violence and literature exclude one another reciprocally because real violence is mute, the prisoner of animal silence, unable to reach the de-realized and surreal peace of the imaginary.

Thus the road is open for a more systematic study of the structures of *rêverie* that Bachelard carries out in a trilogy devoted to water, air and land.[37] What is striking, first of all, is the inorganic orientation of his imagination. Bachelard distinguishes between a 'formal' imagination linked to nature and mimesis, and a 'material' imagination which frees itself from nature and suppresses form in the pure imagination. The first is tied to a vision and reproduces the real, the second, instead, entails a more essential relation to an amorphous, virtual material, susceptible of infinite transformations. The latter could be defined paradoxically as an 'imagination without images' continuously driven by the search for something new and 'other' which can never stop before a form and its outline. Therefore, it is permeated by an extreme dynamism that recoils from any objectification and even from any reality. On this aspect, Bachelard is the opposite of Croce. While the Italian philosopher, in identifying intuition with expression, grounds aesthetic experience solidly to cultural civilization, the French thinker confines it to a sphere which is by definition unreal or, better, surreal, whose ultimate justification is not cognitive but eudemonic. In fact, man the dreamer does not arrive at a more essential and profound knowledge, as in Jung. For Bachelard, the only true knowledge is the scientific one! The reverie has its end in itself, in the joy and in the happiness that gives generously to those who abandon themselves to it. The world to which it guarantees access is 'other' precisely because unreal, because it frees us from the weight, the obligation, the malaise that generates reality, whatever it may be!

At this point one could ask why Bachelard wrote these books instead of limiting himself to dreaming them. In effect, it was never his intention to create a science of the imaginary and not even a philosophy of psychic structures. Differently from Cassirer, he does not claim that there is a philosophical point of view, over and above science and the imagination which can explain the functioning of both. His last works on reverie are introduced as 'poetics'.[38] This term, however, must be understood not in the sense of a poetic programme but, on the contrary, in the sense of an extension of poetic experience, almost as if Bachelard wanted to de-realize poetic texts, that is, free them from their objectuality by returning them to the fluid and dynamic dimension of the reverie. Bachelard's intellectual journey is characterized by the continuous search for an 'alterity' with respect to the real, first discovered in science and then in *rêverie*. Therefore, it would seem that it takes a direction counter to self-referentiality that characterizes both neo-idealism and phenomenology (which, as we have seen, not even Gadamer and Cassirer are able to avoid). Thus, it comes as a surprise to find the self-referential device at work in one of his last works, *The Poetics of Reverie*, which leads him to question himself and to even propose a *cogito* of the dreamer, to identify studying with the object of studying, to make reveries on reveries, that is, to create a 'meta-reverie'. All this makes us think that not even Bachelard has succeeded in avoiding the fate of cognitive aesthetics that brings him inevitably to see in self-consciousness the form of knowledge *par excellence*.

Aesthetics as critical knowledge

We have seen how in the aesthetics of life and form, the second half of the twentieth century brings about a turning point through which the problematic outlined by the founding fathers is reintroduced in distorted ways and unrecognizable at first sight. Cognitive aesthetics is not an exception to this rule. To the *political* turn of the aesthetics of life and the *media* turn of the aesthetics of form corresponds the *sceptical* turn of cognitive aesthetics. It implicates all the four tendencies that we have examined so far: neo-Hegelianism, phenomenology, hermeneutics and the philosophy of symbolic forms.

The sceptical form of neo-Hegelianism is eminently represented by the German philosopher Theodor W. Adorno (1903–69), the author of numerous works on the philosophy of music and literature, as well as of a monumental *Aesthetic Theory*.[39] The term 'scepticism', however, must not be understood in the sense of relativism but as a downsizing of the ambitions of reason, which can no longer claim unduly to account for the entire existing. According to Adorno, Hegel's philosophy represents the highest attempt to comprehend the heterogeneous, what is other with respect to thinking, the non-identical, in a word, the *negative*. Therefore, it is necessary to radicalize the critical aspect of Hegelian philosophy without falling into the temptation of overcoming the contradiction in an autonomous, self-sufficient and self-referential totality. In fact, this is the task of 'negative dialectics' which looks at the non-conceptual as the motor of history and attempts to think it through concepts that will not do violence to its heterogeneity.[40] In other words, there is no longer the possibility of a philosophical foundation of reality, as well of a system that like Hegel's and Croce's identifies a certain number of forms of the spirit which are at the same time determinations of reality. But like Croce, Adorno claims that philosophy, and not science, maintains an essential relation with the knowledge of truth. To be sure, the latter can no longer be thought as something fixed, stable and unchangeable. Truth, like philosophy, is for Adorno something extremely fragile that requires the practice of a continuous critical activity, attentive to the transformations and subversions of things in their opposites, according to that movement of *enantiodromia* of which Hegel and Nietzsche, before Jung, were careful observers.[41] The search for truth is an unavoidable task of thinking. The proposal to abolish philosophy in praxis must be viewed with suspicion as, for the most part, it conceals the intention of silencing the critique of society of which philosophical thinking is the bearer, *par excellence*.

For Adorno too art is knowledge. All aesthetic problems are resolved in questions that revolve around the truth-content of works of art. Adorno has only sarcasm for hedonistic and vitalistic aesthetics that place pleasure or taste before everything else, and defines them as merely 'culinary'. This does not mean, however, that aesthetics must become the refuge of ontology, as is the case with phenomenology and hermeneutics. But it is a fact that to both philosophy and art is essential the relation to its opposite, to the heterogeneous, which lies hidden precisely within itself as doubt of its own legitimacy, as presence of exigencies that cannot be satisfied artistically, as continuous denial of the characteristics that aesthetic reflection attributes to it.

Those who have a soft and sublimated idea of artistic experience make a big mistake. The truth of the work of art is its hard core, which is often impure, outrageous and even incomprehensible. The work of art presents contradictory aspects which are naïve to pretend to overcome in a harmonic and peaceful vision. One of the major contradictions emerges from the opposition between its 'fetishistic' character and the dimension of *apparition* assumed by the artistically beautiful. In fact, if on the one hand, the work of art places itself as a thing among things, on the other hand, it reveals itself with the speed and immateriality of lightening. Thus the work of art appears sometimes as something motionless, sometimes as something dynamic. In fact, its truth becomes eloquent precisely on the strength of the trigger between *res* and *apparition*.

Adorno provides a very acute and penetrating analysis of both these terms. First of all one must not consider fetishism as synonymous of falsehood. Those who see in the 'thing' something radically false are prisoners of a logic of identity that precludes them from a knowledge of the heterogeneous, the negative, what is other with respect to thinking. Thus, they are excluded from any dialectical consideration of reality. The phenomenon of reification not only enslaves men to the logic of capitalism, it also forces a comparison with the real, which idealistic subjectivism avoids.[42] Poets have often spoken of the 'beautiful extraneousness' of the external world, and their love for things makes us reflect on the essential relation between art and fetishism.[43] Adorno goes so far as to claim that the quality and even the truth of works of art depend essentially on the degree of their fetishism, in the sense that the celebration implicit in their status of thing, distinct from useful objects, guarantees them complete liberty, emancipating them from any relation with mere entertainment. Paradoxically, it is precisely fetishism that preserves their 'seriousness'! This fetishism, in fact, represents an exception with respect to the status of commodities and is connected to the characteristic of magic objects, just as artistic production is not comparable to the conditions of economically useful labour.[44]

Nonetheless, art contains an aspect even opposite to reification, which renders it similar to lightening, fireworks or a heavenly manifestation. This is what Adorno understands by the term *apparition*. Even this aspect is strictly connected to the question of the truth of art. In fact, it entails the intrusion of something unforeseeable and unthinkable into reality, comparable to an explosion. It is not up to art to establish the ontological status of what appears, but it is certain that this event entails a spiritualization of the work of art which loses its materiality and almost turns against itself giving way to that process of overcoming that Hegel has described so well in his *Aesthetic*.[45] It is a process similar to the one described by Kant with the name of 'sublime'. Its essence is the claim of the spirit against the excessive powers of sensible experience.

For Adorno, the 'enigma' is the most appropriate notion to grasp the essence of art from a cognitive point of view. Differently from the secret, it cannot be resolved by understanding and interpretation. The truth of the work of art can no longer be resolved in the intentions of the artist. For example, Poe and Baudelaire, who are the heralds of the modern era, opposed society assuming and radicalizing its point of view. Opposition succeeds only through the identification with the point of view of the opponent, otherwise it degenerates into a naïve didactic and hortatory exhortation. This is precisely the Egyptian effect of every work of art. The same weapon both wounds and heals.[46]

The artist is not aware of this paradox. In fact, art is not transparent to itself and that is why it requires the help of philosophy. For Adorno genuine aesthetic experience must become philosophy or it does not exist at all.[47] On this aspect, Adorno is closer to Hegel than to Croce. In his view, the truth content of a work needs philosophy, especially, since art criticism has spectacularly failed in its task. However, we must not forget the essentially critical and questioning character that Adorno attributes to philosophy, so that in the end he is undecided whether it is art or philosophy that maintains a closer relation to truth. If philosophy were to spell out the necrology of art it would pass on the side of barbarism, but if it contented itself with the interpretation of the available works of art, it would not enter into a relation with that other and heterogeneous dimension with which every work of art is constantly confronted.

Art as knowledge of the sensible world

Even phenomenology undergoes a sceptical turn, by equating philosophy and art, with the French philosopher Maurice Merleau-Ponty (1908–61) whose work focuses on perception, that is, on the initial, emerging, genetic moment of knowledge.[48] At first glance, it would appear that we have returned to Croce's conception of art as the initial moment of knowledge, but in actual fact we are far away from Croce, first of all because Merleau-Ponty's thinking implies (like Adorno's) a strong downsizing of the claims of philosophical reason, and, in the second place, because art is thought to be the bearer of a truth not unlike the one we can arrive at with philosophy.

Not unlike Husserl, Merleau-Ponty is very critical of scientific knowledge that he reproaches of unscrupulous operationalism completely devoid of interest with regard to the truth of the individual and collective human experiences. In his view, science is knowledge devoid of depth that glosses over things without grasping their essence. But Merleau-Ponty does not have Husserl's faith in a philosophy understood as rigorous science. For him knowledge or, rather, non-philosophical knowledge, does not consist in an organic whole of acquired knowledge representing a stable patrimony. Philosophy can be nothing more than a critical exercise, a research activity extraneous to any dogmatism, the position of a provisional and temporary truth.[49]

There is a sphere, however, where the philosopher's gaze has paused all too briefly, that of corporeity understood as feeling, as experience of the unreflected, the primordial, what precedes the concept. At this level philosophy resembles art. The knowledge of the sensible, of non-reason, of the state that precedes the distinction between subject and object, still constitute a yet to be explored territory. Between art and philosophy an almost competitive relation is established that excludes aesthetics. In fact, both the former and the latter have a type of cognitive relation that turns directly towards the 'thing itself', towards experience. Aesthetics becomes a superfetation, a useless addition, a mediated knowledge that lacks the excitement of the instant, the sudden apparition of the unknown. This explains the small number of works that Merleau-Ponty devoted expressly to aesthetics. It conceals an actual difficulty that concerns the status of the philosophical discourse on art once that same function is assigned both to art and philosophy. Merleau-Ponty tries to remedy this situation by questioning the work of art directly, which he finds in Cézanne's paintings that for him are paradigmatic of the essence of art in general.[50]

The point of departure of Merleau-Ponty's reflections on art is the benchmark of contemporary cognitive aesthetics: a critique of vitalism and subjectivism. Artistic experience introduces us to a world devoid of familiarity, which prevents any human effusion and makes us strangers to ourselves. The artistic emotion *par excellence* is the feeling of irrelevance with respect to empirical life accompanied by a kind of stupor for an always renewing existence. In the essay 'Eye and Mind', which constitutes his most important contribution to the philosophy of art, Merleau-Ponty claims that the painter gives visible existence to what common existence claims to be invisible, and introduces us to a new experience where seeing is manifested as touching and being touched.[51] The discrimination between sight and touch is obsolete, just as the one between the sentient and what is felt. My body, whose cohesion is that of a 'thing' is caught in the fabric of the world, which is perceived as something continuous. Sensation and thought, sense and intelligence are unified in a cognitive experience that goes to the heart of things. Just as Hartmann and Adorno, Merleau-Ponty also makes use of the word 'enigma' to define art. Art breaks up the superficiality of form, understood as something spectacular, and introduces us to a profound experience of 'exteriority' in which the painter feels that he is akin to things. We are very far from vitalistic sensualism. The painter is engaged in a cognitive activity that looks for the *logos* of lines, lights, colours, reliefs and masses. A promiscuity is established between seeing and the visible for whom to paint entails offering oneself to the miracle of the birth of an always emerging feeling in its novelty and flagrancy.

Nonetheless, not even Merleau-Ponty succeeds, in my view, to avoid the movement of self-referentiality in which every cognitive aesthetic remains imprisoned. Even though philosophy attends the school of art with the greatest humility, it has always an advantage over it, namely, that of communicating and making us aware of experiences that would otherwise remain mute and obscure, buried in the flesh of the world. Even the relation between visible and invisible, which constitutes the topic of Merleau-Ponty's last reflection, appears to be a chiasmus, a relation of reflexive reversibility whereby seeing in its turn is seen, taking in its turn is taken, according to a cognitive dynamic which is satisfied only when it has reached self-referentiality.[52]

Art between the aesthetics of reception and nihilism

In hermeneutics, the sceptical turning point is the work of the German scholar Hans Robert Jauss (1921–97) and the Italian philosopher Gianni Vattimo (b. 1936). Both mitigate considerably the emphasis that Gadamer placed on the intrinsic truth of the work of art and its theoretical meaning.

What strikes one in Jauss is first of all the re-evaluation of aesthetics that Gadamer had radically criticized. In fact, he claims the importance of aesthetic pleasure but does not fall in a sensualistic vitalism. For him, aesthetic pleasure is knowledge. With reference to the religious and philosophical traditions of German pietism, he stresses the character of 'thinking enjoyment' provided by the experience of art which is subdivided in three fundamental moments, each one being the bearer of a specific type of knowledge. The first one is *poiesis*, namely, the production of the work of art which is connected to the technological knowledge implicit in doing. The second is *aesthesis*, namely, the access to a perception of the world different from the utilitarian and instrumental one. It is an intuitive knowledge that deconceptualizes the world and allows access to a cosmological vision capable of establishing connections between its different manifestations. The third one is *katharsis*, namely, the empathy with a character and the social sharing of a judgement. Even this last moment contains a cognitive aspect which is present in the communicability of one's own experiences.[53]

The other major aspect of Jauss' hermeneutics concerns the importance that he attributes to the reception of the work of art. According to him, a work cannot be understood if we do not take into account the effect that it produces. The history of its reception becomes, thus, an essential part of the work. Just as an event cannot be understood if we ignore its consequences, so a work of art requires the knowledge of its effects.[54] The sceptical drift of this position is clear. It shifts the attention from the intrinsic truth of the work (important for Gadamer) to the historical events of its consumption.

Even more theoretically extreme are Gianni Vattimo's views which he outlines in his most systematic and mature work, *Beyond Interpretation: The Meaning of Hermeneutics for philosophy*.[55] Taking into examination recent events in hermeneutics, Vattimo emphasizes the prevalence of aesthetic interest on all the others. The work of art is considered the model *par excellence* of the event of truth. However, to this emphasis on the aesthetic aspect does not correspond an actual in-depth examination of the theoretical meaning of art. Gadamer's assertion of the truth of art leads to rather vague results. The cognitive value of art seems limited to a generic form of wisdom on life and human destiny. It is inane to try to derive philosophical theses from poetry, literature or the arts. On the other hand, differently from

Merleau-Ponty, Vattimo excludes that contemporary poets or artists are truly involved in an autonomous cognitive activity. Art tends to lose 'substantiality' both when it is isolated in the forms of high culture and when it is linked to *mass media*. In an amiable but resolute way, Vattimo, practically, closes a chapter of aesthetics that began at the beginning of the century with Croce who considered aesthetic experience a cognitive activity.

According to Vattimo, the fundamental teaching of hermeneutics can be summed up in the thesis that facts do not exist, only interpretations. By negating any immediate objective evidence (which is the object of phenomenology), hermeneutics discovers its own nihilistic vocation that consists in the refusal of every metaphysical conception and in the assertion of the historical character of all manifestations of being. However, Vattimo distinguishes with the greatest clarity his own hermeneutic nihilism from a generic historicist relativism. In fact, the thesis according to which there are no facts but only interpretations cannot be placed at the same level with the other infinite possible visions of the world. Nihilism is not an interpretation that one places beside the others but is the historical destiny of the West, the meeting point of the techno-scientific dominion of the world and the inessential frivolity of the arts, the historical event of Christianity and the moral disenchantment towards all values. But on what is this philosophy of history based? It seems to me that the theoretical primacy of Vattimo's nihilistic secularism also harks back to the principle of self-referentiality. While all the other interpretations of the world are resolved in dogmatic assertions, nihilism alone has the self-awareness of its own historicity.

Vattimo's point of arrival is also very important for aesthetics, namely, the meeting point of art and religion in a 'sensible religion' where, on the one hand, art has by now relinquished any autonomous value of the cognitive type and, on the other, religion has abandoned any dogmatic and disciplinary claim. But as in Lyotard's case, the entire discourse shifts towards another horizon that has nothing to do with either cognitive aesthetics or with hermeneutics, that is, towards an 'aesthetics of feeling' where aesthetic experience is finally grasped in its difference with respect to knowledge.

Virtuality, the cognitive character of art and meta-aesthetics

Among the four trends of cognitive aesthetics (neo-Hegelianism, phenomenology, hermeneutics and theory of symbolic forms) it is precisely the last one that in its development continues to assign to art a theoretical meaning or, more exactly, a cognitive aspect. To be sure, it is also affected by the sceptical turn but this applies above all to science. In fact, we could say that depending on how minor the value attributed to science, the greater is the value assigned to art.

A strong emphasis on the abstract character of aesthetic experience is already present in the work of the American philosopher Suzanne Langer (1895–1985), *Feeling and Form*, which represents an important development of Cassirer's ideas on art.[56] However, differently from him, Langer places emphasis on the virtual and not on the real character of art which she defines as the creation of the symbolic forms of feeling. The introduction of feeling as the essential element of aesthetic experience does not entail, however, a concession to vitalistic subjectivism. The cognitive value of art is based precisely on the fact that we are not dealing with real emotions but with their symbolic representation. Music, in fact, establishes a virtual time that has nothing to do with the real one, just as the figurative arts open up a virtual space.

The American philosopher Nelson Goodman (1906–98) is the author of a close comparison between aesthetic and scientific experience.[57] In his view, art and science are both disinterested pursuits that exhibit a fundamental cognitive character, although the former seems to have a closer relation to the emotional world. Goodman also rejects vitalistic emotionalism. The feelings connected to aesthetic experience are mute, oblique, even opposite to those experienced in private life, in fact their cognitive use has nothing to do with their intensity. Goodman too, like Merleau-Ponty and Langer, is forced to acknowledge the importance of feeling but in his case he does not see it necessarily in conflict with knowledge. Emotions function cognitively when they are connected among themselves and with other instruments of knowledge. For Goodman it is important not to create gaps between art and science. For instance, it is wrong to think that their difference depends on their relation to truth. The latter counts very little in science. Scientific laws very rarely are entirely true. The truth of a scientific hypothesis is a problem of 'adherence' just as the truth of a work of art is a problem of 'appropriateness'. His conclusion is similar to Cassirer's. The sciences and the arts work with similar symbolic systems, and both fall within the cognitive horizon. However, what has changed with respect to Cassirer is the relation of this horizon with the truth.

Even more sceptical is the Austrian-American epistemologist Paul K. Feyerabend (1924–94) for whom there is no difference between the truth-claim of artistic styles and that of scientific styles of thought.[58] However, the point of arrival of this tendency in contemporary epistemology seems to be the thesis that while science unfolds through a plurality of 'styles of thought',[59] art, instead, requires a relation to 'truth'.[60] And philosophy? It is also a totality of different 'styles of thought' perhaps held together by a propensity towards self-referentiality!

Nonetheless, already a few decades earlier, Anglo-Saxon scholars had dismissed completely the question of the cognitive character of art to focus their attention on the specific character that everyday language assumes when it is employed in an aesthetic context. Among these the Englishman Frank Sibley (1923–96) occupies an important place. In his view, the aesthetic use of language is not at all controlled by conditions, rules or predetermined procedures, but depends solely on taste and the sensibility of those who are doing the evaluation.[61] This way, cognitive aesthetics is transformed in a meta-aesthetics interested not in the study of 'things' aesthetic, but aesthetic words and discourses.[62]

Among these, naturally, the use of the word 'art' plays a very important role. In this regard the position of the American scholar of aesthetics Morris Weitz (1916–81) is the most radical. None of the answers to the question 'What is art?' is true because we do not have necessary and sufficient criteria that correspond to the definitive properties of art.[63] As a result, art becomes an 'open concept' in the sense that the logician Friedrich Waismann (1896–1959) gives to the term 'open texture'.[64] This does not mean that to speak of art is useless. One needs simply to come to terms with the fact that it is 'eternally variable'.[65] Not only the aesthetic is not the bearer of any type of knowledge, but not even discourses on art, that is, meta-aesthetics, have anything to do with scientific knowledge.

4

Aesthetics and Action

'Beautiful action' and conflict

A long tradition that goes back to the Greeks links art to action in various ways. In Homer's *epos* the feats of heroes constitute the content of the poems. In tragedy the action unfolds in the presence of spectators. Both the first and the second exert an effect on the public. Finally, the same poetic, artistic or literary activity has often been thought as a performance, a particular type of action sometime more effective than the military, political or economic ones. In modern thought Hegel is the philosopher who has thought with greater depth the connection between art and action.

In his *Aesthetic*, in fact, in outlining the development of the artistic ideal, he confers the greatest importance on the process through which the spirit entering the world is forced to come out of its own quietness and finds itself exposed to suffering, unhappiness and conflict.[1] When opposite demands of an ideal and universal nature are in opposition to one another within the same subject, a *pathos* is born, which constitutes the very spring of the 'beautiful action', that is, the essential content of rationality and free will that leads to decision and action. The characters of Greek tragedy are full of *pathos, par excellence*, and they welcome, dominate and overcome suffering affirming the primacy of a universal experience over individual interests. Under this aspect they represent the model of rational action of which philosophy constitutes, for Hegel, in the last instance, the greatest development.

A notion widely circulated in the second half of the nineteenth century is that neither the hero nor the philosopher but the artist is the one who performs the 'beautiful action'. Often, as in Wagner and in Nietzsche, it is associated with the idea of a 'return to the Greeks' regarded as the people in antiquity who pursued aesthetic ideals the most, not limited to the production of works of art but extended to the totality of experience. In particular, it asserts the image of the artist as innovator and genius who clashes, by definition, with the incomprehension of the masses and the philistinism of society. Therefore, the function of art is seen as an *agón*, a struggle, a conflict, essentially different from politics and war because animated by a desire for recognition. Artistic action, thus, is represented as essentially agonistic. Here arises a first problem. In what way does the strongly individual character of artistic activity harmonize with the social dimension inherent in approval and praise? Artistic excellence requires to be recognized as such, but for this purpose the search for originality and novelty becomes, in fact, an impediment. Practical reason has two possible outcomes: actuality, which is the aim of politics, and the good, which is the aim of the ethical. Neither one nor the other requires any public judgement. They find their own ratification in themselves. Not so art which finds itself in the unpleasant condition to solicit positive judgement and the admiration of those it opposes! Furthermore, what is striking is the discrepancy between the conflict of artistic action and the irenic, conciliatory dimension implicit in aesthetic experience.

This problematic constitutes the theme of Lev Tolstoy's work, *What is Art?* (1898)[2] where the great Russian writer advances not only a radical critique of aesthetics, of which he sketches a brief history to show its inconsistency, but also of the experience of the beautiful which he considers the object of pleasure and subjective desire. His aim is to break completely the link between the beautiful and art, reserving for the latter a social, moral and religious function. Tolstoy's position constitutes the most vigorous negation of the autonomy of art which he brings back within the sphere of practical reason. In his view, the 'beautiful action' is simply, more or less, an immoral action. Whoever acts can choose between force (which constitutes the basis of war, politics and economy) and the good (which constitutes the foundation of all spiritual, social and cultural values), but he does not have a third practical possibility which is beyond power (and impotence), and faith (and godlessness).

Nonetheless Tolstoy is not blind to the cultural situation of his times, which constitute a clamorous disclaimer of his ideas on 'true' art. The problem is that culture is contaminated by the corruption of society, by the social divisions between rich and poor, and by the spread of atheism. The result is the hegemony of a false and depraved art, entirely devoted to the search for pleasure, whose apotheosis is represented by Wagner and his followers. Wagner's work of art (*Gesamtkunstwerk*) constitutes for Tolstoy the perfect example of a counterfeit art that functions like opium placing the spectators in a state similar to hypnosis. Tolstoy asks himself how is it possible that this false art has succeeded while good art which expresses religious feelings or universal affects, which move beyond social, national and racial barriers, often does not enjoy the favour of the public? Here Tolstoy is perfectly aware of the paradox in which he is falling. If the essence of art is its effect why many good works do not succeed? This depends, according to Tolstoy, from the corruption and perversion of our sense of morality that prevents true art to carry out its function, that is, to excite authentic and sincere emotions.

Tolstoy's thesis in its radicality and simplicity constitutes a challenge to that aspect of aesthetic thought which is sensitive to the problem of the social function of art. In fact, globally, we can consider the pragmatic and socially committed aesthetics of the twentieth century as a series of attempts to confute the ideas of Tolstoy. Their purpose is to distinguish aesthetic, artistic and cultural action from political and moral ones. This distinction, however, does not constitute an autonomous and independent dominion without a link to practical life, that is why the authors we are dealing with in this chapter possess, on the one hand, a total, unitarian and global vision of human experience (which derives more or less directly from Hegel) and, on the other, they cannot help but guarantee in some ways the specificity of the 'beautiful action' with respect to economical and ethical actions.

And yet a clear and convincing answer to this problem was well-known in antiquity. It consists in differentiating between three different forms of active life: work, the production of works of art and real action.[3] It is clear that artistic experience belongs to the second type of *vita activa*. The artist is essentially a *homo faber* and he is the maker of products destined to last well beyond his death. But this solution, which places the artist in his specific activity, without possibility of confusion with the worker and the politician, has not had much fortune in the twentieth century for two reasons: in the first place because it entails a rigid separation between the activities and, therefore, goes in the opposite direction with respect to that total dimension of experience that pragmatic aesthetics pursues, and, in the second place, because it overshadows the element of conflict which constitutes the true motor of socially engaged aesthetics. To be sure, the 'beautiful action' is different from that of the ideologue, the moralist and the politician but the artist is seen from this part of aesthetics as a combatant not any less combative than them.

Aesthetic action as fulfilment

A brilliant solution to the problems raised by the idea of aesthetic experience as action is provided by the North American philosopher John Dewey (1859–1952) whose contribution to aesthetics can be found above all in the volume, *Art as Experience*.[4]

The fundamental problem from which Dewey's discourse unfolds is that of strictly connecting aesthetic experience with ordinary experience. Thus, he criticizes those theories that separate art from everyday life and isolate it by placing it in their own sphere. Instead, it is necessary to establish a continuity between the aesthetic dimension and normal vital phenomena that involve a continuous process of conflict and interaction with the surrounding world. According to Dewey, there is no radical difference between aesthetic and common experience. Any experience can become aesthetic if, instead of being interrupted and abandoned (as it often happens), it is carried out and brought to fulfilment. What characterizes aesthetic experience, therefore, is fulfilment. Action becomes 'beautiful' to the extent to which I engage in it, I devote myself to it, I fight for its manifestation. The opposite of an aesthetic experience is a life that goes adrift, that has no head or tail, neither beginning nor end. Or it is an experience that has a beginning which is abandoned out of sloth, cowardice, disposition to compromise, desire for 'peace and quiet', deference to convention.

Thus Dewey inserts in action a parameter which is independent of success or practical failure, without introducing, however, expectations that are extraneous to the nature of action, such as morality. He undermines the identity established by Kant between practical reason and morality. Fulfilled action, that is, action which is fully and integrally such is not ethical, but aesthetic. At the same time he removes the sphere of action from politics (and from war), because mere effectiveness does not suffice to fulfil an experience. The result in itself does not fulfil the action if it is separated from the process that leads to it. The real man of action is neither the pious man nor the politician (and not even the warrior), but the artist! To be sure the actions of a Caesar or a Napoleon had aesthetic qualities but this does not depend on their practical success but on their specific qualities.

In order for experience to reach an aesthetic dimension a conflict is necessary which, more or less, entails suffering and pain. This allows Dewey to emancipate aesthetic experience from its connection to pleasure, the object of Tolstoy's critique. Pleasure and pain, as all emotions in general, must not be considered separately but connected to the procedural character of experience which unfolds like the events of a novel or a drama. Emotion belongs to a subject who is engaged in a struggle from which it acquires meaning. The suspension, which so many theories consider an essential aspect of aesthetic experience, must not be understood as separation from practice but as expectation, uncertainty over the outcome, tension towards the perfecting of experience. The question of 'how will it end?' is a determining aesthetic factor because it makes possible to understand experience as a movable unity, organized and dynamic, made up of actions and passions. Therefore, Dewey prefers to speak of 'experience' rather than aesthetic 'action'. In fact, acting and suffering alternate and interpenetrate. Every action is in reality an 'interaction' with the external world, a mutual adjustment of the individual to the environment, an exchange of sensations and reflections. Enthusiastic activism prevents access to the aesthetic dimension, that is, to true experience because it does not leave time to think, investigate or re-elaborate cognitively and emotionally, what one is living. Even an excess of receptivity constitutes an obstacle because it distorts experience through an accumulation of fantasies and passive impressions that make you lose contact with the reality of the world and do not lead to resolution.

Even the abyss placed by Tolstoy between aesthetics and art is filled by Dewey with a genial idea. Experience is truly fulfilled (and therefore fully aesthetic) when it materializes in a work of art! Not only because the artistic process forces the artist to a continuous comparison between what he has done and what there is still to do, obliging him to proceed coherently and as a whole but, above all, because it is only from the time when experience is concretized in a work that it becomes communicable and socially relevant. Thus, Dewey provides a very pointed solution to the potential conflict between the individual search for excellence (which is inherent in the pursuit of a fulfilled experience) and social solidarity (which persuades us to shift the axe of our own attention from ourselves towards others). In reality, only those who fulfil their own experience succeed in communicating with others and in being useful to them. After all, we have always known that those who get along with others also get along with themselves! Experience remains unfulfilled if it does not become perceivable to others through its results. According to Dewey, the work of art virtually always belongs to the public domain. The fact that it belongs to a common world does not depend on its publication, exposition or reception but on its physical existence that demands a judgement.

Therefore any tension between the individual and the social is overcome at the same time that one grasps the close intimacy between the aesthetic and artistic dimensions. No experience can ever be fulfilled as long as it remains aesthetic, that is, purely a prisoner of an individual feeling, like a dream or a fantasy! Therefore, those who wish to bring their own experience to fulfilment must they enter necessarily into a literary or artistic production? A scientific or philosophical research, a political or industrial activity, are they not truly fulfilling experiences? According to Dewey, the difference between these and artistic experience consists in the fact that only in the work of art the process is equally important as the conclusion. While in non-artistic experiences it is possible to extract a truth, a formula, a result, an outcome that represents an autonomous value independent of the process that took him there, in art, instead, fulfilment concerns not only the end but also the development, not only the endpoint but also the beginning.

This does not mean, however, that for Dewey the dynamics of experience has a circular progress, as in Hegel, such that the point of arrival is somehow connected to its beginning. Aesthetic action runs towards its actual fulfilment and is terminated in the perfecting of the work. Aesthetic experiences are the only ones on which it is possible, in good conscience, to write the word 'end' because they are, in all of their parts, communicable and transmittable. For Dewey, the essence of action consists in this possibility of closure, of a conclusion. From this point of view aesthetics and art offer more than all the other practical activities, which appear to always be lacking something important. Victory or defeat are not conclusive in themselves. It is also important how one won and how one lost. The fight counts as much as the result. Aesthetic reconciliation does not derive so much from the outcome of the conflict as from the awareness of having done one's best to bring the activity one began to an end.

Aesthetic action as utopian tension

If for Dewey the essential is fulfilment, the thought of the German philosopher Ernst Bloch (1885–1977), on the contrary, revolves around the notion of incompleteness, the unfinished, the undetermined. In fact, only this way human action can be inserted into reality by introducing new elements that do not stay mere fantasies but deeply transform it. However, before the change can occur it is necessary a utopian tension, a creative imagination, a revolutionary enthusiasm which is also manifested in dreams, desires, illusions but above all works of art, religion and philosophy. The relation between action and struggle acquires in Bloch, therefore, a social meaning strictly connected with the grandiose project of the emancipation of humanity elaborated by Marx. His most important work, *The Principle of Hope* (begun in 1938 and completed more than 20 years later), a monumental work in three volumes, constitutes a summa of his thought where the meditation on poetry and the arts occupies a central place.[5]

Art understood as 'visible pre-appearance', of what should be but is not yet, presents a contradictory character. On the one hand, it aspires to that fulfilment that constitutes the pivot of Deweys' aesthetics, on the other, it contains a kind of intrinsic disjointedness that prevents it from being closed in a complete totality. To be sure the artist's greatest fear is not to succeed in completing the work on which he is working, but he does not realize that in art there is a tension towards something that goes beyond it. Nonetheless, Bloch refuses to fall in the trap of transcendence (as is the case with many theorists of form and the sublime). Art is immanence both because it gives itself as something ontologically existent here and now, and because the utopian horizon that it opens is immanent, it is that of social revolution and not of God.

This dynamic and disruptive dimension implicit in art was completely misunderstood by cognitive aesthetics which in the eighteenth century begins by devaluating its object, almost apologizing for its existence, in fact, for Baumgarten, the aesthetic object is only an inferior cognitive faculty. But even moralistic iconoclasm, sometimes animated by a real *horror pulchri*, so well represented by Tolstoy in his will to earnestness against appearance, misunderstands the anticipatory character of artistic experience which is not mere illusion but anticipation of a utopian content. Therefore, it implies a radical decision which in common experience is shown very rarely (*PH*, §17).

Bloch does not limit himself to provide general indications on the utopian character of aesthetic action. He also carries out a detailed analysis of those figures that are symbols of insatiability, restlessness and excess in European literature. These emblematic figures are Dante's Ulysses, Don Juan, the 'strong spirits' of libertinism, Don Quixote, and most of all Faust who is defined by Bloch as the supreme example of utopian man. They are the men of aesthetic action, the sons of the Renaissance who by dispensing with fear act with decision and burst into reality. They are also the sons of the middle class and capitalistic evolution that has produced adventurous and gigantic subjective stimulus. In Don Juan, defined by Bloch as the most splendid image of desire, is displayed an extraordinary and multifaceted Titanism. In him a wretched aspect coexists with a 'utopian drive' expressed in the stimulus towards the unconditional that brings him to prefer death rather than giving in to a confining civility. Master of the moment, Don Juan personifies Dionysian *hubris*. He interprets an essential aspect of the bourgeois revolution which next to the moralistic component embodied by Robespierre also brings forward an excessive sexual component embodied by Danton (*PH*, §49).

But the real master figure of utopian restlessness is Faust. In him utopian action is represented as a striving (*Streben*), which is not contented with any reached result, but appropriates acquired experience to make it the foundation of another step forward. According to Bloch, Faust's progress is similar to Hegel's dialectic whose 'overcoming' is both a preserving and a surpassing. In fact, between Goethe's *Faust* and Hegel's *Phenomenology of Mind* there is a deep affinity for in both works there is no past of which one can be nostalgic. There is only something perennially new which is formed by the expanded elements of the past.[6] Every pleasure is erased by a new desire and every disproved goal is erased by a new movement that goes beyond it. But this infinite productivity, which for its insatiability exhibits a demonic aspect, is not Hegel's 'bad infinity' (the infinite of the abstract intellect that condemns Being in the name of a 'ought to be' which is never present), neither it is a return to transcendence. It is the 'real infinite' of the will to power to transform, which through 'the seven league boots of the concept' struggles and performs in the world.

Faust-ism, however, does not exhaust aesthetic action. There is an artistic experience where hunger for the unconditional reaches its culmination. It is linked to music, which is defined by Bloch as the most utopian and the most social of all the arts. There is in music something essentially incomplete and entirely bent towards moving beyond. The very form of the sound succession points to a strain towards the unconditional. This aspect is greatly in evidence in Bach, Mozart and Beethoven who are for Bloch the real action utopian figures in the musical sphere. Bloch, instead, is very critical of Wagner whose work he does not acknowledge as real aesthetic action, but as the raging of a wild, bestial passion. In Wagner's melodrama we don't reach an authentic dramatic action. Everything remains nebulous, enveloped in a wretched naturalistic narcosis, in a pseudo-ecstasy that plunges one into contemplative passivity.[7]

The same utopian tension that drives the work of Ernst Bloch can also be found in the thought of the French philosopher Olivier Revault d'Allonnes (1923–2009) whose *Musiques. Variations sur la pensée juive*[8] considers music as the artistic form *par excellence*, linked to an inner experience perpetually enriched by hope. This virtue is the essential trait of prophetic Judaism which from the aesthetic point of view is expressed in music and is opposed to the spatial arts, sculpture and painting, considered as the idols of paganism. Music does not refer to anything external and constitutes the only salvation against the distractions of space, idols and futility. With romanticism it succeeds in emancipating itself from a too rigid organization and in introducing dynamic elements of improvisation and transgression consistent with revolutionary action. Jewish aesthetics, therefore, is inseparable from an ethics of hope and justice. It is oriented towards future expectations that surprise for their unexpectedness.

Cultural action as organization

Bloch's critique of melodrama associates him with the Italian thinker Antonio Gramsci (1891–1937). For both (as for Tolstoy), lyric opera represents the strongest form of artistic action before cinema. While Bloch and Tolstoy have in mind Wagner, Gramsci alludes to Italian opera who was in Italy the only truly popular artistic expression. In this country musicians have had the success that other artists and intellectuals did not have, fulfilling a similar function as the novel in other European countries. Lyric opera promoted the spread of a melodramatic taste that in establishing itself onto the traditional tendency for recitation and rhetoric ended up by reinforcing still further a bombastic and inflated sensibility. For this reason, aesthetic taste was not shaped by the profound and close action of reading but by means of the superficial and empty exteriority of public rhetoric, such as those of the law courts, the churches, the funeral orations and artistic performances.[9] According to Gramsci, the salient aspects of this ethico-aesthetic feeling of the Italians of his time are amateurism, fanciful and inconclusive distractions, and absolute lack of sobriety and intellectual rigour. Against these traits it is of the greatest importance to fight in favour of a philosophy that can create moderate and patient men who are not afraid of catastrophes and who do not get carried away by foolishness. He epitomized this programme in the famous motto: 'pessimism of intelligence, optimism of the will' (*PN*, III).

The positive aspect of Gramsci's thought moves in very different ways from Bloch's, that is, not towards utopia but towards a more concrete and realistic horizon. It is necessary first of all to take as point of departure precisely this public who delights in mediocre artistic products. The new literature must try to elaborate what is already in existence even though it is backward and conventional (*PN*, II). It is better to rest on something degraded but strongly felt than on noble and distinguished cultural institutions, but not very effective, like the university. Often, Gramsci writes, a free thinker has more influence than the entire university system (*PN*, XVIII).

To be sure, for Gramsci action cannot be only artistic. The latter has to be set in the context of a much wider and complex action that must be carried out by a different type of intellectual who is capable of uniting theory and practice and mixing actively with daily life, who is not a specialist of just one sphere of knowledge but is also a culture organizer. Gramsci derives from Hegel the belief that intellectuals are very important for the existence of the modern state, but expands greatly the same notion of 'intellectual' including in this category any professional activity (and potentially every human being). Within this context he distinguishes between two basic types of intellectuals: the 'organic' one who believes that his activity is a functional struggle with respect to the establishment of a given social class, and the 'traditional' one who feels, instead, that he is the representative of an autonomous group that enjoys historical continuity independent of the social struggle (*PN*, VIII and XXVIII). This does not mean that Gramsci believed that the struggle should occur between these two types of intellectuals! Traditional intellectuals, the bearers of a specific type of knowledge (for instance, writers and artists) if at the level of the state they do not count for anything, they have an enormous importance at the level of civil society. In fact, Gramsci differentiates hegemony, which is based on consensus, prestige and trust, from direct political power which is based on the exercise of coercion. It follows that they must be both assimilated and not destroyed!

As far as aesthetics is concerned, there are at least two consequences. The first concerns the relative autonomy of art that while tied to a given social situation is not propaganda. Gramsci is extremely critical of those who claim to arrive at a new art from outside, through a self-righteous, hortatory, didactic or, even worse, repressive attitude. A new art is possible only from inside by opening new intellectual and moral horizons (*PN*, XVII). The second consequence, less explicitly stated in the *Notebooks* left by Gramsci, concerns the future of aesthetics and its overcoming by a cultural organization. Gramsci compares the strong influence exercised by popular literature to the failure of both secular and catholic culture in elevating the cultural and moral levels of the masses. The serialized novel, for instance, constitutes a 'real daydream' (*PN*, VIII) that because of its effectiveness does not have equals in the cultural, philosophical and religious literature of its time. It is significant that for Gramsci the philosophy of praxis takes literary and artistic phenomena as its models, however degraded they may be. His diagnosis of aesthetic decadence is not very different from the one provided by Tolstoy but the remedies that he suggests move in a very different direction. To be sure not towards a spiritual revival through art but towards the creation of a new type of intellectual who can be both the heir of German philosophy and of popular literature.

Artistic action as tendency

The Hungarian philosopher György Lukács (1885–1971), the author of a monumental *Aesthetics*, instead, has no tolerance for popular or mass cultural productions.[10] Nonetheless, Lukács shares Gramsci's requirement for an art which is fully aware of its own relation to social reality. His great efforts in many works and essays on aesthetics, history and literary criticism seem driven, in fact, by a dual intention: on the one hand, to ground art firmly to the historical process, in polemics both with utopianism and the literature of escape and mere entertainment, on the other hand, to guarantee full freedom and autonomy to art against any attempt to confuse it with propaganda and rhetoric. As one of the founding fathers of the theory of aesthetic action, he is a great admirer of the great European literary tradition from Goethe on. In his view, there is no need at all for art to be overcome by a new historical experience (a revolution) or an intellectual one (cultural action). Art already puts its action into practice, which is so much the greater the more its specificity and autonomy is preserved and developed.

In fact, the relation between art and reality is not and cannot ever be immediate, direct and spontaneous. Lukács conducts a close and relentless critique of 'naturalism', of that poetics that claims to identify art with reality and is based on a completely false premise, namely, of describing and reproducing reality in a non-critical way without the intervention of the subjectivity of the author. For Dilthey already, naturalism was the greatest challenge that the art world could present to rational aesthetics. Lukács takes up and radicalizes Dilthey's analysis by identifying in the contemporary avant-garde the continuation of the naturalistic trend. He opposes the tradition of 'critical realism' that from Balzac[11] and Thomas Mann represents the real progressive line of contemporary literature. These criteria have an aesthetico-philosophical foundation. According to Lukács there are three different types of 'reflections of reality': that of everyday life, the scientific one and the aesthetic one. The expression 'reflection' must not be understood in the sense of mere photographic reproduction. It points to the rejection of idealism, which reduces reality to a mere spiritual entity, and the affirmation of the existence of the world independently of the cognitive act. Reflection, in fact, is always selective. Even the thinking of everyday life characterized by great fluidity, poor objectification, and the primacy of work over all other activities, functions through continuous discrimination between what is important and what is not.

But what differentiates art from science and everyday life? While in scientific knowledge the categories of singularity and universality play a fundamental role, in aesthetic experience the intermediary term of 'particularity' constitutes the definitive moment. In other words, art represents the 'typical' and not, as naturalism claims, mere singularity isolated from the events of social relations in which every existence is enveloped. Scientific knowledge does not succeed in determining the particular and it is precisely this impossibility that guarantees the autonomy of the concrete artistic creation with respect to laws or general rules. The claim to give artists prescriptions or precepts of an 'aesthetic' nature destroys the aesthetic essence of their work.[12] While scientific reflection is characterized by a de-anthropomorphizing tendency, in the work of art, on the contrary, there is no moment that can be thought without the human being, without the intervention of human subjectivity. What characterizes aesthetic experience is precisely the fact that it requires a subjective stance towards the world and society. Lukács criticizes energetically those contemplative aesthetic theories that consider as true art only those that are born from a non-tendentious attitude and superior to the struggle. On the contrary, for him art is always 'tendentious' in the sense that it implies a stance towards the represented world that takes shape in the work with artistic means. Therefore, art does not belong to the theoretical dimension, as cognitive aesthetics claims. The object of the artistic work is not the concept, in its pure objective truth, but the way in which it becomes action, that is, a concrete factor of life in concrete situations with concrete men. This aspect of the work has nothing to do with the moral or political opinions of the author as long as these remain extrinsic and external with respect to the substance of the work. 'Tendency' implies the inseparable simultaneity of the reflection of an external reality with a stance of objectivity and participation. Even though artistic truth is always a historical truth, nonetheless, it always has as its focus the fate of the entire human species. Therefore, the aesthetic dimension always possesses, objectively and subjectively, a total character, or at least an intention of totality. In Lukács, thus, artistic action is inseparable from the struggle for the emancipation of humanity. The essentially humanistic aspect of art allows Lukács to reassert the difference of art from political journalism. While the latter achieves the immediate mobilization of the most heterogeneous means in view of an immediate practical purpose, art performs, instead, a complex pedagogical function, indirect and mediated on a vast scale that favours the development of self-consciousness and the intellectual and moral growth of the author and his public.

The eminently and immanently practical character of aesthetic experience is analysed by Lukács with reference both to the movement that leads from everyday life to the constitution of an autonomous artistic sphere, and to the opposite movement whereby what was assumed in artistic reflection comes back to flow in everyday life. As far as the first moment is concerned, Lukács argues against the idealistic conception of art that understands it as something original and ahistorical. In his view, art slowly detaches itself from a situation belonging to a primitive everyday life in which it was confused with magic. Initially, the purpose of magic to influence the transcendental powers and the artistic one to produce an evocative effect on the receptivity of men are still not distinct from one another. Similarly, the aesthetic necessity of a more intense life, qualitatively different from the ordinary one, is still united with a search for ascetic and ecstatic states. Art conquers its autonomy through the progressive awareness of the immanent character of its effects, just as aesthetic experience distinguishes itself from the ascetic-ecstatic one starting from the moment when it attributes a temporary and provisional character to the suspension of everyday normalcy. Thus, the essential character of aesthetic feeling emerges slowly, and consists in the conjuring up of affective tonalities and emotional states. This allows Lukács to return once again to the difference between daily life and art. While in the former the communication of feelings, which have their roots in real and objective situations, is essential, in the latter, instead, the essential is the conjuring up of feelings absolutely deprived of foundation in the lived experience of the author. In short, in art affective life must be controlled and evaluated with extreme attention in view of its evocation. Truth and evocative effectiveness have nothing to do with the truth and real effectiveness. Great sensibility is not at all the quality of great genius! After all, as Diderot knew well, if the performance of an actor depended on its emotions, the effect of his performance would be different every time! The origins of art are in magic and not in spontaneous art.[13] Lukács' aesthetics is at the opposite pole of vitalism.

Even for what concerns the second aspect of the problem, that is, the return of art to everyday life, Lukács' focus is centred on the dual action that the work exercises on the consumer. On the one hand it removes the user from his everyday life, allowing him to enter into a new world and keeping him stable. On the other hand, the new horizon in which he enters opens up a relation with reality greatly more essential than the one to which he was used to. Aesthetic fruition is defined by Lukács as the transformation of the whole-man of everyday life in the man-entirely engaged in the reception of the work of art (*A I*, ivi, I, IX). Therefore, it is a question of a total experience that exceeds the distinctions between different faculties. Kant's theory, which regards disinterestedness to be the characteristic of aesthetic judgement ignores the concrete and ensuing consequences of the aesthetic effect. For Lukács, the action of art is profound and lasting. It levels an injunction to the receiver that concerns him directly and personally, and that invites him peremptorily to change his life, to make it richer, more profound and more meaningful. The user finds himself involved in a struggle with himself. Within himself the old and the new man come face to face. This explains the unpleasant effect that works of art provoke sometime. In fact, they often create in the spirit of the consumer a feeling of shame for the fact that he has been unable to perceive and assimilate to that point what the work of art demonstrates with so much artlessness! This powerful action of art was pointed out more by ancient aesthetic thought than by the modern one. The fundamental social finality of art is to transform passions in virtuous habits. This high profile pedagogical function on a large scale is rarely understood by modern thought. In fact, in today's cultural life one wavers between the specialized recognition of art and the propagandistic and moralistic idea of its direct and immediate effect. For Lukács it is a question of a false alternative that misunderstands the concreteness and ethico-pedagogical strength of the artistic message. Naturally, this must not be understood in a conventional and conformist way. What is historically new and progressive is often expressed in the form of a break with the dominant conceptions such as evil, or, in a contradictory way as co-presence of diverging aspects and elements. To conclude, what belongs to the aesthetic sphere is decided on the basis of the breadth and intensity with which the work refers to the essence of man and the destiny of mankind. The result is that art is not at all an illusion but represents the highest cultural power, the only way through which everyday life can be bettered and transfigured. Escape literature, *belletrism*, kitsch, journalism and other productions of the cultural industry, whose aim is to entertain, fall outside art and aesthetics, and they differ from them precisely because of the narrowness and provisional character of their influence.

Lukács' aesthetics is generally considered the most important expression of Marxist aesthetics. In actual fact the thought of Bloch and Gramsci seem to me to be more deeply influenced by Marx. In Lukács' case we have before us a noble and rich theory of the pedagogical function of art, worthy of the greatest admiration and respect but also too much tied to the existence of an educated and intelligent public.

Multifunctionality and the dialogical character of aesthetics

The divergence between aesthetics and art, which Tolstoy pointed out, constitutes the most original theme of the thought of Czech's scholar Jan Mukařovský (1891–1975), the author of numerous essays in large part written in the thirties and forties and collected in two volumes.[14] In his view, while the aesthetic function is present not only in art but also in other extrinsic activities, it also contains many other extrinsic factors that sometime are more important than the aesthetic one.

The point of departure of Mukařovský's aesthetics is a reflection on functionalism, that cultural tendency that regards as the essential aspect of an activity the achievement of the specific end that it sets itself. For Mukařovský this orientation constitutes an inevitable aspect of contemporary industrial society. One can neither refute it nor forget it even if it entails the prevalence of a too specialized and unilateral conception of the work, which does not take into account the multilateralism of the human being and the infinite variety of particular situations. When functionalism is thought through and through one discovers that there is also an aesthetic function whose characteristics are different from all other functions, because it is the dialectic negation of the very notion of function, because it is 'transparent', it has no purpose of its own and refers back to a multifunctional image of the human being. It forces us to break the isolation in which the various functions are enclosed and to consider them as forces correlated among themselves. Therefore, the aesthetic function is not the static property of some things but an energetic component that enters into a relation with all other human activities. There is no living aspect from which the aesthetic component is absent. Mukařovský emphasizes the permeation between everyday living and aesthetics and attributes to the latter a catalytic effect that makes the carrying out of an action more pleasurable and thus favours the attainment of the same specific utilitarian goals.

Art finds itself in a reverse and specular condition with respect to aesthetics, because it is characterized by the prevalence of the aesthetic function. However, when the latter acquires an absolute hegemony such that it excludes any other function (as it happens in the decadent movement), we do not witness an increase of its effectiveness, rather a weakening that can bring about the complete loss of its influence on the public. So while in day-to-day life, the intervention of aesthetics serves to reinforce extra-artistic action, in art the extra-aesthetic functions stimulate and favour artistic effectiveness. Of course, they must not, in their turn, erase the aesthetic function! The optimal situation, Mukařovský writes, is to establish within the work a polarity, a tension, a struggle between aesthetic and extra-artistic functions. So, Mukařovský's attention is focused on borderline cases, on intermediate areas between art and non-art, which he divides into three categories: (1) The arts that also have extra-artistic functions, such as architecture, oratory, the literary essay, the portrait, national hymns, folklore, etc. (2) Activities born independently of artistic intentions but that tend towards art such as crafts, gardening, photography, cinema, etc. (3) The special cases of religious cult and natural beauty. In all these phenomena, the aesthetic sphere does not reach a hypertrophic level but remains in a dialectical relation of opposites with other vital functions. The presence of this internal conflict produces not only the effectiveness of the work of art but also the possibility that it may last in time, developing as it goes a number of diverse functions and satisfying expectations as varied as possible.

With respect to the theories of the founding fathers of aesthetic action (Dewey, Bloch, Gramsci and Lukács), Mukařovský's thesis introduces an element of doubt with respect to the effectiveness of art as art. The Russian literary critic Michail Bakhtin (1895–1975) has also reservations on the hegemonic action of the author as artist. His thinking on aesthetics, formulated in a series of writings between the twenties and the seventies and published posthumously in one volume,[15] constitutes an indirect critique of the aesthetic fulfilment theorized by Dewey and the particularity of art theorized by Lukács.

Bakhtin places at the centre of his aesthetic reflection the need for recognition experienced by the author. Aesthetic experience is not, as Dewey suggested, a phenomenon that finds its finality in the fulfilment of the work of art, as if the author were autonomous and self-sufficient. In reality, man is not capable of completing the perception of himself by himself, but he needs the glance of the other. I cannot become myself without the action of the other. Self-portraits and autobiographies, therefore, have something ghostlike about them. They lack the emotional and affective tension which is born exclusively with relation to the other. Aesthetic experience, therefore, presents an essentially dialogical character. The value of a person depends on the testimony and judgement of others. Without the participation of the other I am unreal to myself. Therefore, Bakhtin rejects the theory of *empathy*, which considers the aesthetic experience as a projection of the 'I' on things. In contrast, he introduces the term *exotopy* which, in fact, designates the condition of finding oneself outside oneself. The centre of experience, therefore, is displaced to the outside, in the conscience and in the feeling of the other.

The emphasis on the pedagogical aspect of art, which the theories of Tolstoy, Gramsci and Lukács exemplify, imply the risk of monologism, of a discourse that attributes to the other a merely passive and subordinate role. The subjects of high literary genre discourse, namely, priests, prophets, judges, leaders, patriarchs, etc. are bearers of monological truths, from which the modern author feels estranged. Therefore, the key word is not 'tendency' but 'responsibility' of the author with respect to the truth of others. According to Bakhtin, even Hegel's dialectic, despite the enormous importance he attributes to the dynamic of estrangement and alterity, remains the victim of monologism, the affirmation of a unique supreme truth. It was rather Dostoevsky who was able to avoid this condition and create a polyphonic and plural work where the characters acquire the freedom and indetermination that the classical novel allowed only to the author. The dialogical disposition must not be confused with scepticism. The author remains profoundly active and involved, but he rejects any didactic role. The creative comprehension does not renounce itself and its own culture but refuses to place it as unique and absolute. In fact, no event develops and is resolved within the sphere of a single consciousness. Every word has an addressee to whom it turns. Culture cannot do without being heard and recognized. When these are lacking, there is the temptation to shut oneself in a proud solitude that pretends to do without the others. One must avoid this error by appealing to a 'super addressee' whose attention and impartial judgement are well beyond empirical reality. This aspiration acquires, according to the period, various ideological identities (God, absolute truth, science, nation, history's tribunal, etc.). Any discourse has as its own essential element the need to be heard.

Imagination and reality in aesthetic action

What is the relation between imagination and aesthetic action? Is the latter destined to remain excluded from actual reality, or the real and the imaginary are inseparably intertwined with one another? Can art and literature have a real influence on society? What distinguishes the writer from the man of action? What is writing? Why does one write? For whom does one write? It is around these issues that the aesthetic reflections of the French philosopher Jean Paul Sartre (1905–80) and the French writer André Malraux (1901–76) revolve.

Sartre's aesthetic thought takes its moves from a philosophical analysis of imagination which he separates completely from any cognitive function. The image is not a copy of reality but the product of the free activity of consciousness, which negates the world.[16] The work of art as the product of the imagination is imaginary and remains such. For Sartre there is no realization of the imaginary in the work of art, which remains an unreal synthetic whole. The sensual pleasure that we derive from the work of art has nothing to do with aesthetics which posits the aesthetic object as essentially unreal. For Sartre between reality and aesthetic experience there is an unbridgeable gap. The work of art posits itself in a perpetual elsewhere, in a permanent absence. Therefore reality is never beautiful and, vice versa, beauty is never real.

This aesthetic theory outlined in *The Imaginary* (1940)[17] appears to exclude at first sight the possibility of aesthetic action over reality. Therefore, it may be surprising that Sartre some years later in *What is literature?* (1947) claimed that language is action.[18] In it literature is considered a secondary act of a certain kind that one could call 'action by disclosure'. This does not mean that now Sartre attributes a cognitive function to art, almost as if it were the copy or the representation of the real. Aesthetic action does not belong to reality in the strict sense, that is, it is not a prisoner of the situation in which we find ourselves, but exceeds it by definition. It is a new event that cannot be explained on the basis of what is given. It is born by an act of freedom and addresses the freedom of the reader. The work of art is not a thing that exists independently of the imagination of the author and the consumer. It is an appeal to others, above all, so that they may read it, look at it and listen to it. It exists only if others take it into consideration and take responsibility for it.

This appeal excludes a direct intervention of the author on the affectivity of the reader. Aesthetic action is not a political discourse or an edifying sermon. It is not a question of moving anyone, or communicating directly emotions of desire, fear or anger. In the passions freedom is alienated. The writer must not impress or condition anyone. He appeals to the freedom of others, and together he presupposes it and establishes it. Aesthetic experience implies detachment and suspension with respect to the real. In order to enter into it and to remain in it a renewed act of commitment is necessary that has its roots in free individual decision. Art avoids the rigid determinism that rules over the real world. It creates an independent sphere from reality that exists only to the extent to which author and consumer offer themselves to it. Every painting, every book recreates the world as if it had its origins in freedom. From this derives the joy that gushes out from the experience of art. This could be defined as an imaginary presentation of the world which the artist and the reader take upon themselves. Therefore, art is intrinsically emancipator and revolutionary because it subverts the given and frees us from the actual situation in which we are imprisoned. Art, therefore, is always action and struggle for freedom against reality. There is no freedom already given. Sartre's thinking moves in a direction opposite to Gramsci. There is no such a thing as an organic intellectual for a certain social class, for a certain economic condition, for a certain nation because as intellectuals we are constituted precisely through a commitment to the imaginary that goes beyond the situation in which we find ourselves. In short, the choice to be an intellectual or an artist places us by definition in opposition to any government or institution. Art is never the expression of a society or the times in which it is produced. It is an action against that society and those times in favour of a society and times to come.

If Sartre began from the ontological status of the imaginary to arrive at a theory of literature as permanent revolution, André Malraux seems to have followed the opposite direction that goes from revolutionary action felt as akin to artistic action to a theory of the museum as a place where the imaginary finds its greatest manifestation.[19] In Malraux, even more than in Sartre, is present the idea of the artist as rival of reality and protagonist of an action much more lasting than any other, even if problematic and susceptible of many interpretations.

Aesthetic action as seduction

We have always known that the purpose of aesthetic action consists in arousing not only approbation and admiration but something more brilliant, more emotionally dynamic and sexually compromising. On this aspect of experience, which we could define with the term 'seduction' have dwelled the Japanese philosopher Shuzo Kuki (1888–1941) and the French Sociologist Jean Baudrillard (1929–2007).

Kuki's work, *Reflections on Japanese Taste: The Structure of Iki*,[20] is completely foreign to the heavy moralistic claims that Tolstoy placed on the aesthetics of action of the twentieth century. It constitutes the example of a philosophical reflection on a notion profoundly rooted in Japanese culture, a notion which is entirely independent of the Western tradition. At the beginning of the nineteenth century, the term *iki*, which is the Japanese pronunciation of the Chinese ideogram *sui*, designated the character of those places where prostitution was practiced, and the typical behaviour of the geisha, namely, that feminine figure gifted with talent and artistic culture whose function as entertainer was sexually intriguing but with an autonomous space of freedom and decision. Differently from the prostitute, it was to the geisha's discretion if she conceded herself sexually. From these premises Kuki develops the notion of *iki* to describe a complex and very organized ideal of aesthetic behaviour.

The first aspect of *iki* is connected to its sexual signification and presupposes the existence of a duality. The establishment of a relation of seduction consists in shortening the distance between the sexes, but this movement does not entail a total abolition of difference, a complete reconciliation, as is the case with love. Essential to the relation of seduction is the establishment of a tension. The geisha, when she denies herself somehow gives herself and, vice versa, by giving herself somehow she refuses herself. Inherent in eroticism is the persisting of a struggle. There is something incomplete in seduction, a kind of Hegelian 'bad infinity', a push towards an action that cannot be concluded. Aesthetic action implies an intermediary condition between peace and war, the presence of combatants who are never definitely winners or losers.

Therefore, the second character of *iki* is the spiritual energy of the warrior which implies a contradictory relation of attraction and reluctance towards the other sex. This aspect derives from the behaviour of the samurai that requires self-assurance and boldness. In the geisha it is manifested as contempt for the commercial value of things, ignorance of their price, an appreciation of cultural and aesthetic values together with disdain for awkwardness, especially when it is paired with wealth. Courage, the ability to overcome a challenge, a taste for danger and provocation, are the attributes of this aspect of *iki*.

But there is also a third dimension that comes from Buddhism: the resignation, the 'nonchalance', the lack of concern for the instability and inconsistency of the world. This aspect is similar to aesthetic detachment which, however, is not resolved in mere contemplative passivity. It is rather a suspended action because it maintains with respect to reaching an end a certain indifference that derives from a knowledge of the world. Therefore one could define it as a kind of 'contemplation in action', a superior glance with respect to subjective passions.

The characteristics of *iki* become even clearer when we compare them to other aesthetic qualities. For instance, those who possess the last two aspects of *iki,* namely, spiritual energy and 'nonchalance' but no sexual provocation, will be refined but not seductive. *Iki* shares with flashiness the active attitude with respect to the world and the thrust towards self-affirmation, but at the same time it partakes of taste, *sabi*, that is, the preference for what is worn out and thus exhibits the signs of time. Therefore, it plays between flashiness and modesty, allowing a brief glimpse of clothing or luxurious linings under opaque and little worn kimonos. Finally, *iki*, is half way between sweetness and harshness. It combines the relative sweetness of coquettishness and the relative harshness of critical consciousness.

Naturally, seduction does not constitute an exclusive prerogative of Japanese erotic culture. The Renaissance and Mannerist cultures of Italy, Baroque Spain, French Classical and Rococo, nineteenth-century England, the German states of the *Jugendstil*, offer similar reflections on the complexities and refinement of seductive action. However, it is certain that in the course of the twentieth century this problematic gradually disappears. The work of Jean Baudrillard, *Seduction*, is devoted to this decline.[21] In his view, more than just a total disappearance we are witnessing a transformation of seduction which is losing the traditional traits of challenge, complicity with evil and rebellion against society. In the age of information and communication it becomes playful, common and indistinguishable from that subtle veneer of pleasantness that seems to accompany the promotion of any electronic commodity. The fate of seduction in contemporary society seems, therefore, paradoxical. On the one hand, as affirmation of appearance over reality, it is in strict adherence with the present hegemony of the symbolic order over the real order, on the other hand, it entails a practice so refined with allusions, evocations and gestures to turn out to be so anachronistic with respect to the search for the 'naked truth', the abolition of all the veils and all the transparencies, to the naturalistic exacerbation that modern revolutions have set in motion and which find their crowning in the triumph of pornography and *trash*.

Communicative and performative action

In the last decades of the twentieth century, even in the aesthetics of action we witness a turning point comparable to the other turns (political, media and sceptical) that we have dealt with in the previous chapters. Issues previously seen and discussed as aesthetic are now viewed as questions having to do with communication. This communicative turn is accomplished by the German philosopher Karl Otto Apel (b. 1922) in *Towards a Transformation of Philosophy*,[22] where the specificity of aesthetic action turns out to be annulled by the absolute prevalence of ethical concerns. Topics such as those of dialogism, engagement and responsibility, which in Bakhtin, and Sartre are discussed as belonging to the aesthetics and philosophy of literature, are now considered to be the exclusive competence of the 'ethics of communication'.[23] Apel's starting point is the critique of methodical solipsism inherent in the philosophical tradition. He rejects the monologism of a critical self-consciousness that proceeds without any consideration of the linguistic and reasoning community. This autonomy of the thinker is illusory because language understood in its essential sociability constitutes the condition of the possibility for the exercise of any interpreting subjectivity. It is not enough that reason acquires a practical dimension and comes to a decision (as in Lukács). If this task is carried out in a monologic way it will be impossible to avoid the risk of dogmatism. For Apel true change occurs only when reason in its course and interaction posits itself as moment and representative of a universal aspiration, ideally identifiable in the boundless community of communication. In short, the novelty consists in the fact that the really important action is no longer the one that the real author exercises on the real addressee (as is the case with the founding fathers of the aesthetics of action) but the one that an ideal subject (identifiable with the entire humanity) exercises on the real author.

Differently from Apel, whose theory of communication entails the absolute prevalence of the ethical dimension, the German philosopher and sociologist Jürgen Habermas (b. 1929) author of a monumental *The Theory of Communicative Action*,[24] places communication in a fourth sphere, beyond instrumental, ethical and aesthetic action. He begins with a critical analysis of the three traditional forms of actions. The first is the teleological action, which has always been at the centre of the philosophical theory of action. It is oriented towards the realization of a purpose and is guided by norms of practical wisdom and is based on an interpretation of the situation. It evolves into strategic action when in the calculation of the agent's success enters the expectation of decisions from other actors who are equally oriented towards that purpose. This type of action is the one that seems more strictly connected to the development of Western rationality. The second is the action governed by norms that have a claim of fairness such as those of a moral or juridical character. They express an understanding existing in a social group about the conformity or deviancy of the group members' behaviour. The third is the dramaturgic action through which the actor represents himself, that is, he turns to the audience for whom he evokes a certain image of himself more or less connected to his own subjectivity. This image is not a spontaneous, expressive performance but entails a stylization of lived experiences in function of the theatrical situation. For Habermas this is aesthetic action in the strict sense. In it the key notions are those of *encounter* and *performance*. Dramatic action can be defined as a social encounter in which the participants constitute a visible audience and represent something to one another. It can even take on a strategic connotation. This occurs when the actor is worried about the effectiveness of his own performance for the purposes of reaching certain ends.

Habermas' basic intention, however, consists in outlining the fundamental character of a fourth type of action that he defines 'communicative', where language is finally applied as a *medium* of comprehension and global understanding. In the previous three models, language is understood in a unilateral way. In the first one it is employed to realize a purpose; in the second one it is only the actualization of an already existing normative understanding; in the third one, finally, it is oriented towards the staging of oneself. Only in the communicative act the actors together make reference to the objective, social and subjective world. It tends essentially towards the establishment of human relations inspired by truth, fairness and truthfulness. Habermas does not hide the difficulties inherent in the realization of this ideal of communication. He remarks, in particular, on the danger of identifying action with speech and communication with conversation. Especially relevant are his reflections on identity and individual self-realization. The common necessity to confirm oneself in self-esteem through performance and outstanding qualities is mostly present in those who like the artist carry out essentially creative activities. Now, for the artist especially, the appeal to a community greater than his real public, inherent in the communicative act, is of fundamental importance for the development of the creative faculty. Partaking of universal discourse, he frees himself from the fetters of concrete and established relations of life that lock him in narrow and traditional situations. Habermas' communicative action, therefore, implies the rebirth of the international figure of the intellectual against which Gramsci had conducted his polemic in the name of the national-popular intellectual.

The contribution of the American philosopher Richard Rorty (1931–2007) to the debate on the society of communication marks the revenge of the artistic dimension over the moral one, supported by Apel, and over the rational-universal one held by Habermas. In his *Contingency, Irony and Solidarity*,[25] Rorty is very critical of the claim that would establish the communicative act on philosophical foundations that refer to the human condition in general, or to metaphysical values such as truth, the good, justice or the like. Any humanistic appeal that prescribes as a rational obligation to feel sympathetic with all other human beings is without coherence and efficacy because the 'us' always presupposes an implicit contrast with a 'them' in whose respect solidarity does not count. The enormous effort made by Habermas to establish philosophically the society of communication is pointless not because man is necessarily evil but because this is no longer the task of philosophy! The sermon and the treatise as main vehicles of the transformation of moral beliefs have become impotent with respect to the novel, film, television programmes, in short, with respect to art! The heroes of contemporary society are neither the priest nor the scientist but the strong poet and revolutionary visionary. Today's philosophy, writes Rorty, is besieged by the conflict between two opposite ways of understanding the relation between theory and reality. On the one hand, metaphysical thinkers pretend to grasp the essence of phenomena, on the other 'ironic' thinkers limit themselves to re-describe them on the bases of historicist and nominalist premises. The former tend to emphasize the weaker and more generic aspects of language (words like 'true', 'good', 'beautiful'), the latter, instead, explore the metaphorical and creative dimensions of expression. The former claim that their vocabulary is closer to reality than the one used by others, the latter have a self-critical and vigilant attitude. The former end up by going along with common sense and with conventional opinions, the latter head in new directions and begin new linguistic games. Among the first, Rorty numbers Marx, Mill, Dewey, Habermas, among the latter Hegel, Nietzsche, Heidegger, Derrida.

What is most striking is his interpretation of Hegel's *Phenomenology of Mind*. In his view, Hegel was not metaphysical at all but the inventor of an ironic philosophy, the author of a commanding re-description of the entire intellectual history of the West, the precursor of the transformation of philosophy in a literary genre.

Ironic philosophers, according to Rorty, are not political thinkers, but private ones. That is, they are not organic towards a political ideal or a social class. They don't have any connection with political issues or with social life. They aim, rather, at the realization of an individual project and aesthetic fulfilment. Therefore, they don't confer power to their addressee, but they widen the canon and above all they change our perception of what is possible and what is important. If, then, the metaphysicians are useless and the ironists are private, should we give up completely on the idea that theory can be social action, praxis, committed activity? Rorty's answer is complex. First of all it is not the task of theory to establish what the values are. While Apel claims to give a transcendental foundation to the society of communication and Habermas a rational foundation, Rorty's argument rests on an empirical-factual plane. The essential is to guarantee the possibility of exercising a free discussion. The values will emerge spontaneously from the contrast with different opinions. Philosophy does not constitute at all a privileged point of view in the determination of what is right. At best it can speak on the formal conditions of the practice of democracy. In the fight against cruelty, which for Rorty constitutes the main objective of political commitment, literature, ethnology or journalism are much more effective because they give a voice to the sorrow of victims and they make us more sensitive to the suffering of others. Social relations, therefore, stand not on a rational order but on a feeling of empathy, identification with the emotions of others, whose origins and whose historical development is in close relation with modernity. In the last instance, Rorty's thinking is focused on an experience that concerns emotions rather than actions. The society of communication emerges as a society of feeling, much more than action. In pragmatic aesthetics, therefore, we observe the same slippage towards a problematic of feeling that characterizes the aesthetics of life (Agamben), the aesthetics of form (Lyotard), cognitive aesthetics (Vattimo). The thinking of these authors, just as Rorty's, has great significance because it marks the actual depletion of the traditional conceptual schemes that go back to Kant and Hegel.

The shift from the aesthetics of communication to the aesthetics of enterprise occurs in the work of the American philosopher Hugh J. Silverman (b. 1945) who reasserts the necessity of action with respect to thinking and feeling, in a very original way, which is that much more significant because it sinks its roots in phenomenology and hermeneutics, that is, in philosophical orientations focused on cognitive problems. For Silverman the key notion is that of 'textuality' which, however, is configured not only as a work of interpretation but also as a crossing the intermediary space that spans theory and practice. Not by chance one of Silverman's central ideas is that of *between*, a term that has a philosophical heritage that goes back to the Greeks (*metaxú*) and to Christian theology (Jesus Christ as *mediator*). In the twentieth century the notion was refashioned by German (*Zwischen*), French (*entre-deux*) and Japanese (*aidagara*) philosophers. With respect to all these inquiries, Silverman's point of view is characterized by the attribution to philosophy of the responsibility *to be a bridge* capable of connecting ideas, concepts, works of art, points of view, as well as practices of the most diverse kind, placing in evidence not only their affinities but also their differences. Philosophy is a passage through differences.[26] Thinking and action are not separated nor is there something like a unity from which they both originate. Silverman inaugurates a kind of *philosophy in act*, by grafting on styles of contemplative thinking an organizational and performative dynamism inseparable from philosophical and literary invention. In other words, it is not enough to do theories of communication or to elaborate an ironic philosophy: philosophical invention must be connected to a socialization, a context, a discussion, an audience, a task, an *interest*. This latter term is to be understood in the literal sense of *inter-est*, of being-between. Silverman's thought, thus, is at the opposite pole of Giambattista Vico who defined philosophy as 'monastic' precisely because it is inseparable from an inter-relational dimension which is not simply 'dialogic' (in Bakhtin's sense), but has 'post-political' ambitions because it emerges from the *disclosure* of action in a world context.

Aesthetic action between influence, interaction and ritual

The communicative and entrepreneurial turn, however, is not the only outcome of pragmatic aesthetics. The American literary critic Harold Bloom (b. 1930), the Sociologist Erving Goffman (1922–82) and the English philosopher of aesthetics Richard Wollheim (1923–2003) follow other directions. In Bloom aesthetic action turns out to be the influence that one poet exercises over a later poet, in Goffman his focus is on aesthetic performance within an institution and in Wollheim aesthetic action is assimilated to ritual. All these instances are examples of very reductive interpretations of aesthetic action especially when compared to that wealth and breadth of functions and purposes that the founding fathers of pragmatic aesthetics attributed to it.

The privileged object of Bloom's thinking is the relation of admiration and dependence that a writer feels with respect to the authors he takes as a model. The creative experience, therefore, is not something immediate and spontaneous but a mediated and complex relation that precedes us. On the one hand, this relation entails great enthusiasm, on the other it generates a malaise which is rooted in the fear to remain dependent on the masterpieces of the past. Hence the title of Bloom's most famous book, *The Anxiety of Influence*,[27] in which he examines in detail the various strategies employed to appropriate the literary past and conquer creative autonomy. Aesthetic action is thus limited to the plot of inter-poetic and inter-literary relations. However, even within these relations there is a process of misunderstanding and misrepresentation, of which the successor is more or less aware, which makes the transmission of messages uncertain and ineffective. This phenomenon is defined by Bloom by the term 'revisionism' which constitutes the dynamic of the cultural process in the West. Any strong author is obliged to rewrite the past and create the taste on whose basis he will be judged. Bloom sheds light on the strategic aspect of these actions which imply a conflict which is dissimulated under the codes of civility and peace. In *Agon*, he emphasizes the essentially agonistic character of aesthetic practice.[28] Every creative spirit is in a struggle with those who have preceded him and that he cannot do without. The plot proceeds through a continuous rewriting of the past. It is not sufficient to be original, one must also show that the works of the predecessors prepare and announce ours which represents, in fact, their overcoming in the double sense of confirmation and suppression.[29]

The work of Erwin Goffman is entirely focused on the strategic interaction within institutions and communities of any kind (from poker players to members of sports societies, from sports journalism to neighbourhood events). He presupposes that in any social group are in use codes, rules or even just non-formalized customs that render it similar to a theatre where everyone recites his own part. In fact, his most well-known work is entitled, *The Presentation of Self in Everyday Life*.[30] The original element of his approach is the idea that in all types of interactions there is an aesthetic aspect which is not merely formal but implies very important practical consequences, and even decisive ones, for one's destiny. Therefore, he attributes to the term *action* a very particular meaning by defining it as an activity which is susceptible of practical consequences and which is undertaken as an end in itself.[31] The interesting aspect is the permanence within this theory of dimensions that belong to aesthetic culture such as honour, challenge, ceremonial order, chivalry, reputation and even virtues such as self-control, composure, exercising mastery over oneself, peacefulness.

A reductive theory of aesthetic action is presented by Wollheim in a short work, *The Sheep and the Ceremony*, based on a Confucian story about an animal sacrifice where the relation between ritual action and art is in question. The ceremony is characterized by four specific aspects: It is felt to be compulsory but not necessary and in any case not by everyone; it is done well or not; as any action it has consequences, but its value does not depend on them; finally, it has the ability to give meaning to the life of those who perform it. However, as art, even ceremony has an external objective meaning that does not depend on the subjective mental states of those who practice it. It is necessary to defend the ritual dimension from the interpretations that condemn it as senseless and futile, or confine it to pathology. However, not any less important is to assert its independence and autonomy with respect to those who consider practical reason as the exclusive sphere of morality. Art and ritual do not allow themselves to be confined to the ethical.[32]

5

Aesthetics and Feeling

Feeling and difference

From the four chapters we have written so far one issue was left out that perhaps ought to be the most pertinent to aesthetics, at least judging from the etymology of the word, feeling.[1] Though feeling can be connected both to knowledge and action, it is also true that aesthetics was constituted as an autonomous discipline when the eighteenth century recognized the independence of the emotions with respect to theoretical reason and practical reason. As for the relation between aesthetic feeling with life and form there is no doubt that notwithstanding all the attempts to situate the aesthetic within a metaphysical and transcendental context, it originates and develops as a type of knowledge tied to experience and immanence, as an essentially worldly and mundane knowledge.

In the twentieth century we are confronted with a paradox. On the one hand, the quasi-totality of aesthetic thought in the strict sense (the one which is identified and self-defined as such) is not very interested in the question of feeling understood in its autonomy and not subordinated to other instances. On the other hand, those who, instead, place feeling at the centre of their reflections have almost nothing whatever to do with aesthetics and, when they do not expressly refuse to be recognized under this label, they claim that its relation to feeling (and art) is entirely insufficient and inadequate.

Where does this lack originate on the part of aesthetics to provide a theoretical interpretation of contemporary feeling? Why does it seem to escape the intellectual grasp of aesthetic experience? Why do notions such as life and form, faculties like knowledge and will, seem inappropriate to catch the peculiar traits of contemporary sensibility? In other words, why do the theoretical instruments provided by Kant and Hegel, judgement and dialectics, reveal themselves to be inappropriate to withstand the impact of an experience that cannot be told either as the subsumption of the particular to the universal or as the overcoming of the contradiction? Implicit within the very notion of aesthetic (understood in the neutral)[2] is the tendency towards a reconciliation of opposites. It is essential to the existence of the aesthetic, at least the prefiguration of an end to the conflict, a peace to come, an irenic moment in which suffering and the struggle are, if not definitely suppressed, at least temporarily suspended. Contemporary feeling, instead, moves in the opposite direction to aesthetic reconciliation, towards the experience of a conflict greater than the dialectic contradiction, towards the exploration of the opposition between terms that are not symmetrically polar to one another. All this great philosophical adventure, which I do not hesitate to consider as the most original and the most important of the twentieth century, goes under the notion of *difference*, understood as non-identity, as a dissimilarity greater than the logical concept of diversity and the dialectical one of distinction. In other words, the access to the experience of difference marks the abandonment of both the Aristotelian logic of identity and Hegelian dialectics. No wonder, therefore, that the thinkers of difference are also extraneous to aesthetics in the strict sense. While in the authors that we have examined so far is always present, albeit in an understated way, the legacy of Kant and Hegel, we are introduced here, instead, to a new theoretical plot which is irreducible to Kantianism and Hegelianism. The philosopher who accomplished this turn at the end of the nineteenth century was Friedrich Nietzsche (1844–1900) who, by introducing in philosophy the notion of *Dionysian* and *overcoming* (*Überwindung*) and by assigning to these concepts a radically subversive character with respect to the entire Western philosophical tradition (beginning with Socrates) has imprinted on Western thought an artistic and a literary vehemence and impulsiveness that anticipates the twentieth-century avant-garde. Not by chance, through reference to the Greek pre-Socratics, he had the courage to write a very important philosophical text, *Thus spake Zarathustra*, and to adopt the literary form of the poem![3] Therefore, the extraneousness of the thinkers of difference with respect to the modern aesthetic tradition does not stem from a disregard of feeling. Rather, it is from the study of feeling that they are led to put aside post-Kantian and post-Hegelian aesthetics as epigonic and belated. Their thinking, therefore, could be defined as 'neo-aesthetic' if this expression were not, in its turn, a source of ambiguity and misunderstanding.

In fact, it is doubtful that the notion of *difference* could be considered a true concept analogous to 'identity' (around which revolves Aristotelian logic) and 'contradiction' (around which revolves Hegel's dialectic). Perhaps more than in the horizon of pure theoretical speculation, its sphere (or at least its point of departure) is precisely the impure one of feeling, of uncommon and uncanny experiences, irreducible to identity, ambivalent and excessive, of which the existence of many men and women of the twentieth century has been intertwined. After all, it is precisely from this type of sensibility, which entertains relations of proximity with psychopathological states and mystical ecstasies, with drug addiction and perversion, with handicaps and disabilities, with 'primitive' and 'alien' cultures, that the arts, the literature and the music of the twentieth century have found their inspiration. This is probably the reason why the problematic of feeling was disregarded in contemporary aesthetics. It had to confront a feeling too different from the one that constituted the reference point for the aesthetics of Kant and Hegel and has preferred to turn back on the more classical themes of life and form, knowledge and action. To be sure something of this feeling, so different from the Kantian sentiment and the Hegelian *pathos*, is noticeable above all in some aesthetics of form influenced by the problematic of the sublime, and in some aesthetics of action obliged to think the conflict. But these instances go against the aesthetic requirement of perfection and reconciliation which, in the last instance, end up by prevailing once again by leading those thinkers back to the river-bed of the Kantian and Hegelian aesthetic tradition. Finally, one understands that the true spokesmen of contemporary feeling, with which we deal in this chapter, cannot recognize themselves in aesthetics even if their reflection has a very close affinity with problems that it has confronted.

Wit and the uncanny

It is a fact that aesthetic experience introduces a separation, a suspension, a distance with respect to conscious subjectivity engaged and involved in the needs and affairs of the world. It is a fact that starting from Kant this has been placed in evidence by so many philosophers and psychologists. From the beginning of the twentieth century, disinterest and psychic distance have been recognized as essential aspects of aesthetic feeling.[4] However, it is only with the founder of psychoanalysis, the Austrian Sigmund Freud (1856–1939) that it was possible to think a psychic instance so extraneous and different from subjective consciousness to establish with it a relation of bitter rivalry. Such psychic instance is precisely the unconscious and the whole of psychoanalysis can be thought as the most grandiose and many-sided theory of conflicting feeling. The psyche becomes the theoretical model of a struggle that exceeds by far the agonistic schema which is based on the comparison between two symmetrical opposites. No correspondence, instead, can be established between the unconscious system and the preconscious-conscious one, because the first one never appears directly on the scene of conflict. It is the scene of *difference*. Its opposition to the preconscious-conscious, however, is not only topical but also dynamic and economical. In fact Freud, in his first theory of the psychic apparatus clearly opposes the drives of the ego, defined as drives for the self-preservation of the individual, to the sexual drive, which because it is removed from the defence of the conscious ego remains unconscious. From an economical point of view, the conflict is presented as opposition between the bound energy of the secondary process, which is held back and accumulated, and the free energy of the primary process which tends immediately towards discharge. The stasis, the blockage of energy, generates displeasure. The movement, the outflow of this energy generates pleasure.

The panorama of psychic instances outlined by Freud is very different from that of the post-Kantian and post-Hegelian tradition where the notion of 'subject' and 'conscience' play an unavoidable role. If the essence of the aesthetic dimension lies in reconciliation, that is, in the tendency to lead back to a unity the relation between man and nature (in Kant), man and history (in Hegel), Freud's thinking seems to move in a direction which is greatly anti-aesthetic. By theorizing so many great conflicts within man himself, he introduces separation and chaos, malaise and ugliness, suffering and abjection into an affectivity that in Kant swayed between the sentiment of the beautiful and the sublime, and in Hegel between the *pathos* of the spirit and the creation of the artistic ideal. By focusing his attention on the absence of conscience (*Unbewusste*), on sexuality (*libido*) and on non-sublimated pleasure (*Lust*), Freud achieves an epochal shift whose importance has not yet been completely understood by aesthetics to this day.

Nonetheless, the difference of the unconscious is not something 'completely other' or is the conflict that opposes it to conscience absolute and total. Between the unconscious and conscience there is an intermediary space characterized by the forming of a compromise in which are satisfied both the demands of the former and the defences of the latter. Neurotic symptoms, dreams, the insignificant psychopathological phenomena of everyday life (such as forgetfulness, slips of the tongue, absent-mindedness) are, precisely, formations of compromise between two fundamental instances of psychic life.

Wit and poetic works also fall in the same category. Freud discusses the former in *Jokes and their Relation to the Unconscious*[5] (1905) which takes up and elaborates the philosophical speculation on laughter. This work constitutes an example of how a traditional aesthetic problematic can be profoundly innovated by the intervention of a reflection which is linked to difference, in this case, seen as unconscious. The object of Freud's analysis is *Witz*, a term that designates both witticism and Wit, the faculty that produces it. *Witz* is something fundamentally different from both the comic and humour which move in the sphere of the preconscious. The conflict which is at the basis of Witz transits, instead, between the preconscious and the unconscious. The comic is born from a degradation of its opposite. It is the outcome of a confrontation in which the subject is constrained by the presence of a new representation that in order to be understood requires an effort which he would rather not make. In other words, the comic is a cheap way to avoid the conflict with a difference. There is nothing which exposed without defence can avoid being ridiculed by comic degradation! In humour, instead, the opposite is assimilated and overcome by the subject. The avoidance of the conflict occurs by neutralizing some of its painful effects. The rise of displeasure is blocked from the start. That is why it is a very valuable mechanism of defence of the ego that believes itself to be superior and transcendental with respect to its opposite, to the different.[6] Wit, instead, is the faculty that eludes a conflict with the unconscious by creating a form of compromise which is, precisely, witticism. Depending on the content of this conflict, we can distinguish two types of witticisms: a tendentious one, where a secret obscene or hostile intention is expressed in a concealed way, or an innocent one, which appears to be without a secret intention and, even more than the tendentious one, is inseparable from the linguistic form in which it is expressed. The character of the witty expression lies, precisely, in its linguistic form, in its literal meaning. Witticism is, so to speak, non-fungible, non-exchangeable. It has no other equivalent. Contrary to the aesthetic explanation of the phenomenon, according to which witticism provokes a pleasure without interest and without purpose, Freud claims that even at the basis of the innocent witticism there is an intention and that it also has an interest in pleasure. Language is also the place where a conflict arises between conscience and the unconscious, identity and difference. A witticism, therefore, is a form of compromise between the drive of the ego which aims at maintaining the linguistic representations, and the opposite drive which aims at dissolving them. By attributing an essential importance to the phonic aspect of the word, the signifier, it treats words like *things*, thus disrupting the intrinsic identity of words. A witticism consists, precisely, in the emergence of an opposite meaning from a similar verbal construct. The latter cannot be stated directly, since the ego inhibits the creation of new meanings, but it can be represented, catching the ego by surprise, so to speak, who is reassured by the phonic resemblance of the words. This explains that absence, the sudden distancing of the intellectual tension that precedes the witty expression as well as the effect of surprise that it creates. Rigorously speaking, Freud writes, we do not know what we laugh about. The ways of wit are twisted because they lead to an oblique laughter, and excludes the representation of conscience. Finally, it is important to remark on the essentially social character of wit with respect to the comic and humour. While the comic implies the presence of two people (the one who degrades and the one who is the object of the degradation) and humour is limited to one person, the witty expression implies the participation of three people (the one who creates the expression, the one who is the object of the sexual or hostile aggression and the one who listens to it). The originality of wit with respect to the other two forms consists not only in the necessary presence of a third person but also in the fact that this is the only person who laughs. The creator of the witticism finds pleasure in it but does not laugh.

Poetic works are equally a form of compromise.[7] They constitute a substitute for the fulfilment of drives that the author had to renounce in real life. Through them an open conflict is avoided with the forces of repression. Differently from dreams they are destined to arouse the interest in other people. Therefore Freud stresses their social dimension. In his essay on *Creative Writers and Day-Dreaming*[8] (1907) he examines the affinity between art and play. Both constitute an intermediary realm between reverie and reality. Play needs the support of tangible objects, just as in art symbols and substitutive forms arise real emotions. The artist is not aware of these processes. If he is asked about it, he does not know how to reply or he replies in ways that are not appropriate. In so doing Freud reinterprets the ancient image of the poet as possessed, similar to the prophet, the Bacchante and the lover, in the light of the new de-subjectivization of feeling carried out by psychoanalysis.

The fundamental oppositions established by Freud in the first phase of his thinking (up to World War I) were organized around the conflict between conscience and the unconscious, the drives of the ego and sexual drives, pleasure and displeasure. None of these oppositions are maintained in the next stage. The unconscious ceases to be a particular instance and qualifies not only the Id (the new term to designate the pole of the psyche's drives) but also the Ego and Super-Ego (also a new term to designate the autocratic instance of the psyche). The drives of the Ego and sexual drives, assimilated in the common project for the self-preservation of the individual and the species, respectively, constitute the life drive. The characteristic of an 'opposite' and 'different' factor is assumed by a 'beyond the pleasure principle' discovered by Freud in some phenomena of 'repetition compulsion'. This new opposite term defined as death drive tends to the reinstatement of inorganic matter and is qualified as the 'Nirvana principle'.

Freud's most important and influential 'aesthetic' essay, *The Uncanny* (1919), belongs to this second phase of his thought.[9] He observes that aesthetics prefers to deal with arguments that correspond to positive states of mind such as the beautiful and the sublime. Thus, it restricts the sphere of its interests which also ought to extend to those aspects of feeling that are characterized by negative states of mind, as in the case of the *uncanny* (*das Unheimliche*) that can be defined as a sort of dread that goes back to what we have known for a long time, to what is familiar to us. The uncanny, therefore, cannot be identified with the 'completely other', the absolutely different, because somehow it is already known to us and in some ways it is even habitual and at hand. By examining the German adjective, *heimlich*, Freud remarks that it has two quite different meanings. In the first place it refers to the familiar, the household, from *Heim*, which is, in fact, home, hearth. But it also means hidden, concealed, secret, dangerous. The adjective *unheimlich* (literally, the non-familiar) is the opposite of the first meaning but not the second, in fact, it tends to identify with it. Therefore, there is a puzzling coincidence between the two adjectives, where one ought to be the negative of the other. Therefore, the definition that the German philosopher Schelling gave of the term *unheimlich* seemed to Freud very perceptive. For Schelling *unheimlich* is all that should remain secret, hidden but, instead, rises to the surface! This could be an excellent definition of the unconscious! But here Freud goes way beyond the identification of the different with the unconscious. In fact, what is truly uncanny is no longer a conflict between two non-symmetrical poles (one of which could never by definition appear on the scene directly) but the phenomenon of ambivalence, the simultaneous co-presence of an affirmation and a negation without the possibility that they may lead to a dialectical overcoming.

A further development of the experience of difference derives from a consideration of the examples of uncanny provided by Freud. One source of the uncanny could be the suspicion that an apparently animate being is in actuality a robot and, vice versa, that an organic entity is not really living. More generally, events are perceived as uncanny that bring back childhood fears or undermine our trust in the identity of living beings, like the double and, in general, the phenomena of the doubling of characters, destinies and actions. Hence Freud concludes that the essence of the uncanny is not to be found in novelty but in repetition, in that particular type of repetition which is not willed and which he defines as 'repetition compulsion', in short, in a different repetition. This is the greatest difference, the farthest experience from identity. Not absolute extraneousness but a familiar one which has its roots in our past, which is and is not itself at the same time. With the notion of uncanny Freud goes beyond the oppositional dynamic that was at the basis of his first system of the psychic apparatus. The difference is no longer a compromise between opposites whose distance is greater than the dialectical contradiction (Hegel) and the polarity (Nietzsche), but it is an ambivalence that unites in itself, indissolubly, identity and alterity. Its movement goes from the same to the same, it is the same that always returns but that in returning it is different from the original model. It undermines all previous polarities established previously, beginning from the most important which separates the pleasure principle from the reality principle. In fact, according to Freud, we find ourselves exposed to an uncanny effect when the boundaries between fantasy and reality become narrower.

Contemporary aesthetics, in the strict sense that we have outlined in the first four chapters of this work, in the last analysis, is a development of Kant's and Hegel's philosophies. Only with the problematic of difference an exploration of unknown areas of feeling can begin that are not reducible to the conceptual devices of previous philosophy and aesthetics.

Abandonment and attention

The de-subjectivization of feeling led by Freud finds its confirmation in an analogous and not less grandiose work by the German philosopher Martin Heidegger (1889–1976). His thinking is an integral part of a wider and general critique of Western metaphysics which Heidegger accuses of having imposed a limiting and inadequate conception of Being which in antiquity, starting from Plato, was thought as substance and in modern times, starting from Descartes, as subject. In the substance as in the subject, the place of Being is taken by beings where the *difference* between Being and beings is forgotten, and a perspective of experiencing and thinking has prevailed characterized by the affirmation of *identity*. This oblivion is present in the calculations of the sciences, the reassuring evaluation of humanism and the lived experience of aesthetics. An important contribution to the development of the metaphysical project was made by Kant, Hegel and even Nietzsche whose will to power constitutes the fulfilment of the identity of substance and subject. In the historical event of the West very few have escaped the rule of metaphysics, namely, the pre-Socratics in antiquity, such as Parmenides and Heraclitus, and some modern poets like Hölderlin and Rilke for whom the thing (*Ding*) returns to its nearing remoteness.

Therefore, even aesthetics, ever since its beginnings, has considered the work of art under the sway of the traditional interpretation of beings, that is, metaphysics. After all, the same distinction of philosophy in various disciplines such as logic, ethics, aesthetics, preserves its own justification only within metaphysics, a thought which has forgotten the difference of Being. According to Heidegger, the essential of art and experience fall outside aesthetics. In it, the hegemony exercised by the subject is present as exclusive attention to the affective state, considered, in fact, as aesthetic state. Wagner's work represents the greatest exaltation of aesthetic subjectivity. The total work of art (*Gesamtkunstwerk*) despite its name does not revive art at all, but liquidates it and dissolves it by reducing it to a pure stimulus of lived experience.[10] The entire world is contemplated and appreciated only on the basis of its effectiveness for the purpose of reproduction of the aesthetic state. The totalitarian and indiscriminate extension of the affective state corrupts and deprives life of any great finality.

The de-subjectivization of experience led by Heidegger takes place as a critique of two central notions of subjectivist aesthetics: the 'expression of lived experience' (*Erlebnis-Ausdruck*) and the 'affective state' (*Gefühlzustand*).[11] As far as the former is concerned, Heidegger opposes it to the essentially linguistic character of poetry and human existence, but language is not at all the expression of a subject, understood individually or collectively, which exists previously and independently. It is not we who possess language but it is language that possesses us! Therefore, it is the most dangerous of our commodities. We cannot make use of it and it does not give us any guarantee because we are presented at the same time with being and non-being, poetry and chatter. Poetry establishes what is permanent but this must not be understood as eternal, divine or transcendental. It is Being as well as non-Being. Language is not only rootedness but also displacement, not only nearness but also remoteness, not only familiar but also unfamiliar. These oppositions are not understood by Heidegger in a dialectical process, but they must be left-together-in front without being identified or overcome in any way. It is not by chance that Hölderlin is within the horizon of thinking opened by Heraclitus who was the first to understand the essence of the logos not as a gathering of unity but as a gathering which holds and brings, keeps and preserves opposites. The greatness and the power of poetic language with respect to lived experience rests, precisely, in the fact that poetry carries within itself Being as well as non-Being, salvation as well as ruin, while lived experience is the most extreme and reactive affirmation of identity.

The second notion rejected by Heidegger is that of the 'affective state'. In fact, the concept of feeling is inseparably connected to the problematic of the subject, that is, to the modern development of metaphysics. In its place Heidegger speaks of a *Grundstimmung*, a fundamental mood which differently from emotion is not limited to carry out a function of mere accompanying but reveals the world and discloses Being as well as its lack. Mood (*Stimmung*) dwells neither in the subject nor in the object, in fact, we are the ones who are transported in the mood that can be defined as an all-embracing power. While emotion claims an absolute identity with itself the *Grundbestimmung* is both joy and grief. Grief can only come from ancient joys, after all, it is a joy that hesitates and wavers. They both have nothing to do with the sentimentality of excitement and melancholy. The power of poetry does not exclude the night of the world, the time of poverty. The poet is rich precisely because he is not divine, if he were divine he would not be able to gather in himself the opposites and preserve them as such. This power and wealth of poetry are not actual but omnipresent. The poets, in fact, according to Hölderlin's poetry, are raised in the gentle embrace of the wonderfully omnipresent, powerful and divinely beautiful nature. She is present in everything which is actual but cannot be reduced to the actual. Omnipresence ignores the one-sidedness of the weight of the mere actual and derives its power from the fact that it keeps and offers one to the other the extreme opposites of the highest heaven and the deepest abyss, Being and non-Being, the familiar and non-familiar, joy and grief. The beautiful, according to Heidegger is not at all impotent or weak, on the contrary, in the simultaneity of enchantment and ecstasy, it is the most powerful and the strongest. Therefore, poets are both spiritual and mundane, but they do not belong only to this century, their way of being is also the most comprehensive and gathering. They are, according to Hölderlin, silent winners over fate because strong from a great weight of happiness.

Thus Heidegger introduces us to a feeling which is inseparable from thinking and action. It occurs before the tripartition of man in knowledge, action and sentiment.[12] This explains the particular emphasis placed by Heidegger on the notion of origin that gives the title to one of his most well-known works on the philosophy of art, *The Origin of the Work of Art*.[13] The original character of art does not imply that something gives origin to art or that art emerges from an absolute nothing. For Heidegger, art has no origin but it *is* the origin or its own essence. This characteristic of origin is precisely what aesthetics has always denied to art. For aesthetics, art has never been present. The works of art exposed to the aesthetic glance of exhibitions and museums, are no longer present, are no longer what they once were. They are before us as having been within the perspective of tradition and preservation.

The notion of origin does not aim at asserting the excellence of the archaic with respect to the modern, or the classical exemplariness of the past with respect to the present, on the contrary, the radical discontinuity of the artistic event with respect to everything that preceded it, surrounds it and follows it. Heidegger aims at freeing the work of art from all relations that it entertains with everything it is not. This does not mean at all to distort them but, on the contrary, to attribute to art the most profound historical dimension, the foundation of history. Art and origin are synonymous because there is no art that is not origin, leap, foundation in the present. The origin is not the point of departure which is followed by a development and an end. The beginning already includes birth and death. If art abandons the experience of the origin it ceases to be art.

To the question, 'What are works of art?', Heidegger's answer is that they are *things* (*Dinge*). However, aesthetics has always avoided this answer. It thinks that there is something else above and beyond thingness which is added to the thing and constitutes the work of art which is thought of as allegory or, more recently, symbol, as the union of spirituality and materiality, of a visible and an invisible element. For aesthetics what is important to the work of art is a kind of addition, supplement, appendix to the thing which remains unthought in its fundamental essence. This falls within a wider and more general inability of the Western metaphysical tradition, of which aesthetics is part, to think the thing. The imposition that metaphysics exerts on the thing takes on various aspects connected by a strict affiliation. The three metaphysical conceptions of the thing (as substance, object perceived by the senses and matter) constitute so many ways of doing violence and aggression to the thingness of the thing, to its essence. Only a meditation on being-thing of the thing can open the way to an understanding of both the utilitarian dimension of being-instrument of the instrument, and the artistic dimension of being-work of the work. The thing is not a symbol, or a synthesis, a being to which something utilitarian or artistic is added. Its utility and artistic character are already inherent in the thingness of the thing. The first is its reliability, the second its presence.

The de-subjectivization of thinking implies an experience of truth completely different from the metaphysical one. Heidegger turns to archaic Greece where truth was called 'aletheia' (a word made up by the privative *a* and the verb *lantháno*, which means 'being obscure' or 'remaining obscure'), which in German could be rendered as *Unverborgenheit*. It is decisive that the word 'truth' is etymologically determined by the failure of a negative dimension and not by an assertion of a positive dimension. It is never a motionless scenario with a constantly raised curtain where the representation of beings unfolds. Truth is not a property of beings, which inheres to it inevitably, or the characteristic of a judgement and, even less, a subjective certainty. All these conceptions of truth fall under the word *orthóthes* (*Richtigkeit*), exactitude, fairness. They lead us to believe that truth is something which we can take possession of by means of a clearer insight, a more correct representation, a more refined perception. In fact, for Heidegger, it is necessary that the thing itself be present to us. The experience of truth implies, on our part, a being already exposed to the whole region, to the clearing in which Being appears and withdraws. It requires an attitude of *Gelassenheit*, releasement with respect to the difference of Being.[14] In other words, truth does not mean possession or unity of a whole that reveals itself to us only in part. The open space, the clearing (*Lichtung*) to which Heidegger refers to explain the special nature of this non-subjective, non-personal, non-psychological feeling, is not thinkable as a unity but as an 'other', as something barely known that opens and guarantees in changing measures the hidden non-Being of beings, as well as its being hidden. In fact, the *Lichtung* is not at all identical with appearance. Non-appearance is equally essential as appearance, hiddenness and concealment are just as important as disclosure and expression.

It is important to understand that *Lichtung*, the lighted clearing, the openness, the lighting, the widening, the *lucus*, is not a metaphysical notion because it is historical, it is an event, an occurrence. Truth is not something eternal but is historicized in the work of art. The *Lichtung* is not even an aesthetic notion because it is not a reconciliation. It presents an essential oppositional element, an element of contrast. This opposition, however, is not dialectical in nature and not comparable to the one between affirmation and negation. The conflicting element implicit in illumination cannot be seen as the opposition between unconcealedness and concealedness, almost as if the former is truth and the latter is falsehood. Concealedness points to the withdrawal, the withdrawing of truth.

One of the important aspects of aesthetic tradition is the distinction between form and matter. Heidegger rejects this distinction and rethinks the two terms in an alternative way. Where tradition writes 'form' he writes 'world', where tradition writes 'matter' he writes 'earth'. However, it is not a question of naming the same thing in different ways but, on the contrary, to think in a completely different way the essence of the work of art. If the work is reduced to form one loses the essential, that is, the historicizing of the truth of the work. The notion of form is connected to the placing of limits: the form is that which limits. The notion of world, instead, is inseparable from the opening of relations. The work of art opens a world and confers to things their aspect and to men their vision of themselves. While implicit in the aesthetico-metaphysic concept of form is the setting of limits, the world refers to the experience of 'openness', which must be understood in the sense of risk. In fact, the 'world' is the greatest of dangers. Similarly, one must abandon the notion of matter which is generally understood as what is limited, forced and contained. Heidegger reproaches tradition for making matter disappear, to subordinate it, not to let it be what it is. Matter is violated, bent, forced into a formal will that can be directed towards usefulness or the artistic. In both cases tradition aims at erasing matter, whether it is a stone, metal, colour, word or sound. Therefore, Heidegger introduces the notion of earth that withdraws in its heaviness and maintains a constant refusal towards any attempt to dissolve it. The earth defers to something safe.

The affinity between risk and security, danger and abandonment, leads to the experience of 'dwelling poetically'.[15] This does not mean to be at one's home. To dwell, for Heidegger, means to have a relation with a place which is not only one of nearness but also of remoteness. The things that are the nearest remain uncanny. Heidegger removes nearness and remoteness as units of measurement that make of them a merely quantitative and metric issue. But this does not mean that space becomes something subjective. In fact, the contrary is the case. Man is *listening*, waiting for nearness and remoteness to show themselves to him. We are on the way: we don't go towards a predetermined goal, we are not led by a project, we don't err without destination and blindly. We are looking for a place in which we can dwell as wayfarers. The 'viaticum' turns out to be an essential trait of the experience of difference. It dissolves both rootedness and alienation. The configuration of Being is not univocal. There is no need to go far in order to find the different: it is always already there where we are. And vice versa, the fact that the regions of Being are connected among each other makes somehow even the most remote places near. Nearness is always already there to greet us.

The term and the notion of region (*Gegend*) seems particularly apt to indicate the complex characters of this experience.[16] It stays untamable, uncanny, different (as it is implicit in the prefix *gegen*, against) and yet it offers itself, meets us (*gegnet*) in its free expanse requesting our abandonment, attention, adherence. Heidegger's thinking is inseparable from the special mood of his language. It introduces us in a region of feeling which is beyond subjectivity and objectivity, activity and passivity. Difference is not something that one can gather exclusively through a conceptual exposition, or through a philological interpretation, and not even thanks to an ecstatic inspiration. These three ways are necessary to access an experience that asks us to bind our destiny to it.

To see something 'as something'

The rejection of aesthetics and the focus on the relation between the familiar and unfamiliar are also present in the work of the Austrian philosopher Ludwig Wittgenstein (1889–1951) who, together with Freud and Heidegger, is the third great thinker of feeling as difference. He subjects aesthetic judgement to a relentless critique showing its logical inconsistency and its practical uselessness. In his view, aesthetics has no cognitive or pragmatic value.[17] Like Herbart, Wittgenstein identifies aesthetics with ethics insofar as they are both evaluative discourses. The words which express the beautiful and the good could be reduced in large part to interjections of praise and blame. What exceeds this dimension is explainable with reference to the concrete occasions in which these judgements are pronounced, or to a set of rules to be applied. Therefore, aesthetic judgements do not possess any autonomy and they can be entirely referred to the local and historical context in which they are uttered.

Wittgenstein is not interested in judging but in feeling, that is, in a particular type of experience that undermines the traditional notions of identity and alterity, and consists in looking at an entity that remains unchanged now as a thing, now as another. In *Philosophical Investigations*[18] he provides a very simple example of this experience, namely, the drawing of a duck which can be interpreted now as the drawing of a duck and now as a drawing of a hare. In actual fact, there are many things that give us this impression of ambiguity. First of all, works of art or musical pieces to which now we listen one way and now another, or works of architecture, sculpture and painting, which arise now an emotion and now another. We find many examples even in daily life. For instance, people and things with which we have been familiar for a long time suddenly appear to us foreign and unnatural, without that the least change has occurred to them. We see a man but we do not recognize him as our friend, we look at a parallelepiped without identifying it with our cabinet.

The phenomenon of seeing a thing now this way now another introduces us to an impersonal dimension of experience. All that remains subjective constitutes an obstacle that perverts, through a conceptual integration, the simplicity of feeling. Wittgenstein even questions that this feeling belongs to someone, that there is a bearer of feeling. Between language and feeling there is a hiatus. The experience of difference turns out to be inaccessible to traditional psychological theories. Wittgenstein finds entirely unsatisfactory the spiritualistic, subjectivist and mentalist theory that goes back to Descartes and is extended to the psychology of form and beyond, according to which feeling is reducible to a mental representation and formation. Wittgenstein considers equally inadequate the behavioural, positivist theory that by eliminating every reference to consciousness and negating any validity to the introspective method reduces feeling to what is observable from the outside. Thus the de-subjectivization of feeling opens new ways to a whole series of new disturbing questions of the type: 'How can one so much as get the idea of ascribing a *sensation* to a *thing*?',[19] or, vice versa, 'I can't imagine that the people around me are automata, lack consciousness, even though they behave the same as usual?'[20]

Usually we believe that in order to understand the facts we need to integrate them through an interpretive mediation.[21] This is the horizon of 'seeing as' where the establishment of a comparison, the allusion to a conceptual scheme, the process of recognition, constitute a guarantee of intelligibility. In the last instance, philosophy consists in large part of this activity of familiarization which is a mixture of seeing and thinking.

To 'seeing as', Wittgenstein opposes 'seeing like this', the sudden and immediate flash of a different vision. Something happens to us, suddenly we remain out of breath and we say, 'look!'[22] There is something like a flash in the face,[23] a beaming, an intensity and an indescribable liveliness. To be sure, this 'seeing like this' seems, for its immediacy, similar to the original and creative intellectual intuition that Kant attributed to God. Therefore, another expression of Wittgenstein is more in keeping with the nature of difference: 'seeing something *as something*'.[24] In fact, the difference is not absolute alterity but a different repetition, a strange and vacillating structure that cannot be grasped in its identity.[25]

The sex appeal of the inorganic

A lot less involved than Heidegger and Wittgenstein in rejecting traditional aesthetics, but like them interested in delineating the traits of the new sensibility, is the German thinker Walter Benjamin (1892–1940) whose privileged subjects of study was the Baroque and Baudelaire.[26] From them Benjamin derives inspiration to outline the essential traits of a feeling centred on three phenomena: death, commodity and sex. Actually these are the three aspects that traditional aesthetics has neglected if not avoided. Benjamin's originality consists not so much in having made them the pivot of his reflection but in placing them in relation to one another, conferring a theoretical dimension to an alternative experience of vitalism which, in taking its cue from one of his remarks, can be defined by the expression 'the sex appeal of the inorganic'.[27]

The theoretical core of this experience is constituted by a mixture of the human and the 'thing' whereby, on the one hand, human sensibility is reified, on the other, things seem to be endowed with their own sensibility. This is a phenomenon already pondered by Worringer, Freud and Wittgenstein. However in Benjamin it is applied to a great multiplicity of situations and acquires not only an essential meaning for the interpretation of Baroque culture and the capitalistic society of Baudelaire's times, but constitutes an extremely fertile key to reading the twentieth century. In fact, the inorganic is not only the mineral but also the cadaveric, the mummified, the technological, the chemical, the commodified, the fetish. Thus it dematerializes itself, becomes somewhat abstract and incorporeal without however changing into something imaginary or unreal. On the contrary, behind these representations of the inorganic operates the paradigm of what is chiefly real and actual, namely, money. It is important to remark that the difference is never an imaginary dimension, neither ideal nor ineffective, weak or secondary. In

Freud it is the primary psychic reality, in Heidegger is Being in the vastness of its his manifestations, in Wittgenstein it is language. In Benjamin it takes on the most disturbing determinations, enveloping in an inextricable relation sexuality, philosophy and economy.

The theoretical starting point of the 'sex appeal of the inorganic' can be located in the failure of identity which, according to Benjamin, is accompanied by trauma, strong emotions or, as he says, by *shock*. In *The Origin of German Tragic Drama*,[28] his only systematic work of a certain breadth, Benjamin sees in the ethics of the Stoics and in the invitation to become nobody and nothing the premise of Baroque feeling, which implies a total distancing from the natural, a complete rejection of subjective expression. The condition for participating to the great play of the world is the abandonment of a fixed and immutable subjective identity. The baroque character views catastrophe as something that has already occurred. His ability to move among the most jarring contradictions derives from a giddy experience of mutations and reversals. Similarly, in Baudelaire, spleen is the state of mind that corresponds to permanent catastrophe. The experience of *shock* occupies the very centre of his artistic work.

Together with identity unity also fails. Everything falls apart and is fragmented in an infinity of parts that gives way to the most disparate combinations. Baroque allegory is based on this phenomenon thanks to which any character, thing and situation can signify any other. It announces and prefigures the commercial condition where everything can be exchanged with everything else. The Parisian *passages* of the twentieth century, galleries and corridors that cross housing blocks expressly destined for commercial activities, constitute for Benjamin the architectural representation of a ceaseless transit that dissolves the notions of internal and external, inside and outside, near and distant.

But it is above all through the category of exteriority that death, commodities and sex pursue one another and are strengthened reciprocally. For Benjamin, the Baroque implies a vision of the world completely secularized and mundane where there is no room for transcendence. The medieval way of indignation is barred and caducity is exalted with provoking tones. In seventeenth-century poetry feminine beauty is magnified through continuous comparisons with jewels, snow and alabaster which associate her with a corpse. A passion for the extreme and a taste for a challenge are essential aspects of the figure of the dandy which in Baudelaire finds its crucial representation: it is interesting only what unites opposites and keeps them in their opposition. What is serious can be expressed only in a frivolous way and, vice versa, vanity has death for its companion. Fashion confuses clothing and body and constitutes the most powerful of aphrodisiacs.

Another figure of exteriority is the *flaneur* for whom sloth has greater value than work.

These determinations reveal themselves to be very fertile in the interpretation of contemporary society which constitutes the object of Benjamin's *The Work of Art in the Age of Mechanical Reproduction*.[29] Here he examines the shift from the traditional work of art, characterized by a unique and unrepeatable identity, to modern forms of artistic expression that like photography and cinema dissolve the *hic and nunc* of the work in a multiplicity of copies deprived of their original. This phenomenon is described by Benjamin as a loss of 'aura' and cultural values. Their place is taken up by their expository value, that is, by an emphasis on the theatrical dimensions of the work that ends up overshadowing its aesthetic specificity. These changes accompany a profound transformation of perception and feeling. The photographic camera and the movie camera capture images that escape the natural eye that finds itself constrained to be identified with a technological device. The vision of the movie camera, writes Benjamin, is similar to that of the unconscious. It captures so many things that remained unnoticed before. This creates an artificial feeling that changes the perception of proximity and distance, as well as the notion of reality which, on the one hand, becomes illusory and, on the other, over-naturalistic. While the actor provides a unified performance in the theatre, in the cinema he is forced into a plurality of takes that externalize his performance. Everything becomes plural and repeated, but we are dealing with a different repetition that creates infinite variations within a common genre. Benjamin emphasizes the revolutionary potential of these perceptive and sensitive transformations. The main thing is not to be afraid of the extent and radicality of the transformations taking place and even though one is without illusions with respect to the new age, it is essential to speak for it without reservation.

Persuasion and estrangement

The search for a non-subjective feeling contrary to vitalism, which breaks from the depressive and defeatist attitude of everyday life, and is deeply impregnated with the experience of opposites, characterizes the work of the Italian thinker Carl Michelstaedter (1887–1910) and the Russian literary critic Viktor Shklovsky (1893–1984). Of very different temperaments, the former was imbued with a kind of heroic rage that led him to attack with vehemence the emotional misery of his age, the latter was endowed with a funambulist and unscrupulous irony that dissolved all literary conventions and opened new horizons to artistic research. In common they shared an attitude of dare with respect to social, philosophical and aesthetic traditions and the commitment to venture on the uncharted roads of sensibility and thinking.

Michelstaedter's point of departure is a critique of vitalism in *Persuasion and Rhetoric*,[30] his most important work and one of the most brilliant examples of philosophical writing in Italian literature. A feeling which lets itself go to the flow of desire, illusions, and hopes, and which lets itself be pulled along by the spontaneous course of life, cannot produce any self-esteem in those who feel it. The mere love for natural life is defined by Michelstaedter as *philopsuchía*, synonymous of cowardice! In fact, cowardice is letting oneself be swept by a desire for life that always looks for something new, who is never satisfied with the situation in which one is in, who experiences the present as a non-existent moment between memory and anticipation. Cowardice means to suffer one's own need to live. It is to be appeased with a chronic deficiency that can never be healed. In this perspective life is similar to a hook, it always tends towards the lowest point and can never stop. Cowardice is the pain of life that can never be sated. The hedonistic conception of life, according to which pleasure is what counts, is prey to an insatiable hunger that leads those who trust it to dissolution.

However, there is another attitude even more deplorable than vitalism. Michelstaedter calls it 'rhetoric'. While cowardice, so to speak, is spontaneous, rhetoric is a reactive formation. It consists in wanting to affirm an absolute certainty to oppose to the experience of nothing. Rhetorical man feeds on lies and deceit. Social life becomes a 'league of wolves', a place of general fawning that by means of an inconclusive verbosity conceals the total absence of experience. Rhetoric is also the negation of historical sense because it purports to abolish time and promises access to an absolute and eternal dimension. If the life drive is an illusion, rhetoric is illusion squared. In rhetorical man we find a groundless claim of stability, an inadequate and, under all aspects, a very fragile affirmation of individuality, of certainty. There are many types of rhetoric: of authority, of pleasure, the artistic one and the philosophical one but they can all be brought back to a will to transform the present in something eternal.

In opposition to cowardice and rhetoric, Michelstaedter lays claim to a different type of feeling that he defines with the term 'persuasion' whose character is a converging of opposite dimensions, energy and peace, intensity and exteriority, movement and immobility. Michelstaedter does not believe in the unity of consciousness, the identity of the ego, the continuity of inner experience. To avoid the insatiable hunger for life means to break the never satisfied desire for the future and to consider every instant of time as already fulfilled and perfect. This way, he introduces us to a feeling where, on the one hand, the situation asserts itself with a compelling radicality which is impossible to avoid, on the other, it does not give rise to a passive resignation, but to strongly emotional and affective states that aspire to complete autonomy and self-sufficiency. On the one hand, we must not ask what cannot be given, on the other hand, precisely this descent in the abyss of one's own insufficiency generates a very intense sentiment that Michelstaedter defines as 'becoming flame'.

An impression of spirited nonchalance pours out of Shklosky's *Theory of Prose*.[31] In it the experience of difference is manifested as estrangement (*ostranenie*).[32] It consists in transposing the object of its perception in a new unforeseen and surprising perception. Against the blindness and the deafness of everyday life, Shklovsky lays claim to the importance of wonder. Things pass by us as if they were packed in boxes. Art has the task of making us feel them as if we were perceiving them for the first time. It has affinity with eroticism which feeds equally on allegories, discontinuities, 'dissimilarities of similarities'. Thus, he describes an experience similar to the one characterized by Freud and Wittgenstein: aspects of life traditionally considered insignificant acquire a fundamental importance and, vice versa, usual associations reveal themselves to be completely ineffective. The opposite of estrangement is identification. We avoid it with the 'Knight move' as in chess.[33] The Knight is not free, it moves according to a strange rule which precludes it from advancing directly.

Eroticism, the neutral, the simulacrum: The stupor of reason

The French writers Georges Bataille (1897–1962), Maurice Blanchot (1907–2003) and Pierre Klossowski (1905–2001) constitute a triad of adventurous explorers of the feeling of difference. With essays, short stories and novels they have covered and explored the unknown territories of sensibility and affectivity, transposing their discoveries in theoretical terms.

According to Bataille, Hegel has subordinated the negative to an historical positivity that by transcending it abolishes it. Therefore he lays claim to the autonomous existence of a 'use-less' negative, irreducible and sovereign, which is manifested in the causality of birth and death, in the revelation of one's own finitude, in laughter, in eroticism, in poetry and in art. All these experiences throw man outside himself and remove him from his subservience to work and knowledge. What matters are no longer the demands and the needs of the subject closed in his cognitive and moral certainties but the excess of a flow of energy which is transmitted as a whirlwind.

Between poetry and the negative exists a deep relationship. The poetic word, and the work of art in general, is constituted as such precisely in the rejection of the positive and servile language of economy and logic, and it is free of utilitarian and designing intentions. Therefore, it can be defined as the 'perversion' and the 'sacrifice' of words. Poetry destroys the things that it names and makes possible the access to the unknown, to non-knowledge. It is similar to minority states. A fine bond links it to the various manifestations of the logical negative (nonsense, antinomy), moral (evil), economical (loss, extravagance), legal (crime), psychological (infancy, madness), physical (death). The essays contained in *Literature and Evil*,[34] devoted to various poets and writers which are said to be exemplary from this point of view, demonstrates the meaning of destinies that are fulfilled under the sign of transgression.

Even more radical than poetry and art in the pursuit of the negative is eroticism which in Bataille is represented as the real experience of sovereignty,[35] and must be distinguished from mere sexuality. In fact, eroticism is a psychic activity connected to the experience of the negative and transgression. It marks the shift from animality to humanity. In fact, while the animal lives in the identity of the natural instinct, the human being is constituted as such in the conflict between work and play, seriousness and laughter, taboo and transgression. Eroticism is the contradictory experience of prohibition and its violation. It suspends the former without getting rid of it and therefore it can never assume the character of a return to nature or the reconstitution of a positive totality.

For Maurice Blanchot what characterizes the border-line experience is not the negative but the neutral. It is irreducible to a unity as well as a duality, a presence as well as an absence. Its space is the *in-between*. It cannot be attributed to either an individual or to a consciousness because it implies precisely the dissolution of one and the other. It is not someone's experience but the access of the ego-that-dies to the space where, by dying, he does not die as an 'I', in the first person. This is the space of literature[36] which identifies with the neutral because it is the only language that, by putting itself into play, creates within it not a relation of identity or alterity, but one of infinite difference.[37] Literature, through self-reference, suspends the sense of what it says. It does not assert or deny but establishes a neutral sphere that leaves out of consideration the author and the reader. In the end, literature is constituted and is destroyed in the self-questioning of its own nature.

The different repetition is the problem of Pierre Klossowski to whom we owe the philosophical elaboration of the *simulacrum*. It constitutes something which is irreducible both to reality and appearance. In their essence things are copies of a model that never existed. Experience is always repetition, the eternal return that dissolves the identity of the real and takes away from history any meaning or direction.[38] In such cases nothing else is possible but *amor fati*, as Nietzsche had already pointed out.[39] It is not the internalization of a blind and unknown necessity but, on the contrary, the loss of identity and the greatest externalization that leads man to devote himself to the existence of a universe that has no other purpose than being what it is. On the other hand, the eternal return is not a real theory but rather a test through which the philosopher must pass. He is the *Versucher* in the double sense of experimenter and tempter. Klossowski's work also opens dizzy and unprecedented perspectives in the sphere of sexual feeling. In his *La monnaie vivante*,[40] he asks what it means to consider the body not as a commodity (as is commonly the case with prostitution) but as currency.

An even more daring experience of limits and an even more extreme exploration of the negative than that of Bataille can be found in the thinking of the Italian philosopher Luigi Pareyson (1918–91). The author of numerous works on aesthetics,[41] in the last years of his life he left behind academic aesthetics and focused his attention on the problem of evil that has its roots in the analysis of conflict, duplicity and difference.[42] He reverses the classical opposition between atheist and libertine 'strong spirits' and pious and devout 'beautiful souls'. In his view, contemporary society offers examples of a pacific nihilism in its quiet and modest happiness. The new 'beautiful soul' is an atheist, a nihilist, completely reconciled with life, affable and sociable. Under the guise of unconventionality he craves a good and comfortable life which lies at the pole opposite of challenges and risks, that is, philosophy. The characteristic of reality for Pareyson is its lack of conceptuality, its being completely independent of thinking. The pure existent asserts its presence and creates a perpetual dismay that could be defined, the *stupor of reason*. Whoever is possessed by it appears bewitched and possessed by an alien force. This state is not without similarity with the abandonment inherent in the listening to Being of which Heidegger speaks, or Blanchot's experience of limits. But Pareyson confers an enormous importance to suffering. Suffering and evil are so unfathomable that they seem unable to be contained in a vision of serene acceptance and religious piety. He rejects the metaphysical identity between God, good and Being. God, in his view, is not only a solid positivity, rounded on itself, motionless in its closed identity, in God there is also the presence of evil that can always be reawakened. In the description of this reawakening as frenzy of treason, rage of self-annihilation, impulse of destruction, de-creation, 'disfaction', Pareyson make use of a very effective and passionate eloquence. Beside the 'daring discourse' of the theological kind, he brings forward an equally daring anthropological discourse that has to do with the incredible co-presence in human experience of pain and pleasure, suffering and sensual pleasure, torment and delight. Thus, he introduces us to a feeling indeed excessive which opens up horizons where coldness and theatricality, negation and expectation, subjugation and revenge, humiliation and rebirth are inseparably joined together.

Sexual feeling and difference

The psychoanalyst Jacques Lacan (1901–81) is responsible for explicitly transferring the philosophical problematic of difference to the study of sexuality. Between the male sexual feeling, characterized by phallic pleasure and that of the female, which emerges as a relation to the Other, which not even those who feel it are able to say anything, exists a radical dissymmetry.[43] Therefore, it is deeply wrong to imagine the sexual relation as the achievement of a unity. The male and the female sex are not at all complementary and harmonious with respect to one another. The aesthetic paradigm of harmony is mystifying. The pleasure of the male, viewed as activity, and the female, viewed as the opening of something completely Other, never meet. The sexual relation is a blind alley that leads nowhere.

On these bases Lacan develops a reading of medieval courtly love, which is presented as a refined way to supplement the lack of sexual relation, by pretending that the partners are the ones who stand in its way! Also interesting are his thoughts on the beautiful of which he emphasizes the ambiguous nature which prohibits desire and solicits abuse.[44]

Even for the Belgian philosopher Luce Irigaray (b. 1932) there is no symmetry between male and female. In her view, feminine sexuality cannot be reduced to identity and, for this reason, it cannot be thought adequately as long as philosophy remains the prisoner of metaphysical categories. By means of a very subtle analysis, Irigaray shows that these categories are subsumed by a phallocentric structure of thinking, whereby the woman is not thought in her autonomy but in her subordination to man.[45] Nonetheless, one could conjecture a feeling of difference that would belong both to the experience of men and women. It is rooted in the admiration before the unknowable, before the other that differs sexually. This is the aspect of sexuality which is closer to art and aesthetics. This is how one avoids the logic of possession and metaphysical reductionism. Admiration respects and exalts the difference because it keeps an open and attractive space between male and female. According to Irigaray, this space could also be thought to be neutral as long as one was prepared to welcome the advent of difference.[46]

In an analogous direction moves the French critic Roland Barthes (1915–80) who establishes a close connection between pleasure and the literary work. He subjects both notions to a deep transformation making the pleasure as well as the work pass from the logic of identity to the experience of difference. Beyond pleasure he discovers joy (*juissance*), beyond the work he discovers the text. Joy is a feeling that goes beyond the distinction between pleasure and pain. It even engulfs what is unpleasant, boring and even painful.[47]

The deconstruction of aesthetics: Disgust

The problematic of opposites, alterity and difference has been rethought with great perseverance by the French philosopher Jacques Derrida (1930–2004). In his *Of Grammatology*,[48] the author reproaches the Western philosophical tradition for having subordinated writing to discourse, to the *logós*, understood as the origin of truth. In fact, it attributed to it a relation of essential proximity to the soul. With respect to the voice, *phoné*, writing seems to be a failure of the exteriority of the sign. In short, the text, understood as a system of signs, is always secondary because it is preceded by a truth or a meaning already constituted in the *logós*. Then, 'grammatology' seems to be at first sight an assertion of the anteriority of writing against the logocentrism of Western philosophy. However, it is not a question of overturning the order of dependency or to pose objections to phonologism by maintaining the current concepts of language and writing, but to radicalize the alternative to the logic of identity and dialectics, as it was begun by Freud and Heidegger.

This intention plays out in a tireless activity of *deconstruction* of philosophy. This shift occurs, as the others, in the sixties and marks a break from the previous ways of feeling. Aesthetics being part of philosophy, it is also the object of deconstruction. For instance, Derrida places under scrutiny the Kantian notion of taste. But what does it mean to deconstruct taste? First of all one locates the opposite of taste.[49] Now Kant admits the possibility of some negative pleasures which, in fact, is the sublime that goes against the interest of the senses. But the sublime is connected to an idealizing experience where the negative dimension is completely sublimated and overcome. The same is the case with the representation of evil which can be assimilated and purified by art. Only one dimension for Kant cannot be assimilated by aesthetics, *disgust,* which is not a negative value redeemed by art. Therefore disgust seems to be the non-representable and the unmentionable, the completely different, the absolute other of the system. Nonetheless, the experience of disgust has still some relation to pleasure: vomiting entails a relief in being free of something repellent. Does this mean, therefore, that logocentrism is so powerful to recover and incorporate even vomit? Is it possible to forego the logic of identity and the logic of dialectical contradiction? To find an answer to this question it appears necessary to pass from aesthetics to anthropology, that is, from an a priori and formal consideration of feeling to an empirical consideration. It is precisely in *Anthropology* that Kant examines the human senses and distinguishes between the objective senses (hearing, sight and touch) and the subjective ones (taste and smell). Perhaps it is in the latter sense that we can find something more disgusting than vomit, something non-representable, unnamable, unintelligible, inassimilable, obscene, something on which the hierarchizing authority of logocentrism holds no sway. In fact, Kant observes that breathing through the lungs entails a swallowing deeper and more internal than eating. Therefore, it is the sense of smell that makes possible a more disgusting experience of disgust: it is the vicarious, temporary, substitute feeling of disgust; it is the double of disgust. In other words, we can reach the different, not through its opposite (with the risk of reverting to dialectics) but through duplication, repetition, the simulacrum! The greatest opposition is not yet sufficiently different from what it opposes. Only the simulacrum, the repetition of the greatest opposition can reach the difference.[50]

At this point we must make an almost final observation. With the last two thinkers we have discussed, Irigaray and Derrida, we witness a slippage from the sphere of the psychic and the phenomenological to the sphere of the empirical and the physiological. The feminine and the disgusting (or rather, the feminine difference and vicarious disgust) are notions that one can reach exclusively through thinking and acting. They require a *feeling* or, rather, a feeling that does not remain at the level of an idealizing spirituality like Kant's sentiment, Hegel's *pathos,* Bergson's *élan vital*, Riegl's will of art, Croce's intuition and Bloch's utopia. They require a different and uncanny feeling, bright and estranging, not ascribable to the quiet harmony of the aesthetic beautiful soul. But all this still does not suffice because it remains at the psychic and phenomenological level. Irigaray and Derrida, instead, describe a feeling which is not inscribed in an exteriority reducible to the spirit, but in the folds of the feminine sex or in the pulmonary cavity, in an unpronounceable writing or in a prosthesis, in a chemical substance or in an incomprehensible ritual, that is, in 'things that feel'. Therefore, because of them, the feeling of difference takes a *physiological turn* on whose importance and meaning we must question ourselves. It can be added to the other four turns of which we have already spoken (political, media, sceptical, communicative). In actual fact, it is not just added to them but it transforms them into something that we still don't know and on which theorists, men and women, are now working, in various parts of the world, more or less in isolation. But here my task of historian is almost over.

Schizoanalysis and the blocks of sensation

The French thinkers Gilles Deleuze (1925–95) and Félix Guattari (1930–92) are the authors of a vast work, *Capitalism and Schizophrenia*, divided into two volumes *The Anti-Oedipus*[51] and *A Thousand Plateaus*[52] that can be considered the summa of all aesthetic perspectives of the twentieth century. Within the framework organized around the fundamental opposition between paranoia, tied to the logic of capitalism and the affirmation of identity, and schizophrenia, tied to the movement of emancipation and the emergence of multiplicity, all four major lines of aesthetics are subject to revision: the notions of life, form, knowledge and action. At the same time Deleuze and Guattari are involved in the four turns (political, media, sceptical and communicative) that have marked the aesthetic event of the second half of the century.

However, the most important aspect of their reflection concerns feeling whose de-subjectivization is further pursued and promoted in all spheres. Still this does not lead Deleuze and Guattari to dissolutive and chaotic conclusions. In their next work, *What is Philosophy?* the problem of the relation between feeling and art is discussed with great clarity and lucidity. First of all it is necessary to distinguish the subjective, personal, dimension of feeling, which is manifested in perceptions and emotions, from the de-subjectivized and impersonal one which congeals in *percepts* and *affects*. These exceed both the subject and the object and can be reached only as autonomous and self-sufficient entities that do not owe anything anymore to those who have tried them. They are the non-human becoming of the human being. Percepts and affects open areas of sensible and affective indiscernibility between things, animals and people, equatorial or glacial areas, which are removed from the determination of genders, sex, orders and realms. Works of art play a fundamental role in stabilizing and maintaining these entities. In fact they are *blocks* of sensations that challenge the caducity of living and are handed down as monuments to future generations. According to Deleuze and Guattari, art must be differentiated both from philosophy, which is explicated in concepts, and from science, which develops through functions.[53] Still the three spheres of art, philosophy and science find their connection in the brain. Even they, therefore, in the last instance, outline the turn from the level of the psychic and phenomenological to the physiological.

Aesthetics and Culture

Aesthetic education and culture

Each of the first five chapters of this book have their roots in theories elaborated in previous centuries. The problematic of form and the sublime have their most important reference point in Kant; cognitive and pragmatic aesthetics in Hegel; the theories of post-aesthetic feeling in Nietzsche. There is still a sixth trend of contemporary aesthetics that does not recognize itself in any of these tendencies because its chosen object of study is not only the beautiful, the sublime, art or feeling but culture, above all.

The identity of culture and aesthetics finds its most coherent formulation in the philosophical writings of the German writer Friedrich Schiller (1759–1805), in particular, *On the Aesthetic Education of Man* (1759).[1] In his view, only through aesthetics we move towards political freedom, eluding the opposing dangers of the state and nature, where violence reigns supreme, and of barbarism, where abstract intellectual principles are imposed as laws of the state. The process of civilization must avoid coarseness and savageness as well as the idolatry of the useful and of work. Schiller inaugurates a strategy that will be pursued by many thinkers in the twentieth century. The way out of the despotism of the *Ancien Régime* and modernization are not achieved by means of a great leap forward towards a future completely unknown and unforeseeable, but through a step backward towards the rediscovery of the origins of civilization from which we come. Schiller has no doubt that the highest form of aesthetic culture was reached in ancient Greece which, therefore, remains the fundamental standard of reference of any excellence.

Some ten years after Schiller, the identity of culture and aesthetics is taken up by the Swiss historian Carl Jacob Burckhardt (1818–97). Although he never wrote a book expressly devoted to aesthetics in the strict sense, he paved the way for an extraordinary expansion of the aesthetic horizon by including in it all the manifestations of private and collective existence. This aestheticization of the entire history of humanity occurs through the adoption of a detached and disinterested point of view with respect to the historical events of the West, which are, so to speak, made smaller and miniaturized.[2] After all, Burckhardt is simply applying to history the characteristics that Kant characterized as the essential aspects of aesthetic judgement: disinterestedness, absence of preconceptions, independence with respect to reaching a purpose and emancipation from the particularity of the single individual. After all, these were already the aspects that Schiller singled out when he considered play (*Spiel*) as the essential element of aesthetic education.

The questions that Burckhardt poses are the following: What is the most important thing that has occurred in the history of the West? Who were its great men? What is the criterion on whose basis we can tell that something has succeeded or failed? At first, these questions belong more to the philosophy of history and civilization than to aesthetics. However, if they are approached with that attitude of disinterested contemplation that characterizes aesthetics, they free the entire philosophical horizon from the dominion of passions and fanaticisms that hinder its knowledge.

As for Nietzsche, who was a friend of Burckhardt, the ancient Greeks were the people who gave aesthetics the greatest expression. This occurred in very exceptional circumstances that were never to be repeated in the history of the West and, perhaps, in the history of humanity: the absence of a religious caste, a weak political power and the overwhelming authority of Homeric poetry. However, differently from neo-Classicism, Burckhardt does not idealize the ancient Greek world at all: the powers are weak and uncertain, but not for this reason less violent![3] The study of sources is essential to an understanding of civilization but the originality of the West with respect to other civilizations was its dynamism that allowed it to be radically modernized twice: the first time with the Roman Empire and the second time with the Renaissance[4] without, however, breaking its connection with the Greek cultural heritage. The Romans had the ability to make of every conquered city an outpost of Rome. The Italians of the Renaissance transformed the state in a work of art and reduced the power of the clergy.

For Burckhardt the truly historical crises are rather rare. Even phenomena that create a great sensation for a long time do not succeed in producing real changes: even the Reformation could have been avoided and the French Revolution placated. The aesthetic point of view manifests itself in this looking at things from afar which proceeds, on the one hand, by making actual remote events and, on the other hand, by minimizing so-called novelty. The only true crisis known by the West is the one caused by the barbarian invasions, as for the rest, continuity prevails over novelty. Naturally everything comes to an end. This happens when the idea that things have to change prevails and that the past must be forgotten and destroyed. For Burckhardt this is the situation in which the West finds itself. We are witnessing a total devastation of the spirit caused by journalism and an unprecedented network of communication that together stun people completely! At the same time, excessive scientific specialization creates scholars very well prepared in very small areas of knowledge who, nevertheless, remain for the most part uncouth and ignorant. One must always ask: how much of my life can I devote to this topic?

On the question concerning the excellence of historical figures, Burckhardt has no doubts: only with the great philosophers the dominion of authentic greatness, uniqueness, invaluableness, exceptional energy and the relation to the universal begins. Finally, for what concerns historical success or failure, the judgement on their fortune or misfortune, these belong to the cumbersome baggage of public opinion who are the real enemies of historical knowledge.

The importance of Burckhardt is not limited to the fact of having been among the first to realize the decline of the West. He also contributed three fundamental intuitions: the first concerns the acknowledgement of the multiplicity of cultures. The decline of a civilization does not imply the end of the world: something new begins in some other part. Under this aspect one can consider him the precursor of global aesthetics.

His second important contribution concerns the same notion of culture which he regarded as one of the three great powers next to state and religion, which are basically always hostile to it, because in it is manifested the world of liberty and movement, of what is not necessarily universal, of what does not lay claim to any coercive validity. For Burckhardt culture is the total sum of the manifestations of the spirit that occur spontaneously and do not claim any universal and necessary validity. Therefore, culture has a disruptive function with respect to state and religion. From any material action, if executed with zeal and not purely out of subservience, a spiritual *excess* originates which, even though initially frail, represents the point of departure of every work of art. The origin of culture, therefore, is to be sought in the ornament, in the non-utilitarian, in what is done in a completely disinterested way. Culture, therefore, is identical with aesthetic attitude.

Burckhardt's third and perhaps most productive contribution concerns the invention of a method of emancipation from the cultural colonialism of the West that will be applied by the founders of extra-European aesthetics starting with the Japanese, followed by the Chinese, the Muslims, the Brazilians, the Koreans and so on. It consists in breaking up the relationship between modernization and Westernization and in rethinking in new terms their own cultural tradition, just as the West had done in the Renaissance. Cultural modernization does not occur, therefore, in the colonial form of an uncritical and passive adoption of Western mentality, but through a *step back* towards one's own past, which makes it possible to present it in a new and appropriate form to withstand comparison with the West. The traditional interpretations of Western thought do not grasp the fundamental aspect of this process that occurs for the first time in Japan in 1868 with the Meiji renewal.[5]

Eastern modernization versus colonizing Orientalism

Orientalism (1978)[6] by Edward Said (1935–2003), a scholar of Arabo-Palestinian origins, constitutes an epoch-making turning point. For the most part Western culture, with respect to Eastern civilizations, has been inclined to prevent any process of autonomous modernization, emphasizing and even extolling precisely the most backward aspects of those cultures. Orientalism reveals itself in many ways: in the first place, in the organization of a series of negative stereotypes on the Orient which is said to be characterized by an imprecise and illogical style of thinking, by a refusal of progress, and by a tendency to despotism. Only the commercial, political, cultural and military intervention of the West could have remedied these flaws by lifting these people to democracy, the respect of the individual, tolerance, in short, civilization.

This *racist* view of the East, however, is complementary with the opposite one that shows itself as fanatically pro-Oriental and in opposition to Western rationalism, repudiating the entire cultural heritage from which it comes. It is enthusiastic and even claims to appropriate some of the aesthetic and religious aspects of the East, ignoring completely the complexities, tensions and conflicts that affect them. Most often the same Eastern thinkers facilitate and even promote this uncritical and reactionary view of their own culture, in the hope of gaining that recognition which is precluded by the racist view. Thus, in the last three centuries of the Second Millennium, simultaneously with the colonialism of pillage and plunder, an anti-Western movement developed and spread which, combined with esoteric traditions of various origins, created an Oriental aesthetic-religious style which, for the most part, knows very little of either the East or the West. Countering artificially the economic materialism of the West with the aesthetic spiritualism of the East, and spreading false and conventional stereotypes of both that are harmful to both, as if the West never had a great spiritual tradition and, vice versa, as if the East never had a very refined technological knowledge! One can only agree with Said when he claims that Orientalism is the triumph of prejudice and ignorance, more or less concealed.

Finally, there is a third obstacle to the process of autonomous modernization of traditional societies that derives from syncretistic universalism according to which there are ideal models or archetypes common to cultures the world over. This orientation focuses its attention exclusively on the conflict between tradition (very often written with a capital T), the bearer everywhere of universal ideals and truths, and modernity which disrupts communities and corrupts every form of morality. This is the danger of comparative studies when they avoid the scientific study of single cultures.

Since the nineteenth century, the challenge for non-European countries has been simple: their modernization is absolutely necessary to avoid being completely colonized by the Euro-Americans, but this process must not follow slavishly the cultural models proposed and imposed by the Euro-Americans, but must invent new forms of modernization which, by maintaining a relation with their past, are capable of withstanding on all points of view the attack that comes from the West.

The first Asian country to become aware of this situation in the first half of the nineteenth century was Japan which, through an extraordinary and particularly fortunate series of circumstances, succeeded in passing, without unleashing a civil war, from a premodern condition, which would have caused it to be colonized, to a modern, autonomous and extraordinarily effective condition, on all points of view, without having to renounce to its own traditions.[7]

Japanese aesthetic culture versus political power

Japanese modernization depended on entirely exceptional political circumstances and on extraordinarily fortunate events. The socio-historical premises of this success are essentially two: the fact that this nation was a 'closed country' (*sakoku*) to foreigners from 1639 to 1868, that is, until that deep and radical political transformation of the country known as the 'Meiji renewal'; and in the second place that it happened in a relatively peaceful way and it was led by a new 'enlightened' class formed by *samurai*, that is, warriors of middle income who had already abandoned arms more than 200 years before and had become technicians, administrators, bureaucrat scholars, often inventing devices and mechanisms quite different from European ones. In other words they had already modernized the country independently of European technology.

This period of Japanese history, the Tokugawa era, also goes by the name of *Edo* from the name of the city that later in 1869 will be re-baptized with the name *Tokyo*. The Edo era saw great artistic and aesthetic developments that found its expression in the production of beautiful prints known as *Ukiyo-e*, as well as in the spread throughout the population of an extremely refined aesthetic sensibility whose remote origins go back to the Heian era (794–1185), the ancient name of Kyoto. These brief preliminary historical facts are necessary to understand that in Japan aesthetics, understood as appreciation of natural beauty and excellence in craftsmanship, has behind it a 1,000 years history. At the beginning of the Second Millennium, when Europe was struggling to emerge from barbarism, in Heian flourished an aesthetic and ritual culture of the highest level.[8] It is natural that many Euro-Americans in the last three centuries of the second Millennium have been seduced by it. However, it is precisely this attitude that Edward W. Said calls *Orientalism*. One admires and identifies precisely with those same aesthetic aspects that prevent Japan from succeeding in standing up to Western colonialism and economic exploitation!

The genius of the authors of the Meiji renewal was to have understood that without abolishing the feudal system and a deep understanding of the West, inspired by the principle of incorporating the good things and rejecting the bad things, Japan could not have resisted the colonial imperialism to which most of Asia had succumbed. This is how the famous diplomatic mission Iwakura was born (1871–3), made up of influential men from the government, high diplomats and representatives of various disciplines and specializations with the purpose of studying the political, administrative, educational, industrial systems of the Western powers. The mission, which consisted of 107 people, lasted a year and ten months and visited 12 countries in the attempt to assimilate and appropriate what could be useful to the modernization of Japan. Among the good things there was also Western aesthetics. The Emperor himself took lessons of Western aesthetics from Nishi Amane (1829–97) who had studied for a few years in Holland and had translated the term 'aesthetics' with the Japanese word *zenbigaku* which means literally, 'science of the good and the beautiful'.[9]

It is only years later that a thinker appears on the scene, Okakura Kakuzō (1862–1913), the author of a small book, written in English, *The Book of Tea,* in which he asserts the independence of Japanese aesthetic culture with respect to the West.[10] Tea, which originated in China, became in the fifteenth-century Japan the object of a cult, *Teaism*, based on the worship of the beautiful in contrast to life's squalor. The fundamental idea behind this cult consists in the awareness that even in an ignorant and unjust world, like the one in which we live, it is possible to accomplish something of value, however contingent and impermanent. In Japan, aesthetics soon allied with religion and ethics. In fact, Shintoism is a kind of religion of nature deeply imbued with a profound aesthetic sensibility. In other words aesthetic feeling is not a theory elaborated by the philosophical tradition independently of popular feeling, but a way of being that permeates everyday experience for more than a millennium. The cult of tea, therefore, is for Okakura the authentic spirit of Eastern democracy because it transforms all those who devote themselves to it into aristocrats of taste. In the common idiom, Okakura writes, a person insensitive to the tragic-comic aspects of individual existence is defined as 'without tea'! The aesthetic and superficial way in which Westerners look at the tea ceremony is a projection of their materialistic and hedonistic ways. Teaism could be defined 'the smile of philosophy'.

Nonetheless, the modernization of Japanese aesthetic culture is not without its conflicts. Of the three powers evoked by Burckhardt – the state, aesthetic culture and religion, the conflict between the first two in Japan, which goes back to the end of the sixteenth century, was above all disruptive. Paradigmatic was the conflict between the most influential tea master Rikyiū Sen no (1522–91) and the military man Toyotomi Hideyoshi who was also his friend. Alarmed by the slanderous insinuations of a conspiracy against him, to which Rikyiū presumably had taken part, he condemned him to death, leaving him with the only privilege of dying by his own hand. The last pages of *The Book of Tea* describe a situation very much like that of Socrates' death. The suicide of the tea master has the same symbolic value as that of Socrates' death in Western philosophy. In fact, we are not dealing with a chance occurrence but with the logical consequence of a radical conflict between two conceptions of the world, one based on the power of arms and the use of violence, the other on an ethico-aesthetic one, which was not limited to the elaboration of a poetics, but left remarkable evidence in the arts of the period (for instance, the universally known Katsura's villa[11]). It had succeeded in finding adepts at all levels of society, creating an alternative lifestyle that conditioned all aspects of everyday life. As the major historian of Japanese literature Katō Suichi writes, the tea ceremony could not exist if its practitioners did not regard life as art. Rarely in the history of humanity have aesthetic culture and politics reached such a radical and irreconcilable opposition.[12]

The problem faced by the Meiji era was how to modernize the state, the army, the economy, education, the industry but also aesthetic culture independently of the West. Okakura has the merit of showing the world that a millenary and autonomous Japanese aesthetic culture exists, which is in no way inferior to the West.[13] Nonetheless, it is doubtful that the Meiji era was favourable to artistic creation and to the birth of a modern aesthetic thought, since it had the tendency to squash the figure of the intellectual and the artist on that of the bureaucrat, creating in the brightest men a deep discomfort.

In the decades that followed many aesthetic categories belonging to the Japanese aesthetic tradition were identified and studied, at the same time that many Japanese scholars and philosophers became familiar with all Western aesthetic and philosophical trends. However the danger that still remains today consists in the wavering between a conservative Orientalism and the capitulation before Euro-American colonialism.

The concept of modern art in Japan is also something very complex. There are three different notions that are perceived and developed in completely independent ways, according to a logic of juxtaposition, and not hybridism or *melting pot.*[14] The three categories are *nihonga*, *yōga*, *gendai bijutsu* which refer, respectively, to the traditional Japanese artistic production, to Western style painting and to contemporary art (*happening*, installations and such). But already the first notion, that of *nihonga*, is problematic. The term and the notion come from the Meiji era and are part of the cultural politics of modernization of the country together with the creation of museums and the valorization of the national heritage. As is well-known, the problem which confronted the Meiji reformers was dual: to halt first of all the anti-Buddhist iconoclasm of the early years (1868–75) and, subsequently, to try to bring the artwork out of the temples (something which even today is very difficult).[15] That is why the museum in Japan has a different meaning than in the West. It is part of the process of modernization against traditional resistance that would not like these works to be visible at all or very rarely. Furthermore, the artistic activity implied in the notion of *nihonga* has also undergone a deep transformation and evolution from 1868 to the present.

Not any less problematic is the second notion, *yōga*, which includes Western style painting from 1868 to 1960. Under this term are included many Western trends from impressionism to abstract art, from informal to academic painting. The case of the Japanese avant-garde (*zen'ei*), where the Buddhist influence is present since its beginnings, is paradoxical. Exemplary is the case of the great writer Mori Ōgai who translated in Japanese Filippo Tommaso Marinetti's *The Manifest of Futurism* (1909), a few weeks after its publication, in a classical language that makes use of rare Chinese terminology, already obsolete then! Significant are also the encounters between Dadaism and Buddhism, Surrealism and Eastern forms. Differently from what occurred in the West which considered the applied arts an inferior manifestation with respect to real art, or even as kitsch, in Japan the works that belong to the category *nihonga* have always enjoyed public recognition and even the interest of avant-garde artists.

As for the third category, *gendai bijustu*, there is debate whether it began with the Anti-art movement (*Han-geijustu*), that is, between 1958 and 1964 (connecting it with the *Yomiuri Independent Exhibitions*), or with Osaka's Universal Expo of 1970, visited by 50 million people. In the first case the emphasis is on the transgressive aspect of contemporary art, in the latter, instead, on its alliance with the institution.

An important exception to the always latent conflict between Eastern traditionalism and Japanese modernity is *mingei*, a movement promoted by the scholar Yanagi Soetzu (1889–1961) who introduced a local production of handicrafts in a world movement. The *Studio Craft* is still flourishing today in many countries of the world.[16]

Ren, a Chinese ethico-aesthetic notion

Although aesthetics had already made its appearance in China with Zhu Guangqian and Cai Yuanpei, these authors were still very much influenced by European aesthetics. Only with Liang Shuming (1893–1988) there was a real critical emancipation from Western thought, oriented towards the aesthetic and cultural modernization of the aesthetic heritage of his country. He can be considered one of the great global aesthetic thinkers since he does not limit himself to lay claim to the autonomous character of Chinese culture with respect to the other two global cultures of humanity, the Euro-American and East Indian ones, but he asserts its universal validity, namely, the possibility of being acknowledged and accepted in any part of the world. He is critical of both the Western way of thinking, which privileges economic evolution and is obsessed by an excessive ambition to master nature, and Indian thought, which is guilty of the opposite flaw in attributing sole importance to religion and in considering as its primary purpose the rejection of life and parting from this world. These conclusions, which seem drastic and simplistic, are the result of Liang's in-depth study of Western and Indian philosophy. It is obvious that within the West and in India there are trends that move in the opposite direction to the fundamental orientation of the way of thinking of their civilizations, but these, in the end, seem destined to remain marginal.

Liang's ideas are outlined in his work *Les cultures de l'Orient et de l'Occident et leur philosophies* (1929),[17] which is the definitive result of the transcriptions of his lessons made by his students between 1919 and 1927. In this work we find an answer to the problems raised by Burckhardt. In the West, politico-economic power puts aesthetic education aside, just as in India the power of religion is so strong to prevent aesthetics from developing independently (as we saw in Chapter 2 of this work with respect to the great thinker Ananda K. Coomaraswamy).

Liang is critical of both economics and religion since they are exclusive modes of thinking. Only Chinese culture succeeds in joining in an indissoluble bond ethics and aesthetics thanks to Confucius (551–479 BC) whose teachings, without neglecting material and spiritual needs, place at the centre of his own thought the notion of *ren* (an untranslatable Chinese term which is very close to what Schiller called *aesthetic education*). It could be defined, approximately, as the concern that we have for one another based on the practice of rituals and music. It introduces in Chinese thought the idea of the perfectibility of man and the obligation to pursue it. Under this aspect it is not too far from the Western idea of *magnificence* understood by Thomas Aquinas as the search for the *arduous* and the *difficult*.[18] The notion of *ren* has been the object of infinite interpretations that occupy 2,500 years of history. We are interested in Liang Shuming's interpretation which mainly stresses the aesthetic aspect of this idea, characterized in some of its fundamental traits. First of all, *ren* has nothing to do with the state of passivity and abandonment promoted by Indian thought. Confucianism is praise for life in all its aspects. In the second place, it implies a state of balance and communion with Nature, where the sensible aspect is a fundamental factor. In the third place, in Liang's interpretation *ren* turns out to be something a lot closer to what in the West is called aesthetic *disinterestedness*, that is, a rejection of interested and petty calculations. In the fourth place, the enormous importance given to ritual, music and filial piety recall the aesthetic idea of *form*, understood as a guarantee of equilibrium. Finally, it must not to be understood as something static. On the contrary, Confucian thought inherits a fundamental idea of Chinese culture, formulated in *The Book of Changes* (Yijing) which is the canon *par excellence* of Chinese thought, because its origins go back to the most remote antiquity. In fact, there is not a single important Chinese thinker who has not made reference to it.[19] The same Confucius does not see himself as an innovator but only as the interpreter of five or six Classics, whose origins are lost in the most remote antiquity: the *Book of Changes*, *The Book of Rites*, *The Book of Documents*, *The Book of Odes*, *The Annals of Spring and Autumn*, to which we should add *The Book of Music*.

A fundamental aspect of Chinese thought, since its prehistoric origins, is the idea that everything changes constantly: nothing is static. The fundamental dualism on which this dynamism rests are the notions of Yin and Yang, which are neither opposites nor harmonious. When one of them has reached a certain expansion, the opposite principle takes over until it acquires hegemony in its turn. To understand the dynamic of things is to grasp the *lowest beginning*, the imperceptible emergence of a movement that goes in the opposite direction to what is evident and obvious.

One last very important aspect of Confucian aesthetics is the *rectification of names*. Liang compares Chinese thought to that of Heraclitus (535–475) for whom 'everything changes'. Even for Heraclitus, agreement on the meaning of words was of the greatest importance and this could occur only through the logos, that is, a reason common to everyone, where one sets aside personal interests and passions. For Heraclitus, generally, this does not happen, and that is why he has the impression to be living among people who are asleep, who live in a world of their own, and with whom it is impossible to communicate.[20]

Even though the origin of language is said to be conventional, in order to maintain the balance and harmony of social relations, it is of the greatest importance that there is concurrence on the meaning of words. For Xunzi (340–305 BC), a pupil of Confucius, this concurrence is guaranteed by *writing*, which represents the first among the duties of sovereignty. To fall short of this fundamental principle means, sooner or later, to fall into anarchy and civil war.[21]

Modernization of Islam as the reconstruction of the three powers

Even Islam is faced with the same problem that confronted the Asian cultures between the nineteenth and twentieth centuries: how to invent a modern, autonomous and independent aesthetic society without falling in the apathetic and indolent traditionalism, which had made possible the triumph of European colonialism almost everywhere and especially in the Middle East, in India and in Asia? The thinker who posed himself this question, with total devotion and immense erudition, was Muhammad Iqbal (1877–1938), philosopher, poet and political organizer: a Muslim of East Indian origins, a profound expert of Classical Persian literature, gifted with a very vast store of cultural experiences both Eastern and Western, with the knowledge of many languages and an admirer of Dante, Goethe, Nietzsche and Bergson. Iqbal believed that a complete and radical political, philosophical and cultural reform was necessary in order to wake up the Asian populations drugged by the torpor and indifference in which false and disastrous versions of Hinduism, Islamism and Buddhism had submerged them for centuries. In their different ways, these have brought about the annihilation of every energy and every form of struggle, through the tightening of ritual practices, the resignation in the face of injustices, iniquities and horrors of colonialism, as well as the naïve and obtuse preaching of universal love. Nevertheless, Iqbal does not advocate violence but doing. In his fundamental theoretical work, *The Reconstruction of Religious Thought in Islam* (1934),[22] written directly in English and based on six talks he gave previously in some Indian cities, his use of the term *deed* (from the verb *to do*), instead of *action*, is very striking. In his view, armies, prisons, chains, tortures are banditry. The real government is the one that is able to do without this machinery. The *deed* implies an *inner* experience of one's own individuality with relation to God which represents the main and most important element of the modernization of Islam. In other words, external doing – pragmatism and materialism, typical of Western thinking are equally inadequate to the invention of a Muslim modernity just as much as the passive mysticism of Sufism.

The three individual powers identified by Burckhardt – state, religion and aesthetic culture, must be rethought in completely different ways. Their reconstruction is based on a return to the democratic origins of Islam, the rejection of mystic quietism, the theology of Asharita of the ninth and tenth centuries, and the loyalty to the way of feeling of Persian poetry. Furthermore, Iqbal claims, as all Asian thinkers who aspire to the emancipation of their cultures, that in order to stand up to European colonialism it is necessary to know, first of all, the theoretical premises on which it was founded since Greek antiquity. Typical of his way of thinking is Iqbal's definition of Plato as a sheep in man's clothing because of his misplaced trust in the tyrants of Syracuse.

Iqbal's masterpiece, *Book of Eternity* (*Javid Nama*) is neither a treatise nor an essay but a poem written in Persian,[23] published in 1932. It is really a singular philosophical work which employs a genre not often used in the West, except for Nietzsche's *Thus Spoke Zarathustra.* Nevertheless, it takes as its model Dante Alighieri's *Divine Comedy* and is structured as a voyage to the otherworld in which Iqbal (who appears under the pseudonym of Zinda-rōd) is accompanied by the medieval Persian poet Jalāl al-Dīn-Rūmī, who has the role of Virgil in Dante's poem.

The three powers identified by Burckhardt – state, religion and aesthetic culture, are in need of radical reform. As far as the first one is concerned, Iqbal is decidedly hostile to the idea of a plurality of states, according to the European model and the examples that already existed in his time (Turkey, Egypt, Iran), which brought about the fragmentation of Islam, making it weak and at the mercy of European colonialism. The political form of Islam is the *Ummah*, a unique community which originally (Medina's Constitution of 622) included even people of different cults, such as Jews and pagans.

As for religion, the clergy with its ultra-conservative defeatist attitude can only promise a paradise where one eats, sleeps and sings. The abolition of the clergy is the inevitable premise to the renewal of Islam. In fact, religion does not consist of dogmas, clericalism, liturgy and the observance of external practices and duties, but in the discovery of one's own personal individuality (*selfhood*) in relation to God. Iqbal introduces in Muslim thought the notion of *khudi* a Persian term meaning *self* or *ego*, which is already present in the title of his first poetry collection, *Secrets of the Self* (Asrar-e-Khudi). From the beginning, Iqbal places at the centre of the modernization of Islam the necessity to become aware of the uniqueness of one's own existence because this is the only possible way to gain the strength to oppose injustices and iniquities. However, he avoids falling into Western individualism because *khudi* is related to God who, in turn, has a personal way of being. Iqbal refuses energetically the Aristotelian conception of God understood as a motionless motor not subject to becoming, and introduces in the thought of Islam an extreme energy and an unlimited dynamism. In fact, God himself changes constantly and is always engaged in a ceaseless creative activity that manifests itself in creating new worlds and transforming constantly the one in which we live. Another key word in Iqbal's philosophy is *ardour* in which religion and poetry reinforce one another. The motor of this incessant work is *dil*, a Persian and Urdu word which is commonly translated *heart*. The West does not have a heart and the East has forgotten, which was exemplified above all in Rūmī's poetry and in other Persian poets, but not in the work of Hāfiz, whom he considers the expression of the hedonistic decadence of Islamic élites. The *dil*, however, is not irrational. It is the locus of right intuition and contains within itself, together with the affective dimension, also an intellectual aspect.

Iqbal attributes to poetry a fundamental role where the aspect of acting is inseparable from doing. Here Iqbal seems to integrate in his own aesthetic conception an important aspect of Indu thought, foreign to the Islamic world, namely, the concept of *karma*, which is used in many regions of India with various meanings to refer to the idea of acting and doing. The sense that Iqbal attributes to it appears to be related to the etymology of the word. The term *karma* takes its origin from the Sanskrit root-word *kṛ*, which has the meaning of 'doing' or 'to cause', which presupposes the notion of 'creating something by acting'. This is precisely the task of poetry. Its Indo-European root corresponds to **kwer* (sacred act, prescribed act), and we find it in the Latin *caerimonia* from which we get, for example, *ceremony* in English.

Iqbal's poetics goes beyond the opposition between a hermetic poetic art accessible only to a restricted circle of learned readers and a popular production comprehensible to everyone. On the one hand, in fact, it has its place among the *trobar clus* of the great poets who wrote in Persian and Urdu (as Ghalib), on the other, a few of his verses have had great success among the illiterate masses who have great appreciation for sung verse. This is the miracle, unconceivable in the West, of a very refined literary production which is popular at the same time.

Brazilian modernization as tropicalism

The fourth culture that wanted to be emancipated from Westernization and invent an original form of modernization presents two completely different characteristics with respect to the three of which we have written so far (Japanese, Chinese and Islamic). It does not have a millenary past, it has European origins and preserves a few of the aesthetic aspects of the country that colonized it: Portugal. I am alluding to Brazil that for a series of exceptional historical events tied to the decision of the Emperor Pedro I to declare the secession from Portugal in 1882 and create an independent Brazilian Empire. Brazil was later governed by the son Pedro II who abolished slavery in 1888 and resigned a year later thus making possible the birth of the Brazilian Republic.

Brazilian modernity is founded on four apparently contradictory cultural trends and difficult to define with a single notion: arcadism, positivism, a type of experience which is at the same time poetic, philosophical and religious, similar to the one that thinkers of Classical antiquity and the German philosopher Edmund Husserl (1859–1938) referred to with the term *epoché* (bracketing), as well as the phenomenon of *trance*, which in Brazil is taken to be a continuation of African rituals. Therefore, Brazilian modernity is neither a syncretism, nor a hybrid, nor an indiscriminate melting pot, but the confluence of four precise cultural orientations. Each one has found one or more exceptional representatives who have succeeded in creating an aesthetics autonomous and independent of Euro-American colonization which can be defined with the general term of *tropicalism*.

Arcadian aesthetics has its great interpreter in the Pernambucan sociologist Gilberto Freyre (1900–87), a student at Columbia University of the anthropologist Franz Boas (1858–1942), author of a gigantic portrayal of the traditional life of North-eastern Brazil, from which emerges an aesthetic conception of the greatest emotional impact. His most important work is *The Masters and the Slaves: A Study in the Development of Brazilian Civilization*,[24] which was followed by many other works, some of them devoted to art.[25]

Freyre describes with extensive documentation and an enormous abundance of details a model of aesthetic society which is the necessary condition to understand Brazil. The aesthetic aspect of this culture consists of some aspects that were lacking in the other types of colonization (especially the English one). The first of these is the absence of racism, despite the structural character of slavery and the existence of an enormous economic disparity between rich and poor that lasts to this day. The Portuguese, from the beginning, reveal themselves to be completely devoid of racial prejudices and rigid principles. They do not destroy the culture of the natives or the

African diaspora but promote an incredible quantity of original and fertile grafting, even if at times logically aberrant. Brazilian society is among the most fluid and dynamic in the world. It was constituted by means of an intense circulation of elements both vertical and horizontal, and the most disparate origins. Of course, this does not exclude the existence of strong antagonisms of every type, reducible in the last instance to the fundamental one of master and slave. Nonetheless, this opposition is thought and lived in Brazil, for the most part, not as an absolute conflict, but according to a familiar mentality that often finds its meeting point in a compromise, an aesthetic point of reconciliation.

The second aspect of Brazilian culture for Freyre is a consequence of the first. The production of wealth was not managed by international business companies, not even by the state but by the families and, therefore, it remained within the nation even though its distribution was unfair. From the beginning, modernization did not mean colonialism and globalization. It also entailed a negative element: an autarchic vision of the country which found its extreme form in the so-called *ufanismo*, a fanatic nationalism that constitutes to this day the greatest obstacle to Brazil's claim as a world power.

The third aspect is properly aesthetic in the true sense of the term: the care of the body. It derives from the women of the aboriginal populations: cleanliness and hygiene of the body, the habit to wash oneself very often and extreme care of one's physical aspect. The comparison is with the cult of beauty in ancient Greece and with Japan, cultures that share with Brazil a century of pagan feeling.

Few years after the publication of Freyre's work, another work makes its appearance which is fundamental to the understanding of the specific character of Brazilian modernity, *Racines du Brésil*[26] by the historian Sérgio Buarque de Holanda (1902–82). Differently from Freyre, who represents the point of view of the North East, whose economy is based on the production of sugar cane, Buarque expresses the point of view of San Paolo and the entrepreneurial and industrialized South. His characterization of the specific traits of the aesthetic way of being Brazilian not only coincides with but deepens Freyre's analysis. Even for Buarque, the model on which Brazilian society is constructed is that of the family. He develops the notion of *cordiality*, as the specific trait of Brazilian style, contrasting it to European *politeness* (*urbanità*) or *courtesy* (*polidaz*). While the latter is based on the defense of individual intimacy, on interpersonal relations based on distance, on work as vocation (*Beruf*) and, for this reason, it is connected with that conception of the spirit of capitalism elaborated by Max Weber (1864–1920),[27] the way of being Brazilian is completely the opposite.

Cordiality, whose etymology derives precisely from *cordis* the Latin for 'heart', establishes among people a relation of immediate sociability and amiability, which is manifested in the language and in customs: the use of the pronoun *você*, an intermediate form between *tu* (too confidential and rarely used, except in some regions of Brazil) and the third person *o senhor*, *a senhora* and *senhorita* (considered very formal), the omission of the family name, the use of diminutives, as well as a tendency to reconciliation, a general optimism, an absence of racism. Obviously *cordial* does not mean *good*. Enmity can be as cordial as friendship, in the sense that both derive from the sphere of the familiar.

Differently from Freyre, Buarque also emphasizes the negative aspects of cordiality. These are present in the absence of a disciplined personality, in the inability to devote oneself to a project that goes beyond the lives of individuals, in a superficial religiosity that saves the believer every effort, in the bitter incomprehension of any true intellectuality.

In what way is the road of Brazilian modernity different from the rigorist one of Protestant derivation which to Buarque also seems unrealizable in Brazil? Buarque's answer is surprising and opens a path to arrive at the second fundamental aspect of Brazil's aesthetic way of being. All this emotional and intellectual disorder finds a compensation in the love of forms, ceremonies, rituals, which on the one hand prevent society from falling into chaos, and on the other hand, exempt the individual from a truly autonomous intellectual and emotional commitment, which obviously requires effort, a self-critical spirit and irrevocable choices.

This brings us to the second fundamental aspect of Brazilian modernity: the philosophy of the French thinker Auguste Comte (1798–1857) and the philosophical trend which he represents: positivism.[28] The fluidity and mobility of Brazilian life are framed within a system of ideas and institutions that confer the greatest importance to scientific knowledge, progress, the preservation of the social order, professional education, the religion of humanity and the power of technology. It is significant, furthermore, that Brazil's entrance on the scene of modern political culture does not pass through Jacobinism (as is the case of other Latin American countries), but through the positivism of Auguste Comte from whom derive the central notions of 'order and progress' printed in 1890 on the Brazilian flag. The Arcadian attitude, therefore, finds its development in *altruism*, namely, in the development of a conduct inspired by sociability and attraction, and not by individualism or deference. The aesthetic style that derives its inspiration from rustic Arcadism and a positivist harmonic ideal find a common point in the fact that both are pre-established and ritualized forms. In other words, Brazilian cordiality is not at all a spontaneous manifestation and not even a return to nature *à la Rousseau*, but a ritual of Mannerist origins inspired by Arcadian models. Its prototype can be found in the 'manuelino style' of Portuguese origins, characterized by an exuberant decoration of floral and vegetable motifs.

The third element of Brazilian aesthetic modernity is not something conceptual. Beside Arcadian cordiality and positivistic altruism there is another component that belongs not so much to the history of Brazil as to its geography. To employ the terminology of the French philosophers Gilles Deleuze (1925–95) and Félix Guattari (1930–92),[29] it is not so much a concept as a *percept*, which is why it lends itself better than the previous ones to confer a deeper sense of tropicalism beyond the ideological interpretations that have been given to it. I am alluding to that experience of estrangement and bracketing generated by the contact with tropical nature that some Brazilian poets and writers have represented very well, which places Brazilian literary culture at the same level as European modernist literature. For example the poet Carlos Drummond de Andrade (1902–87) writes: 'The contemplation alone/of a world huge and still',[30] or the writer Clarice Lispector (1920–77): 'a big moment, still, without nothing in it'.[31] This cosmic feeling is not an alienation but an appropriation, and not different from the *oikeiôsis* of the ancient Stoics when they referred to the relation between men and nature. In this Greek word (which was translated in Latin as *conciliatio* and *commendatio*, and in English as *attraction*) is inherent both the emotional aspect of cordiality and the social one of altruism. This experience has little to do with the Portuguese *saudade*, solitude and the nostalgic recollection of the past. Therefore, *suavidade, gentleness*, is the most pertinent term for Brazilian tropicalism. It has the same root as *persuasion* though it is not a question of persuading or communicating an idea. It is something non-conceptual that can only be expressed through poetry which, by the way, is one of the best products of Brazilian culture.

The fourth aspect of Brazilian aesthetic culture derives from the African diaspora, the result of the slave markets that in three centuries brought to Brazil almost two million blacks. Their culture, together with the indigenous one, constitutes an essential aspect of the so-called Brazilian spirit. In fact, differently from the countries where racial discrimination exists, Brazil was always characterized by a strong sexual promiscuity that favoured the universalization of this mode of feeling. Its ancient origins go back, probably, to the Dionysian and Apollonian religion of ancient Greece. But the phenomenon of *trance*, sometimes included in the wider category of *Altered States of Consciousness* (ASC), can be found under various forms practically the world over. In Brazil it is connected to the Afro-Brazilian religions (referred to with various names according to the region: *candomblé, xangô, macumba,* etc.) where it has developed deeper roots than elsewhere.

Although the experience of *trance* proper is limited to a small number of followers in these regions, it has produced a very commanding scientific literature of the aesthetico-psychological type that characterizes the entire twentieth century influencing writers, musicians and artists of many countries who were the representative figures of the European and North American avant-garde. Therefore, we are not dealing here with a local phenomenon, of strictly ethnological interest, but with a modern manifestation of autonomy with respect to Western aesthetics.

The scholar who has contributed the most to the knowledge of the Afro-Brazilian religions is Roger Bastide (1898–1974) with his monumental work, *Les Religions Africaines au Brésil. Contribution à une Sociologie des Interpretations.*[32] The interpretations of *trance* as liberation or as spectacle do not grasp its full meaning. These are typically Eurocentric categories and perspectives which are applied to phenomena that imply completely different conceptions. According to Bastide, *trance* understood as a form of protest and opposition against the world is a *failed trance*, which moves towards hysteria, epileptic seizure or satanic epidemic. Although these possibilities are not ignored in African and Afro-Brazilian cults, their efforts are directed towards bringing it back within a context of rules and rituals rigorously ordered, in an aesthetic liturgy admirably conducted. The conception of *trance* as pure effervescence, pathological overexcitement, wild rampage, belongs to the European imaginary. As for its spectacular character, it is a secondary function that considers only the public aspect and ignores the private, the everyday, the domestic and the ritual. The ludic function is subordinate and additional to the phenomenon of possession that must be considered in its specificity. The African and Afro-Brazilian *trance* belong to the realm of the *serious*. Its experience consists in the fact that the believer places himself, his own body, at the disposal of a divinity that possesses him, that 'rides' him. Individuality is bracketed. Therefore, it is not a question of subjective liberation but of displacement, a becoming nothing and nobody in order to provide the god with a garment of flesh, a tunic of skin, a corporeal receptacle to the god or the goddess that could not otherwise be present in the world. The one possessed feels his own body as something that does not belong to him, which is other, external and different.

The *trance*, however, is not only an experience of difference but also of *repetition* at the same time. In fact, possession is achieved in a ceremony in which music plays an essential role under the direction of a priest or priestess who function as director. Therefore, it has the character of an aesthetico-religious ritual of the highest level: something essential and decisive occurs, supervenes, is accomplished. Possession, however, does not mean mysticism understood as the union of the human and the divine. Incarnation does not imply any anthropomorphism: the divinity does not bond with this or that human form. It is not an idol but an icon: it is left without a face or a definitive form.

Edward W. Said's critique of *Orientalism* can be extended to *primitivism*, that is, the way in which the West has understood African culture which possesses a very profound and completely independent aesthetic vision. It was conceptualized by the African scholar Janheinz Jahn (1918–73), the author of a brilliant work, *Muntu. The Modern African Civilization*[33] where he also extends his analysis to the *Vodu* of Haiti, the *Santeria* of Cuba, the North American *blues* and to other manifestations of the African diaspora. The title of his work, *muntu*, refers to humanity, both living and dead. The aesthetic dimension of the human condition is defined by the notion of *kuntu* which presents two aspects: the relative formal arbitrariness of the work and rhythm. In African art, the relation between form and content is not determined in an univocal and definitive way. The same image can have completely different meanings or it can also mean nothing. In order for it to mean anything it is necessary the conferring of a name and its artistic configuration. This process becomes immediately clear when we keep in mind that the cultural model *par excellence* of the African experience of the sacred is the *trance*.

As it was stated earlier, there is no essential relation between the divinity and the physical aspect of the person possessed. This model applies also to sculpture: the single statue acquires a meaning and value only on condition of being determined by the *nommo*, that is, by the magical power of the word that relates it to this or that divinity of the black pantheon. At the same time, the activity of the sculptor reduces the field of indetermination by sensitizing the name of the statue, and materializing it in an object. As in the *trance*, the materialization of the divine has a limited duration, beyond which the bodies and the statue fall back in their profane condition. The consequence of this experience is a strong intensification of the tactile aspect over the visual. What matters is not the shape of the body but its being cloth, garment and skin.

The second aspect of *kuntu* is rhythm. It is an essential component of any African art-form and, not by chance, one of the fundamental ritual conditions in which *trance* appears. The model from which all African art-forms take their inspiration is the rhythm of percussion instruments. The language of the drum is language in the proper sense, the *nommo*, the word of the ancients. The various parts of an African work of art are always articulated rhythmically and related to one another: rhythm is generated by repetition whose ultimate function is to prove and guarantee the articulated unity of the cosmos.

It is very important to note that the focus of Jahn's work is modern African culture. Differently from what happened in the West, there has not been a complete fracture between the premodern and the modern. To demonstrate the existence of such continuity in the past of the West is the basic aim of the English historian Martin Bernal (b. 1937) who, in a monumental work in three volumes, *Black Athena: The Afroasiatic Roots of Classical Civilization*,[34] claims that ancient Greek civilization has had an intense exchange with Afro-Asiatic cultures: Egyptian, Phoenician, Canaanite, etc. This crossbreeding has been expressly ignored and denied by the 'Aryan model' which, in attributing an exaggerated importance to the relation between Greece and the Indo-European world, presented Greek culture as the only true mother of Western civilization. On these premises the racist ideology of the 'Aryan model' has its bases which assert the supremacy of the white race over all the others. For instance, it radically disregards the Egyptian civilization that was highly esteemed from the Renaissance up to the Enlightenment. The 'Aryan model' has survived World War II and in recent times it is experiencing an impressive come back, full of evil omen. Its analysis leads one to suspect that postmodernism, the hegemonic cultural movement of the eighties and nineties, was an attempt to destroy the relation between premodern and modern, the sole guarantee of a culture and of an aesthetic education. So far the non-European cultures have tried to preserve it because on the preservation of this relation depends not only their survival but the last dyke to the spreading of global barbarism.

Aesthetics and ethics of the Japanese environment

A fundamental contribution to the aesthetics of the environment, which questions Heidegger's thought and connects it with an ethical vision of wider implications, can be found in the work of the Japanese philosopher Watsuji Tetsurō (1889–1960), author of two works, *Climate and Culture: An Anthropological Enquiry*[35] and *Rinriraku (Ethics in Japan).*[36] In his view in *Being and Time* Heidegger has neglected the dimension of space in favour of time. For Watsuji, spatiality and temporality are inseparable. To deal with the question of the environment as *landscape* is a very superficial and hedonistic way that does not touch the deep cords of the soul. As to the Western way of thinking nature, Watsuji believes that it is almost always directed by technological concerns. He transforms the Japanese word *fūdo* (wind and earth), which comes from the Chinese word *suido* (water and earth), in an aesthetic category. Through *fūdo* humanity understands itself in its intimate relation to nature, in the awareness of its cohesion, as well as of the historical stratification which is at the basis of this experience. The Japanese character, characterized by a 'calm passion and a martial selflessness', is expressed through it.[37] Watsuji believes that *fūdo* is everywhere threatened and that it is difficult to imagine in what other completely different form it could be reborn. Even more interesting is the ethical development of Watsuji's thinking that can be considered a further development of his aesthetic ideas. The *fūdo*, in fact, has an inter-subjective character and implies the existence of a relation between myself and others which is aptly expressed by the notion of *aidagara*. With the introduction of this word, Watsuji rethinks in Eastern terms one of the great philosophical questions of the West, *intermezzo*. Therefore, Watsuji represents one of the most important examples of global aesthetics for his ability to modernize, in original ways, European thinking without being colonized by it.

The question of *intermezzo* is one of the most complex of Western philosophy both because various philosophical languages employ different terms and because it has been the subject of profoundly different reflections on the part of some of the greatest Western philosophers. The Greek term is *metaxú,* a term already ambiguous in itself because it contains two antithetical terms: *metá* (in the middle, between) and *sún* (with, together, together with). Its ambiguous nature was already pointed out by Plato who attributes it to the demonic. In Augustine, who uses the word *mediatio,* it characterizes the nature of Jesus Christ. The French use *entre-deux* and it ushers a semantic-conceptual field of its own. In German, the term *Zwischen* constitutes one of Heidegger's key philosophical terms. In English, *between*, implies a sliding towards a pragmatic orientation that emerges clearly in the American philosopher Hugh Silverman.[38]

In Watsuji, this question, which in the West has been dealt with mostly in philosophico-theological terms, takes on a cultural meaning both ethical and aesthetic. *Aidagara* is the basic social relation that connects people among themselves. It cannot be thought in simply utilitarian and materialistic terms, as is mostly the case in the West. Watsuji's ethics are aimed neither at the individual nor at the community because they are based on another Japanese notion, *ningen*, a term which is commonly translated as 'human being, person'. These translations, however, are misleading because in the West the notions of subject and individual are strictly connected. The *ningen*, instead, is both immediately individual and social. It is not an isolated person who is in contact successively with others, but is the *aidagara* itself, that is to say, that which is in between people without uniting them inseparably, and not even without dividing them irrevocably. This is the environment. Neither agreement nor harmony are taken for granted, or rivalry and permanent negotiation. The *aidagara* implies a space among people that divides and unites them simultaneously. The *ningen* is never a *tabula rasa* or something autonomous, but presupposes for the same existence a spatio-temporal position, a social conditioning, the mediation of another. Within the *ningen* there is already an impersonal and external point of view, which is relational. On the other hand, a completely utilitarian society which annuls the *ningen* completely could not exist. It would collapse. Society is not a substance independent of the individual conscience, but consists of reciprocal relations between an individual conscience and another. As Robert Carter has remarked, *aidagara* implies a spatial distance that separates things from things (*aida*), indicating, at the same time, that we can meet in the intermezzo while we remain at a distance from one another.[39]

Between the aesthetics of harmony and the aesthetics of conflict exists, therefore, another, the aesthetics of the environment, of spatio-temporal relations in which we are immersed ever since birth. In other words we are not autonomous individuals of a society but not even members of a community.

An interesting development of Watsuji's ideas can be found in the work of French Geographer Augustin Berque (b. 1942) who represents the rare case of a Western thinker who, taking its starting point from Eastern conceptions – the ideas of *fūdo* and *aidagara,* develops a general theory of the environment aimed at overcoming the aporias in which Western thought fails when it thinks it in ecological terms. His is not at all a form of Orientalism, in the sense that Said gives to the word but, on the contrary, it is an attempt to emancipate the West from its cultural imperialism, according to a strategy of multiple modernities.[40]

In his first work *Climate and Culture*, Watsuji includes in a single type, defined as monsoonal, India, Japan and South East Asia.[41] However, what is striking is the disproportion between the multi-sided wealth of the first three aesthetic cultures and the difficulty of identifying an aesthetic culture of South East Asia. In other words, is there a *fūdo* or an aesthetic idea that could assimilate countries as diverse as Thailand, Vietnam, Cambodia, Laos, Myanmar, Malaysia, Brunei, Philippine and Singapore (which, however, constitutes a case apart)?

An attempt in this direction has been tried by David Chou-Shulin (b. 1955) according to whom there is only one mode of feeling which is common to all these countries and is called *semangat* in Indonesian.[42] It is a word that can be translated in almost 15 different Western languages: spirit, soul, zip, team spirit, flush, spunk, fervour, ginger, gust, life, passion, perkiness. The *semengat* creates a climate of joyous acceptance of existence and makes its appearance in ways that vary according to the different foreign influences that these countries have undergone.

The *semangat*, which becomes an aesthetic notion only at the end of the nineties, is characterized by a tendency to fill spaces with all kinds of things, animate or inanimate, without differentiating among them. At the musical level, it manifests itself equally as abolition of silence by playing at the same time different kinds of music. The *semangat* is connected, therefore, with an experience of excessive plenitude in which every person and object, living or dead, have equal dignity. To express this experience in Western terms, it would be a kind of cosmic animism in which different and opposite cultures are absorbed like the Indian, the Buddhist, the Confucian, the Taoist and the Islamic. Chou-Shulin makes a point to clarify that this aesthetic tendency has nothing to do with the postmodern melting pot of the West. This part of Asia has not known Western rationalistic modernity and, therefore, despite appearances, it is not very receptive to Euro-American tendencies. What is at issue, once again, is the search for a modernity different from the Western one.[43] According to the Japanese philosopher Ken-ichi Sasaki (b. 1943), while the West claims to look at, judge and analyse the single works of art, the Eastern point of view, always more watchful of the environment and the processes undergone by the artistic work, is less professionally oriented and, therefore, it has a more collective idea of aesthetic experience.[44]

The inner dualism of the Chinese official man of letters

The Chinese philosopher Li Zehou (b. 1930) is among the great thinkers of world aesthetic culture in the twentieth century whose work, *A Path of Beauty. A Study of Chinese Aesthetics*[45] constitutes neither a pessimistic nor a defeatist response to the problems posed a 100 years earlier by Burckhardt. His work constitutes proof that the same fundamental question posed by Burckhardt concerning the relation between the three powers: aesthetic culture, political power and religion, reached in Chinese civilization a self-awareness without compare with respect to Western civilization. After a gestation of 2,500 years, the same problem has acquired in China a centrality and a depth without compare with other civilizations and reappears in our day in ways not very different from those that it had at the time of Confucius and Zhuangzi. We could even go so far as to state that cultural aesthetics is a Chinese problematic *par excellence* because it reached there the greatest possible level of conflict, finding between the two most extreme solutions (the death penalty for the man of letters and his greatest politico-bureaucratic elevation) many intermediary solutions, extremely subtle and refined.

Ever since the Warring States Period in China (475–221), there were at least four philosophical tendencies absolutely different from one another: Confucianism, Pragmatism (Mozi), Taoism (Zhuangzi) and Legalism (Han Feizi) that proposed different conceptions of morality and politics arriving, nonetheless, after a long debate, at various ways of compromise and eclecticism.[46]

Absolutely central to the entire duration of the Empire (which was unified in 221 BC) is the figure of the official man of letters to whom are assigned administrative, legislative, judicial, bureaucratic and military tasks of the greatest importance, to which corresponded, according to periods, an economic position, social prestige and a very high standard of living. One gained access to this social condition, which reached its greatest development in the Tang (618–907) and Song (960–1269) dynasties, by the so-called system of Imperial exams that became more and more democratic in the sense that even candidates without an eminent background could be admitted. The essential aspects of the official man of letters are two: the first is the precariousness of his condition whereby according to the orientation of the various dynasties he could be dismissed and put to death. The second was a kind of internal division whereby, on the one hand, he was a faithful servant of the State and, therefore, a Confucian who ruled by means of rituals and music, on the other he was a man of letters, which in the West we could define a 'humanist', most often a poet, writer, calligrapher, usually influenced by Taoism.

The aesthetic and political question, therefore, were so entangled with one another throughout the duration of the Chinese Empire as in no other civilization. Sometimes when the Emperor gained power he made a slaughter of all the intellectuals; at other times, one of the first laws he would issue was that: 'officials and intellectuals must not be put to death!' There was even an Emperor, Cao Pi, almost a contemporary of Marcus Aurelius, who stated in his *Discourse on Literature*, that the brief duration of honours and pleasure cannot be compared to the infinity of literature! The inner dualism of the official man of letters is manifested in glaring fashion in the poetry of Ruan Ji (210–63), a great lord and shrewd politician, and goes like this: 'Behind the clouds I would like to hide / where no net can capture me./ Why waste time with petty people / and shake their hands and drink with them?'

The virtues of Li Zehou are many. Through a concise and detailed historical analysis of the whole society, all the great problems involving the relation between aesthetics and culture are examined with extremely rare intellectual tact and refinement that reveals a profound knowledge of the Chinese mind and its subtleties. Of the three powers specified by Burckhardt, only the first two have had a determining role in China: culture and state. None of the four fundamental tendencies native to China (Confucianism, Taoism, Buddhism and Legalism) can be considered religions. The essential character of the Chinese way of thinking is not transcendental. Buddhism, a true religion, arrives in China only at the beginning of the first millennium and even though it exerted an enormous influence on its philosophical thinking,[47] it did not even dent, according to Li Zehou, the most profound Chinese way of feeling which remains aesthetic in its two complementary orientations: Confucian and Taoist, the first interested in art and the second in nature. Even though Chinese thinking is always aware of the precariousness and impermanence of human life, it never arrives at nihilistic or fideistic conclusions. It continues to be interested in the vicissitudes of existence and in the betterment of oneself and others. The spread of Buddhism in China corresponds to a politico-social situation of extreme poverty and hardship (Dynasties of the North and South, 420–581), which forced quite a few people towards fanaticism that led to massacres and atrocities of every kind. Therefore, many saw in religion the promise of an illusory world. Nevertheless, a little at the time, Buddhism underwent a process of Sinization: on the one hand, in resenting the influence of Taoism, it became more rationalistic and pragmatic, on the other hand, Buddhist priests were assimilated by Confucian men of letters. These transformations were also and above all aesthetic: the enigmatic smile of the Buddha statues, the construction of pagodas according to an architectural and rationalistic poetics, the abolition of the terrifying figures of the Indian gods, gradually created a new world where religion was displaced by a realistic and secular art, and Buddhism became part of the sphere of aesthetics.

With the Tang dynasty (608–907) begins the happiest period of the Chinese Empire. The official man of letters acquires a much greater role, which also entails the theory and the practice of military science; poetry reaches its highest level, so far unequalled, becoming a *poetry of poetry*; friendship is recognized as the highest virtue. A relation of affinity is established between dance and calligraphy, as well as between poetry and music. All these arts reach the highest levels of perfection and serve for many centuries as standards of excellence.

The Song dynasty (960–1279) follows and institutionalizes the cultural politics of the Tang dynasty. The system of the 'imperial exams', to which everyone has access, is perfected. The criterion of 'aesthetic disinterestedness', as the foundation of aesthetic experience, is perhaps enunciated for the first time. This notwithstanding, the inner torment of the official man of letters, who is an administrator, on the one hand, and a poet, on the other, does not disappear. This inner duality makes its appearance in striking ways in the figure of Su Shi (1037–1101), who wielded great power but felt a deep *tedium vitae* towards his career and poetry. He is the example of someone who although withdrawn from politics remains extremely attentive to social transformations. In other words, an intelligent person can withdraw from politics, if he is disgusted with it, but must not withdraw from society: *none can escape history and the world*, not even monks!

When the Mongol dynasties come to power (1271) for the Chinese empire begins a phase of progressive decadence and decay which, through various dynasties, concludes with the collapse of the Manchu dynasty of the Qing (1636–1911). Even in this long period, Li Zehou detects a few positive aspects that concern aesthetics and the arts. With the arrival of the Mongols, the official men of letters become marginal and devote themselves to painting succeeding in making extremely refined aesthetic observations such as the importance of the line, the suggestion of the non-represented, the idea of beauty independent of the represented object, the unity of painting, calligraphy and poetry. When in the middle of the nineteenth century photography became an issue, the Chinese never had any doubts: painting is beauty that does not exist in nature and therefore it has nothing to do with photography!

Even in the last Ming and Qing dynasties important works are being produced, above all, in the theatre (the creation of the Peking Opera), in narrative (the rise of the notion of sentimental love), the novel *The Dream of the Red Chamber* (1791) by Cao Xueqin, which is a kind of encyclopaedic document of the end of an Empire, full of stories (*pinghua*) similar to Boccaccio's *Decameron*. In other words, for Zehou, there is no determinist relation between economic conditions and artistic production. In this final phase of the Empire, the philosophers are those who count the most because they focus on the real problem of Chinese civilization between the nineteenth and the twentieth centuries: the invention of systems of modernization independent of European colonialism but, in some ways, heir of the great multi-millenarian past of Chinese civilization. Starting with the seventeenth century is born a kind of 'enlightenment', an attitude of 'critical realism' with respect to life, accompanied by a refined taste similar to French 'rococo', and one realizes that human nature finds its meaning only in art. Rationality settles in the emotions which find their expression in form.

This is the fundamental point of Li's aesthetics: culture has tried for at least a century to point the way to the modernization of China but, unfortunately, they were opposed and fought at every turn by the Qing dynasty, a government of backward and ignorant Manchurians who followed with obstinacy a conservative and reactionary line in the political, economic and social spheres.

The figure of Li Zehou stands among the greatest aesthetic thinkers of the second half of the twentieth century not only for the keenness with which he focused on the problem still unresolved of the relation between aesthetic culture and politics, but also for the splendid pages with which his book begins that describes with an intensity of feeling and aesthetic enthusiasm the prehistory of Chinese civilization (6000 BC), populated by dragons, phoenix and a quantity of extraordinary imaginary animals, as well as the cruel, vigorous and dynamic beauty that appears in the first mythic dynasties (Xia, Shang, Zhou, from 2100–770 BC). Contrary to the nihilistic and populist tendencies that existed in the West at the same time that Li's work was published (1994), he believes that the way of beauty and aesthetic education has a future, on condition that we know how to treasure the past.

The choking of Western aesthetic culture

While many non-European cultures have produced modern aesthetic reflections, independent of the Western tradition (but almost always with a profound knowledge of its nature and with subtle conceptual sophistication), in the West in the sixties a shift takes place in each of the five fundamental issues that we have previously identified (political, media, scepticism, communication and deconstruction) which radically alters their original nature.

The same phenomenon also occurs in aesthetic culture with greater and more relevant consequences from the social point of view. In fact, the shift does not only occur within philosophical theories but also undermines the relation of consonance and essential co-appurtenance between society and the interpreters of its way of feeling and benefiting from aesthetic and artistic experiences. What is at issue is the continuation and development of the process of civilization, aesthetic education and cultural progress begun in the eighteenth century and continued in the next century. In other words, it would seem that the twentieth century interrupted the modernization of the West through two terrible and unpredictable catastrophes: World War I (1914–18), which disrupted with millions of dead and barbaric cruelty the existence of many people, and World War II (1939–45) which set back the conditions of life in many European countries of many years, and led to unthinkable, unprecedented atrocities and savagery such as concentration camps and the atom bomb.

According to the German historian of ideas Reinhart Koselleck (1923–2006), one of the principal elements of the Western crisis of modernity is to be found already in the Enlightenment's emphasis on utopia. If the emancipation from absolutism had happened with greater attention to concrete problems than to projects of perfection, perhaps the experience of modernity would not have resulted in the politico-social crisis of the twentieth century.[48]

When the very deep wounds of World War II were healed, as best as they could, we were left with a world in which it was impossible to take up the severed threads of modernization and civil progress. In other words, there was no longer any place for aesthetics, not the philosophical discipline taught at the university, but a collective way of life of which thinkers could be the interpreters. An abyss was created among peoples always more enslaved by the cultural industry, the mass media, the logic of profit at all costs, the illusion of well-being made possible by technology and the heirs of the project of aesthetic modernization.

Among the first ones to be aware of this rift early on, which kept becoming wider and wider, were the English poet Thomas Stearns Eliot (1888–1965) and the Polish philosopher Władyslaw Tatarkiewicz (1896–1980). It was clear to Eliot in his *Notes towards the Definition of Culture*,[49] that the conflict established by Burckhardt between culture and religion had no longer any reason to be. Either one was about to be swept away by social change that tended to do away with them. Ours is an age in decline and there is no sign of change or reversal. Those who have an interest in our civilization, all they have to do is improve what we already have because we cannot imagine a different one. In Eliot's view, when we compare our culture as it is today to that of non-Christian nations we must be prepared to realize that it is inferior! Both culture and religion presuppose not only writers and priests who are aware of their own actions, but also a public capable of comprehending them. Even though religion and culture have been in conflict in the past, today we realize that no culture has ever been completely separate from religion. Their alliance gives life a meaning and shields us from boredom and despair. The survival of a cultural *élite,* which is still capable of an aesthetic and religious sensibility, of conducting brilliant conversation and behaving according to *good manners*, is not something that interests the group which is visibly affected but the entire nation.

As regards the second point on which Burckhardt had laid out his scheme, that of the relation between culture and state, it had to be completely revised in the light of the exploitation of political ideologies that occurred in the first half of the twentieth century. Even in this case, it seemed necessary to reach a compromise between aesthetic culture and the uneducated classes, as well as with those who claimed to be speaking in their name. It seemed necessary to widen the notion of aesthetics tied to the philosophies of Kant, Hegel and Nietzsche, which appeared too difficult to comprehend to those who didn't have a philosophical background. To sense this need was the polish philosopher Władyslaw Tatarkiewicz author of a vast *History of Aesthetics*,[50] which unfortunately stops at the eighteenth century, and a *History of Six Ideas*,[51] which introduces the idea of an *implicit aesthetics* beside an *explicit aesthetics*, which is about the work of philosophers and theorists. In his view, aesthetics is present also in the ideas of artists, in the predominant conceptions and in the *vox populi*. Before finding explicit expression in the work of scholars, a large part of aesthetic categories have made their appearance in ordinary taste, customs, emotions and in popular sensibility. As a result, he is the author of an extensive history of aesthetics that ends precisely when aesthetics in its true sense as a philosophical discipline is born, which deals with the beautiful, art, sensible knowledge and lifestyle. His position is a moderate one: though he acknowledges that a large part of concepts and aesthetic theories are a collective work, we must recognize that someone has formulated them in a more accurate and more profound level than others! It is to them that we must turn if we want to understand the relation between society and culture.

The real turning point with respect to Burckhardt's scheme occurs only at the beginning of the sixties with the work of the English scholar of literature Raymond Williams (1921–88), *Culture and Society 1780–1950*.[52] Beside religion and state, a third factor comes into play destined to condition culture in capitalistic countries more than the other two: the market. By means of a very detailed study of English literature starting from the 1780, Williams shows that the industrial revolution reduces the power of religion and state, and becomes the true antagonist of culture. William's originality consists in the fact of having pushed back the origins of this factor by a century and half.

At the beginning of the sixties it is clear that in capitalist countries the market tends to condition culture more than religion and the state, but only a sophisticated socio-literary analysis could have demonstrated that this process was already present at the beginning of the nineteenth century. Since then, with the decline of patronage, the decisive relation between culture and society passes through the market. A large number of readers of the new middle class are born and the lucky writer becomes a respectable 'professional'. Culture is now up against something impersonal and unpredictable, the public, which soon reveals to be not a very reliable judge. Aesthetic appreciation and cultural recognition become something very uncertain, fortuitous, subject to factors entirely extraneous to knowledge and art. A consequence of this turning point is the contempt that the romantic artist has for this not very qualified judge. He has no other choice than imagine an 'ideal reader' who is above the real readers. This situation produces a strange dichotomy. On the one hand cultural production is considered subject to the same conditions as industrial production, on the other hand, aesthetic education acquires an always more elitist and separate character from the processes of transformation of society. The reader becomes a customer, the cultured person an enemy of 'democracy' because what counts is the opinion of the majority which is generally oppressed by the logic of utility.

The difficulty in which aesthetics finds itself today consists in the fact that it deals with experiences, modes of feeling, acting and knowing, lifestyles, freedom from the world of profit, empathy for the suffering of others, which do not find a very strong and sincere echo in public opinion. The commitment to a 'good cause' turns out to be always instrumental and sectarian, functional to aims that have nothing to do with it, in fact, they are really antithetical with respect to that 'disinterestedness with respect to the existence of the object' that for Kant constitutes the essence of aesthetics. It is not even thinkable that aesthetic modernity could find a compromise with those powers that Burckhardt considered its historical enemies, state and religion, which have lost all ties to culture. The state can completely do away with ideologies that forced it into some kind of coherence,[53] just as religion silences its entire theoretical apparatus to better be able to attract the greatest number of illiterate, superstitious and ignorant people.[54]

The self-destruction of Western aesthetic culture, which many had foreseen in the period between the two World Wars, takes on staggering acceleration after the sixties. After all, the five turning points that we have identified in the previous chapters (politics, media, scepticism, communication and deconstruction) are the aspects of a single crisis of Western culture that seems incomprehensible to those who are only concerned with the astonishing progress of technology and the extraordinary betterment of the living conditions of Euro-Americans. It seems as if these conquests concealed within them an accelerated and irreversible process of internal disintegration from which none seems to be completely immune.

Not even art is immune to the devastation of aesthetic culture. The American philosopher Arthur C. Danto (b. 1924) was among the first to realize that the status of the work of art following the advent of Pop Art was deeply changing. In his article 'The Artworld'[55] he points out that to define an object as a work of art its simple vision is not sufficient. It must be immersed in the atmosphere of an artistic theory, in a historico-social context that can be defined as 'Artworld'. It follows from a classification point of view that a work of art is an *artifact* to which one or more people, who act on behalf of certain social institutions, prepared in advance to recognize works of art, confer the status of candidate for an evaluation. This problematic has been taken up by the American philosopher George Dickie (b. 1926). In his *Aesthetics. An Introduction*,[56] he asks Danto two questions. The first is: how do we know that the status of a work of art has been conferred to an object? The second question concerns the modalities through which this status is conferred.

According to Dickie, traditional aesthetics makes the mistake of attributing to the expression 'artwork' an immediately positive meaning and, in so doing, it excludes the possibility that there could be an ugly work of art. It attributes to art, surreptitiously, an aesthetic value, almost as if there was an essence of art. The entrance to the 'world of art' is not in itself an evaluation. It only means that someone, or more people, is presenting something as 'a candidate for appreciation'. The number of proponents does not matter, at best it could be just the artist. What matters is that someone baptizes the thing in question as a 'work of art'. This way, he assumes a responsibility and becomes an officer of the world of art. Dickie provides a very clear example: in a zoo, a monkey paints pictures which are exhibited inside the institution as monkey-productions. If the same pictures were exposed in a museum or in art gallery they would acquire the status of 'work of art'. In other words, it all depends on the *institutional setting* in which they are placed. This is why Dickie's theory is known as the 'institutional theory of art'.

The second question has to do with the difference between legal institutions, which entail precise formalities for conferring the status to which they are prefixed (for instance, marriage or the university), and informal institutions like the Artworld, precisely, where no procedure is required to access it. Dickie, therefore, is against transforming the world of art into a formal institution because it would take freshness and exuberance away from art.

Arthur C. Danto's *The Philosophical Disenfranchisement of Art*[57] constitutes probably the most advanced and most profound reflection of American philosophy on aesthetics both for the complexity of the arguments dealt with, as well as for the extraordinary breadth of the erudition of his author. His fundamental thesis is the death of art, a theme he takes up from Hegel but to give it a different meaning. For Hegel the death of art begins with Christianity. Art is sublated by philosophy because the new religion breaks the balance between form and content that constituted the greatness of classical art. For Danto, the death of art is a recent event that took place in the eighties and is the result of Pop Art. Beginning from the moment in which the international art market becomes hegemonic, the idea that there is a progressive history of art constitutes an obstacle and a limitation to the total freedom and independence to which it aspires. There are no longer movements that interpret the spirit of the time but everything becomes possible all at the same time. Aristotle's principle of non-contradiction on which Western logic is founded no longer applies. Even in art we can do without history. Of course, people will continue to paint, sculpt, make installations, and so on, but their works will be placed in a post-historic context that confine them in an ephemeral hedonism deprived of that theoretical support which philosophy had guaranteed to it, though in a very ambiguous and tendentious way.

The relation between philosophy and art constitutes, actually, the most problematic aspect of Danto's book. The very term, 'disenfranchisement', which means to deprive someone of his own rights, is in itself very strange. For Danto, philosophy, ever since Plato, is hostile to art. The Greek philosopher reproached it for being two stages detached from the truth. This critique has been passed on through the centuries and even those who in the modern era like Schopenhauer (1788–1860) attributed to art a function that gave us access to the most profound sense of existence, did not assign a cognitive value to it. Therefore, for Danto, art is not the carrier of any knowledge and cannot even have any impact on society. The fact that it was feared and not just by Plato, and that during the centuries it was the object of censorship and control by politics and religion, remains paradoxical. If art has nothing to do with truth and has no influence, why did it create so much hostility to the point of being stripped of its rights, yesterday as today, if it ever had any? An answer could be sought in its uselessness and ineffectiveness. In a world which is entirely dominated by practical interests, connected to power and the economy, art introduces us to the aesthetic experience which is, in fact, disinterested and extraneous to needs. But Danto strongly rejects this answer that would bring art back under the umbrella of aesthetics and, furthermore, it would be anachronistic and irrelevant at the highest level, since from Pop Art onwards it has become a market of luxury goods, if not something worse. Perhaps it is precisely in this disenchantment and degradation of its supposed powers that rests its disenfranchisement. Not only art does not serve any purpose but not even this uselessness affords some indirect advantage. Its identification with the enemy is total.

Not all artists share or abide by this view of the self-destruction of Western aesthetics and artistic traditions. There is an opposition that Danto defines with the term 'disturbation' that moves towards self-harmful artistic actions that seem extreme while, in fact, they are only pathetic and futile. A case in point is the artist who put himself in a plastic bag to be left on a California highway. This experiment was his work of art from which he was lucky to come out alive. This type of performance has nothing to do with that disturbing and alarming aspect that has always constituted an important aspect of Western art. 'Disturbation', a term Danto chooses for its phonic affinity to masturbation, is only the last pang of agony that precedes death.

The last stand of Western aesthetics: Interested disinterestedness

The last attempt to save Western aesthetic culture from destruction is made by French Sociologist Pierre Bourdieu (1930–2002) in *Practical Reason* and *Pascalian Meditations*[58] by transforming and greatly stretching the concept of *aesthetic disinterestedness*.

If for Burckhardt the state and religion were the enemies of culture, for Bourdieu the state has an enormous importance because it is the guarantor of the cultural capital. Furthermore, cultural work implies a true and proper vocation-profession (in the sense of the German word *Beruf*), for which, as in religious life, one must be always ready to die. Aesthetic culture, strictly speaking, is only the transformation of an attitude with respect to life typical of pre-modern societies that attribute to honour and disinterestedness a peremptory importance. In the modern age, this attitude has led to the formation of *fields* in which disinterestedness and generosity constitute the basis of an economy of symbolic goods within which money and power have a subordinate role. Kant's notion of 'aesthetic disinterestedness' acquires an extraordinary breadth which includes not only all the fields of cultural production (literary, artistic, moral, scientific, religious), but also legal and bureaucratic. The fundamental characteristic of these fields is their relation to the universal. For Bourdieu, therefore, the state and the church are no longer the enemies of culture but, on the contrary, they constitute the bastions against the utilitarianism that purports to reduce all motives of human actions to a desire for money and power.

The acquisition of this disinterested attitude implies, however, a *habitus*, that is, a way of being that ever since birth shapes the individual as an initiate to the logic of the economy of symbolic goods: he is the product of a family and scholastic education. The complicated rules that are at the basis of the exchange of gifts are part of this mentality. One must not think, however, that the *field* is a community or a class (a notion especially criticized by Bourdieu). It is rather the space of a game made of conflicts, alliances, compromises within which are situated those who have deeply assimilated the rules and the strategies. It is built on an *illusion,* that is, a belief shared in an almost ludic way which entails expectations, interests, emotional investments, objective opportunities and, above all, recognition. The *illusion* is something completely different from a mere subjective fantasy or individual mirage. Every field has its rules of the game that result incomprehensible to those who are on the outside: for instance, the commitment, the disinterestedness, the enthusiasm and the determination of those who operate within an intellectual, religious or artistic field are inexplicable to those who belong to another field. The field must not be thought as something static but as the place in which a game takes place where the positions and the symbolic values of each change constantly in function of the positions and the values of others. For Bourdieu, therefore, contemporary society does not signal at all the end of *illusions*. On the contrary, under certain aspects it multiplies the number of fields and, therefore, *illusions* and opportunities. Generally, however, especially in the intellectual sphere, there is a lack of awareness that one belongs to a field, and a fierce internal competition prevails over the common interest to preserve the autonomy of the field within which one operates.

Without these *illusions* life is meaningless. People need *distinction* which is guaranteed by the possession of a symbolic capital which is also manifested in family life (i.e. to be recognized as a good mother, a good father, a good son). At the scientific and artistic levels, only the state has at its disposal the means to impose and instil lasting principles of vision and division conforming to its structures. It is the place of concentration and exercise of symbolic power, *par excellence*. Bourdieu, therefore, is extremely critical of aesthetic populism. None will ever be able to prove a disinterested sentiment if all his energies are concentrated exclusively on the satisfaction of basic life needs. Therefore, populism can only consolidate the *status quo*. It denounces the inhuman conditions of millions of needy people at the same time that it claims to attribute to them the gratuitous dispositions that are connected to aesthetic culture. Exceptional historical situations have made possible a process of collective liberation which is at the origin of the rarest conquests of humanity: the order of knowledge, the order of ethics and the order of aesthetics.

For Bourdieu it is of fundamental importance to save the autonomy of all fields (from the artistic to the legal, from the scientific to the bureaucratic). This autonomy is threatened not only by the instruments of mass communication and the puerile level of Western societies, but by the *tycoons* who try in every way to marginalize and annihilate even the political field. With the idea of an *interested disinterestedness* and, therefore, not merely subjective, but integrated in a social field that recognizes an economic value even to symbolic goods, contemporary Western aesthetics comes to an end.

Notes and Works Cited

Chapter 1

1 Wilhelm Dilthey, 'The Three Epochs of Modern Aesthetics and its Present Task' (1892), *Poetry and Experience*, Vol. 5, ed. Rudolf A. Makkreel and Frithjof Rodi. Princeton, NJ: Princeton University Press, 1985.
2 Immanuel Kant, *Critique of Judgment*, trans. J. H. Bernard. New York: Hafner, 1951. Henceforth cited as *CJ*.
3 Georg Wilhelm Friedrich Hegel, *Lectures of the Philosophy of History* (1837), trans. E. S. Heldane. Lincoln: University of Nebraska Press, 1995.
4 Wilhelm Dilthey, *Poetry and Experience*, Vol. 5, ed. Rudolf A. Makkreel and Frithjof Rodi. Princeton, NJ: Princeton University Press, 1985.
5 Wilhelm Dilthey, *Wilhelm Dilthey: Selected Works, Volume III: The Formation of the Historical World in the Human Sciences*, ed. Rudolf A. Makkreel and Frithjof Rodi. Princeton, NJ: Princeton University Press, 2002.
6 George Santayana, *The Sense of Beauty* (1896). New York: Modern Library, 1955.
7 Ideas closer to Santayana on the relation between the quality of experience and the importance of evaluation, understood as the central point of aesthetics and art, can be found in Ivor Armstrong Richards (1893–1979) in his work *Principles of Literary Criticism*. London: Kegan Paul, Trench, Trubner, 1924.
8 George Santayana, *Reason in Art* (1905). New York: Dover Publications, 1982.
9 Henri Bergson, *Time and Free Will: Essay on the Immediate Givens of Consciousness*, trans. F. L. Pogson. London: G. Allen & Unwin, 1959.
10 Henri Bergson, *An Introduction to Metaphysics*, trans. T. E. Hulme. Indianapolis: Hackett, 1999.
11 Henri Bergson, *Creative Evolution*, trans. Arthur Mitchell. London: Macmillan, 1911.
12 Kant, *CJ*, §17.
13 This similarity never appears in Bergson who even though compares his work constantly to Kant's *Critique of Pure Reason* and its neo-Kantian interpretations, he completely disregards his *CJ*. However, the connection between Bergson and Kant's aesthetic thought is emphasized by V. Jankélévitch in *Henry Bergson*. Paris: Alcan, 1959, 137 ff.
14 Henri Bergson, *La perception du changement*, in *La pensée et le mouvant*: *Essais et conférences*. Paris: Alcan, 1934.
15 Henri Bergson, *Laughter: An Essay on the Meaning of the Comic*, trans. Cloudesley Brereton and Fred Rothwell. New York: Macmillan, 1911.
16 Kant, *CJ*, §54.

17 Henri Bergson, *The Two Sources of Morality and Religion*, trans. Cloudesley Brereton, R. Ashley Audra and W. Horsfall Carter. London: Macmillan, 1935.
18 Luigi Pirandello, *On Humor* (1908, 1920), trans. Antonio Illiano and Daniel P. Testa. Chapel Hill, NC: University of North Carolina Press, 1974.
19 Georg Simmel, *The Conflict in Modern Culture and Other Essays*, ed. and trans. Peter Etzkom. New York: Teachers College Press, 1968.
20 Georg Simmel, *Zum Problem des Naturalismus* (pubblicato postumo), in *Fragmente und Aufsaetze*. München: Drei Masken Verlag, 1923.
21 Georg Simmel, 'The Metaphysics of Death' (1910), *Theory, Culture & Society*, 24, 7–8 (2007): 72–7.
22 Georg Simmel, *The View of Life: Four Metaphysical Essays with Journal Aphorisms*, trans. A. Y. Andrews and Donald J. Levine. Chicago, IL: University of Chicago Press, 2010.
23 Henri Bremond, *La poésie pure*. Paris: Grasset, 1926.
24 Henri Bremond, *Prayer & Poetry, A Contribution to Poetical Theory*, trans. Algar Labouchere Thorold. London: Burns, Oates & Washbourne, 1927.
25 Miguel de Unamuno, *The Tragic Sense of Life*, trans. S. De Madariaga. New York: Cosimo, 2007.
26 José Ortega y Gasset, '*Adán nel Paraíso*' (1910), *Obras Completas*, Madrid: Revista de Occidente, 1966–71.
27 Karl Jaspers, *Philosophy*, trans. E. B. Ashton. Chicago, IL: Chicago University Press, 1969–71.
28 José Ortega y Gasset, 'An Essay in Esthetics by Way of a Preface', trans. Ph. W. Silver, *Phenomenology of Art*. New York: W. W. Norton & Co., 1975.
29 José Ortega y Gasset, 'The Dehumanization of Art' (1925), *The Dehumanization of Art and Other Essays on Art, Culture, and Literature*. Princeton, NJ: Princeton University Press, 1968.
30 José Ortega y Gasset. 'In Search of a Goethe from Within', trans. W. R. Trask, *The Dehumanization of Art and Other Writings on Art and Culture*. Garden City, NY: Doubleday, 1956.
31 Karl Jaspers. '*Leonardo as Philosopher*.' *Three Essays: Leonardo, Descartes, Max Weber*, trans. Ralph Manheim. New York: Hartcourt, Brace & World, 1964.
32 Herbert Marcuse, *Eros and Civilization. A Philosophical Inquiry into Freud*. Boston: Beacon Press, 1955.
33 The English critic Herbert Read (1893–1968) has provided a strong reformulation of the issues of anarchist aesthetics in many works among them *Icon and Idea: The Function of Art in the Development of Human Consciousness*. Cambridge, MA: Harvard University Press, 1955. Read claims that a separation between art and life is artificial. In any epoch there are works capable of influencing our sensibility and to communicate their vital impulse.
34 Karl Marx, *Capital: A Critique of Political Economy*, Vol. I, trans. Ben Fowkes. London: Penguin Books, 1990.
35 Sigmund Freud, *Civilization and Its Discontents*. London: Penguin, 2002.

36 Wilhelm Reich, *The Sexual Revolution* (1945), trans. Theodore P. Wolfe. New York: Noonday, 1969.
37 Herbert Marcuse, 'The End of Utopia'. *Five Lectures*. Harmondsworth, UK: Penguin, 1970.
38 Herbert Marcuse, *The Aesthetic Dimension: Toward a Critique of Marxist Aesthetics*. Boston: Beacon Press, 1978.
39 Gregory Bateson, *Mind and Nature. A Necessary Unity*. New York: Hampton Press, 1979.
40 Michel Foucault, *The Order of Things: An Archaeology of the Human Sciences*. New York: Pantheon Books, 1970.
41 Michel Foucault, *The History of Sexuality Vol. 1: The Will to Knowledge*. London: Penguin, 1976.
42 Michel Foucault, *The History of Sexuality Vol. 2: The Use of Pleasure*. London: Penguin, 1992.
43 Michel Foucault, *The History of Sexuality Vol. 3: The Care of the Self*. London: Penguin, 1990.
44 Martha Nussbaum, *The Therapy of Desire: Theory and Practice in Hellenistic Ethics*. Princeton, NJ: Princeton University Press, 1994.
45 Giorgio Agamben, *Homo Sacer: Sovereign Power and Bare Life*, trans. Daniel Heller-Roazen. Stanford, CA: Stanford University Press, 1998.

Chapter 2

1 Heinrich Wölfflin, *Renaissance and Baroque*, trans. Kathrin Simon. Ithaca, NY: Cornell University Press, 1966.
2 Heinrich Wölfflin, *Principles of Art History: The Problem of the Development of Style in Later Art*. New York: Holt, 1932.
3 Immanuel Kant, *Critique of Judgment*, par. 57, note 1, ed. Nicholas Walker, trans. James Creed Meredith. Oxford: Oxford University Press, 2007.
4 Alois Riegl, *Problems of Style: Foundations for a History of Ornament*, trans. Evelyn Kain. Princeton, NJ: Princeton University Press, 1992.
5 Alois Riegl, *Historical Grammar of the Visual Arts*, trans. Jacqueline E. Jung. New York: Zone Books, 2004.
6 In the emphasis that Riegl places on the organic and the inorganic is evident Schelling's influence who seems to be the philosopher who has exercised the greatest influence over him.
7 Alois Reigl, *Late Roman Art Industry*, trans. Rolf Winkes. Roma: G. Bretschneider, 1985.
8 Wilhelm Worringer, *Abstraction and Empathy; A Contribution to the Psychology of Style*. New York: International Universities Press, 1953.
9 In his lessons on aesthetics, Hegel provides a philosophical justification of iconoclastia. He claims that following the Reformation the Spirit feels the need to be satisfied by its own interiority alone and therefore rejects

any sensible representation. In this fashion art finds in religion its own overcoming. This shift, after all, is already present in the third and last form of art identified by Hegel as the Romantic one which, ever since Christianity, has its fundamental principle in the elevation of the spirit to itself.

10 Wilhelm Worringer, *Form problems of the Gothic*. New York: G. E. Stechert & Co., 1920.

11 Hans Prinzhorn, *Artistry of the Mentally Ill; a Contribution to the Psychology and Psychopathology of Configuration*, trans. Eric von Brockdorff. New York: Spinger-Verlag, 1972.

12 Kitaro Nishida, *Nishida Kitarō Zenshū* (Opera Omnia), Vol. III. Tokyo: Iwanamishoten, 1965.

13 Ynhui Park, *Man, Language and Poetry*. Seoul: National University Press, 1999; '*Meot. In Search of Korean Aesthetics*,' *Asian Aesthetics*, ed. K. Sasaki. Kyoto-Singapore: Kyoto University Press, 2010. See also, 'Is Intercivilizational Dialogue Possible?' *Korea Journal*, 41, 3 (Autumn 2001): 5–29.

14 Pavel Florenskij, *Ikonostasis* (1922), trans. Donald Sheehan and Olga Andrejev. Redondo Beach, CA: Oakwood Publishers, 1996.

15 Sergei S. Averincev, *Poétika rannevizantijskoj literatury*, 1982.

16 Pavel Florenskij, 'Obratnaja perspektiva' *1922+, *Trudy po znakovym sistemam* III [Sign Systems Studies], 198 (Tartu, 1967): 381–416.

17 Erwin Panofsky, *Idea: A Concept in Art Theory*, trans. Joseph J. S. Peake. New York, NY: Harper & Row, 1968.

18 Andre Chastel, *The Sack of Rome 1527*, trans. Beth Archer. Princeton, NJ: Princeton University Press, 1983.

19 A conception of *living form* understood as the language of emotions is suggested by the English art critic Roger Fry (1866–1934) in 'An Essay in Aesthetics' *1909+, *Vision and Design*, London: Chatoo & Windus, 1920, 16–38.

20 Henri Focillon, *The Life of Forms in Art*, trans. C. B. Hogan and George Kubler. New York: Wittenborn, 1957.

21 Georg Kubler, *The Shape of Time: Remarks on the History of Things*. New Haven: Yale University Press, 1962.

22 Norbert Elias, *The Court Society*, trans. Edmund Jephcott. Oxford: Blackwell, 1983.

23 Norbert Elias, *The Civilizing Process*, trans. Edmund Jephcott. Cambridge, MA: Blackwell, 1994.

24 For instance, the present-day interest in thinkers like the Jesuit Balthasar Gracián, the author of the most famous treatise on the art of living well of the Baroque era, *The Art of Worldly Wisdom* (trans. Joseph Jacobs. New York: Macmillan Co., 1956) can be placed in relation to the importance that advertisement and the elaboration of a competitive image has assumed in today's capitalist society.

25 Norbert Elias, *The Society of Individuals*, ed. Michael Schröter, trans. Edmund Jephcott. Cambridge, MA: Basil Blackwell, 1991.

26 Rudolf Arnheim, *Art and Visual Perception: A Psychology of the Creative Eye*. Berkeley-Los Angeles, CA: University of California Press, 1954.
27 On the study of *pattern* in decorative art, see also E. H. Gombrich (1909–2001), *The Sense of Order. A Study in the Psychology of Decorative Art*. Oxford: Phaidon, 1979.
28 Rudolf Arnheim, *Visual Thinking*. Berkeley-Los Angeles, CA: University of California Press, 1969.
29 M. C. Beardsley, *The Aesthetic Point of View*. Ithaca: Cornell University Press, 1982.
30 A singular encounter between aesthetics and religion, united in an experience of form similar to ecstasy can be found in Clive Bell's (1881–1964) *Art* (New York: Capricorn Books, 1958), which has had great influence even outside Western aesthetics, for instance, on the work of the Chinese philosopher Li Zehou.
31 Hans Urs von Balthasar, *The Glory of the Lord: A Theological Aesthetics*, trans. Erasmo Leiva-Merikakis, ed. Joseph Fessio and John Riches. Edinburgh: T&T Clark, 1982–c1991.
32 Within Protestantism Balthasar differentiates at least three different attitudes with respect to aesthetics: the pro-aesthetic one, in the classical sense, the humanistic and liberal one of Hegel; the anti-aesthetic one of Kierkegaard and finally the pro-aesthetic one in the anti-formal and dynamic sense of K. Barth and G. Nebel. Only the latter tendency gets partial recognition in Balthazar's work.
33 Ananda Kentish Coomaraswami, *Selected Papers: Traditional Art and Symbolism*. Princeton, NJ: Twayne Publishers, 1977.
34 Even in the East (in ancient Indian art, in Buddhism and in Persian art) one can find aniconic orientations but, according to Coomaraswamy, they do not show that character of harshness and absoluteness that they have in the West, precisely because the notion of form as *nama-rupa* excludes any opposition between sensible and supersensible world.
35 Marshall McLuhan, *Understanding Media*. New York: McGraw-Hill, 1964.
36 A similar claim of participation addressed to the consumer can be found in the poetics and critical works that Umberto Eco (b. 1932) examines in *The Open Work*, trans. Anna Cancogni. Cambridge, MA: Harvard University Press, 1989.
37 Marshall McLuhan and E. McLuhan, *Laws of Media: The New Science*. Toronto: University of Toronto Press, 1992.
38 This attitude is expressed with the greatest energy by G. Debord (1931–94) in the *Society of the Spectacle*. Detroit: Black and Red, 1983.
39 Jean-François Lyotard, 'After the Sublime: The State of Aesthetics', *The States of 'Theory': History, Art, and Critical Discourse*, ed. David Carroll. Stanford, CA: Stanford University Press, 1994.
40 Jean-François Lyotard, 'Anima minima', *Postmodern Fables*, trans. Georges Van Den Abhcele. Minneapolis, MN: University of Minnesota Press, 1997.

41 Jean-François Lyotard, *Enthusiasm: The Kantian Critique of History*, trans. Georges Van Den Abbeele. Stanford, CA: Stanford University Press, 2009.
42 Slavoj Žižek, *The Sublime Object of Ideology*. London-New York: Verso, 1989.

Chapter 3

1 Immanuel Kant, *Critique of Judgment*, ed. Nicholas Walker, trans. James Creed Meredith.Oxford: Oxford University Press, 2007, §15 e 23.
2 Alexander Gottlieb Baumgarten, *Aesthetica* (1750–58), *Theoretische Ästhetik*, trans. H. R. Schweizer. Hamburg: Felix Meiner, 1988.
3 F. D. E. Schleiermacher, *Estetica*, trans. Paolo D'Angelo. Palermo: Aesthetica Edizioni, 1988.
4 Georg Wilhelm Friedrich Hegel, *Aesthetics. Lectures on Fine Art*, trans. T. M. Knox, 2 vols. Oxford: Clarendon Press, 1975.
5 E. Cassirer, *The Philosophy of the Enlightenment*, trans. Fritz C. A. Koelln and James P. Pettegrove. Princeton, NJ: Princeton University Press, 1979.
6 Benedetto Croce, *The Aesthetic as the Science of Expression and of Linguistic in General*, trans. Colin Lyas. Cambridge: Cambridge University Press, 1992; henceforth cited as *A*. *Problemi di estetica e contributi alla storia dell'estetica italiana*. Bari: G. Laterza, 1910; *Nuovi saggi di estetica* (1920). Bari: G. Laterza & figli, 1969; *Poetry and Literature: An Introduction to its Criticism and History*, trans. Giovanni Gullace. Carbondale: Southern Illinois University Press, 1981.
7 Benedetto Croce, *Breviary of Aesthetics*, trans. Hiroko Fudemoto. Toronto: University of Toronto Press, 2007. Henceforth cited as *BA*.
8 Benedetto Croce, *The Character of Totality of Artistic Expression* (1917), *The English Review*, 1918.
9 Benedetto Croce, *Poetry and Literature: An Introduction to its Criticism and History*, I, 1 e 2.
10 Starting with the *Logic* (1908), history, instead, is considered identical to philosophy.
11 Benedetto Croce, 'Le due scienze mondane. L'estetica e l'economica' (1931). *Ultimi Saggi*. Bari: Laterza, 1935.
12 The English philosopher R. B. Collingwood (1889–1943) and the Chinese philosopher Zhu Guangqian (1897–1980) are thought to be close to Croce's thought. The former, in *The Principles of Art* (Oxford: Clarendon Press, 1938) clearly separates art from crafts and claims that the imagination is an intermediary form of knowledge between feeling and thinking. The latter, who introduced with Cai Yuanpei (1868–1940) modern aesthetics in China, creates a theoretical system within which aesthetic appreciation is represented as pure intuition. See *Psychology of Literature and Art*, the English translation of Yuanpei's *Wenyi Xinlixue*, Hefei: Anhui Jiaoyu Press, 1996.

13 Gabriel Scaramuzza and Karl Schuhmann, *Ein Husserlmanuskipt über Ästhetik* (*Husserl Studies*), 7, 3 (1990): 165–77.

14 Roman Ingarden, *The Literary Work of Art*, trans. George G. Grabowicz. Evanston, IL: Northwestern University Press, 1973. Henceforth cited as *LWA*.

15 Nicolai Hartmann, *Aesthetik*. Berlin: de Gruyter, 1966.

16 Hans Georg Gadamer, *Truth and Method*, 2nd rev. edn., trans. J. Weinsheimer and D. G. Marshall. New York: Crossroad, 2004. Henceforth cited as *TM*. See also the integrative volume, *Wahrheit und Methode. Ergänzungen*, Tübingen, 1986–93.

17 Dilthey, according to Gadamer, does not belong to the aesthetics of life, since his concept of *Erlebnis* has a purely gnoseological and hermeneutical meaning.

18 The idea of the world as play without players constitutes the main thesis of the work by Eugen Fink, *Spiel als Weltsymbol*. Stuttgart: Kohlhammer, 1960.

19 Hans Georg Gadamer, 'Dichten und Deuten,' *Kleine Schriften II*. Tübingen: J.C.B. Mohr, 1967.

20 Hans Georg Gadamer, *Reason in the Age of Science*, trans. Frederick G. Lawrence. Cambridge, MA: MIT Press, 1983.

21 E. Cassirer, *The Philosophy of Symbolic Forms. Volume One: Language*. New Haven: Yale University Press, 1955; *The Philosophy of Symbolic Forms. Volume Two: Mythical Thought*. New Haven: Yale University Press, 1955; *The Philosophy of Symbolic Forms. Volume Three: The Phenomenology of Knowledge*. New Haven: Yale University Press, 1957.

22 E. Cassirer, *An Essay on Man: An Introduction to a Philosophy of Human Culture*. New Haven: Yale University Press, 1944.

23 Cassirer acknowledges his debt to Friedrich Theodor Vischer (1807–87), author of a work, *Das Symbol* (1887) in *Philosophische Aufsätze Eduard Zeller zu seinem fünfzigjährigen Doktorjubiläum gewidmet*. Leipzig: Zentral Antiquariat der Deutschen Demokratischen Republik, 1962. 151–93.

24 Cassirer is referring to Hermann Helmholtz (1821–94) and to Heinrich Rudolf Hertz (1857–94).

25 E. Cassirer, *Philosophie der Symbolischen Formen*, III, 2, 5. Cfr. Also the important conference paper, '*Das Symbolproblem und seine Stellung im System der Philosophie*', *Journal for Aesthetics and General Art History*, 1927.

26 E. Cassirer, 'Language and Art. I and II (1942)', *Symbol, Myth and Culture. Essays and Lectures of Ernest Cassirer 1935–45*, ed. D. Ph. Verene. New Haven, CT: Yale University Press, 1981.

27 Even the English philosopher Alfred Whitehead (1861–1947) in *Adventures of Ideas* (New York: New American, 1933) and in other works, starting from mathematical and physical premises, attributes a great importance to the notion of *harmony*, a concept which, for him, is not only at the basis of beauty but also of truth and goodness.

28 E. Cassirer, *Philosophie der Symbolischen Formen*, III Intr. 4.

29 Carl Gustav Jung, 'On the Relation of Analytical Psychology to Poetry', *The Spirit in Man, Art, and Literature*. Princeton, NJ: Princeton University Press, 1978.

30 Carl Gustav Jung, 'On Psychology and Literature,' *Art and its Significance: An Anthology of Aesthetic Theory*, ed. Stephen David Ross. Albany, NY: State University of New York Press, 1994. 507–20.

31 Carl Gustav Jung, *Psychology of the Unconscious*, trans. Beatrice M. Hinkle. New York: Dodd, Mead and Co., 1949.

32 Cfr. Gaston Bachelard, *The Formation of the Scientific Mind: A Contribution to a Psychoanalysis of Objective Knowledge*, trans. Mary McAllester Jones. Manchester: Clinamen, 2002; and *Le matérialisme rationnel*. Paris: Presses Universitaires de France, 2000.

33 Gaston Bachelard, *The Formation of the Scientific Mind: A Contribution to a Psychoanalysis of Objective Knowledge.*

34 Gaston Bachelard, *The Psychoanalysis of Fire*, trans. Alan C. M. Ross. Boston: Beacon Press, 1964.

35 Gaston Bachelard, *Lautreamont*, Dallas: Dallas Institute of Humanities & Culture, 1998.

36 I follow here the excellent analysis of Bachelard's thought by Giuseppe Sertoli in his highly documented volume *Le immagini e la realtà. Saggio su Gaston Bachelard*. Firenze: La nuova Italia, 1972, where he analyses the various stages of his intellectual journey with particular attention to aesthetico-philosophical problems.

37 Gaston Bachelard, *Water and Dreams: An Essay on the Imagination of Matter*, trans. Edith R. Farrell. Dallas: Dallas Institute of Humanities and Culture, 1999; *Air and Dreams: An Essay on the Imagination of Movement*, trans. Edith R. Farrell and C. Frederick Farrell. Dallas: Dallas Institute Publications, Dallas Institute of Humanities and Culture, 1988; *Earth and Reveries of Will: An Essay on the Imagination of Matter*, trans. Kenneth Haltman. Dallas: The Dallas Institute Pub., 2002; and *La terre et les rêveries du repos*. Paris: J. Corti, 1948.

38 Gaston Bachelard, *The Poetics of Space*, trans. Maria Jolas. Boston: Beacon Press, 1969; and *The Poetics of Reverie: Childhood, Language, and the Cosmos*, trans. Daniel Russell. Boston: Beacon Press, 1971.

39 Theodor W. Adorno, *Aesthetic Theory*, trans. and ed. Robert Hullot-Kentor. Minnesota, MN: University of Minnesota Press, 1996.

40 Theodor W. Adorno, *Negative Dialectics*, trans. E. B. Ashton. London: Routledge, 1973.

41 Theodor W. Adorno. *Philosophische Terminologie*. Frankfurt (am Main): Suhrkamp, 1973, §1 e 2.

42 Theodor W. Adorno, *Negative Dialectics*, London: Routledge, 1973.

43 Theodor W. Adorno, *Aesthetic Theory*, Minneapolis: Minnesota University Press, 1997.

44 Ibid.

45 G. W. F Hegel, *Aesthetics: Lectures on Fine Art*, London: Routledge, 1973.

46 Theodor W. Adorno, *Aesthetic Theory*, Minneapolis: University of Minnesota Press, 1996.
47 Ibid.
48 Maurice Merleau-Ponty, *Phenomenology of Perception*, trans. Colin Smith. London: Routledge, 2002.
49 Maurice Merleau-Ponty, *In praise of philosophy and other essays,* trans. John Wild, James M. Edie and John O'Neil. Evanston: Northwestern University Press, 1970.
50 Maurice Merleau-Ponty, 'Cézanne's Doubt,' *Sense and Non-Sense*, trans. Hubert Dreyfus and Patricia Allen Dreyfus. Evanston: Northwestern University Press, 1964. 9–25.
51 Maurice Merleau-Ponty, 'Eye and Mind,' *The Merleau-Ponty Aesthetics Reader*, trans. Michael Smith, 1993. 121–49. Evanston: Northwestern University Press, 1993.
52 Maurice Merleau-Ponty, *The Visible and the Invisible, Followed by Working Notes*, trans. Alphonso Lingis. Evanston: Northwestern University Press, 1968.
53 Hans Robert Jauss, *Kleine Apologie der Aesthetischen Erfahrung*. Konstanz: Universitätsverlag, 1972; and *Aesthetic Experience and Literary Hermeneutics*, trans. Michael Shaw. Minneapolis, MN: University of Minnesota Press, 1982.
54 Hans Robert Jauss, *Literaturgeschichte als Provokation der Literaturwissenschaft*. Konstanz: Universitätsverlag, 1969; and *Toward an Aesthetic of Reception*, trans. Timothy Bahti. Minneapolis, MN: University of Minnesota Press, 1982.
55 Gianni Vattimo, *Beyond Interpretation: The Meaning of Hermeneutics for Philosophy*, trans. David Webb. Stanford, CA: Stanford University Press, 1997. Of his previous works, we should note: *Poesia e ontologia*. Milano: U. Mursia, 1967; *The Adventure of Difference: Philosophy after Nietzsche and Heidegger,* trans. Cyprian Blamires with Thomas Harrison. Baltimore, MD: Johns Hopkins University Press, 1993 and *The End of Modernity: Nihilism and Hermeneutics in Postmodern Culture*, trans. Jon R. Snyder. Baltimore, MD: Johns Hopkins University Press, 1991.
56 Susanne Langer, *Feeling and Form: A Theory of Art developed from 'Philosophy in a New Key.'* New York: Scribner, 1953.
57 Nelson Goodman, *Languages of Art*. Indianapolis: Bobbs-Merrill, 1968.
58 Paul Feyerabend, 'Science as Art: A Discussion of Riegl's Theory of Art and an Attempt to Apply it to the Sciences,' *Art & Text*, 12/13 (Summer 1983–Autumn 1984).
59 The idea of science as 'style of thought' goes back to Ludwik Fleck (1896–1961) and his work, *The Genesis and Development of a Scientific Fact*, ed. T. J. Trenn and R. K. Merton. Chicago, Ill: University of Chicago Press, 1979.
60 Gerd Buchdahl (1914–2001), '*Verità e stile nella scienza, nell'arte e in filosofia,' Nuova civiltà delle machine,* 4 (1983): 14–22.
61 Frank Sibley, 'Aesthetic Concepts,' *Approach to Aesthetics*. Oxford: Oxford University Press, 2001.
62 From a development of this problematic emerges the notion of *aesthetic supervenience,* elaborated by Jerrold Levinson in 'Aesthetic Supervenience'

(1984), in *Music, Art, Metaphysics*. Ithaca, NY: Cornell University Press, 1990. According to Levinson, aesthetic attributes are not reducible to structural ones (merely perceptive), or to sub-structural ones (not immediately perceivable as such) and not even to contextual ones (i.e. endowed with a relation that can be appreciated within the artistic context).

63 Morris Weitz, 'The Role of Theory in Aesthetics', *Problems in Aesthetics*. New York: Macmillan, 1959. 145–56.

64 Friedrich Waismann, 'Verifiability', *Proceedings of the Aristotelian Society, Supplementary*, 19 (1945): 119–50.

65 Morris Weitz, *The Opening Mind: A Philosophical Study of Humanistic Concepts*. Chicago, Ill: University of Chicago Press, 1977.

Chapter 4

1 G. W. F. Hegel, *Aesthetics. Lectures on Fine Art,* trans. T. M. Knox, 2 vols. (Oxford: Clarendon Press, 1975), I, 3, B, II .

2 Leo N. Tolstoy, *What is Art?* trans. Almyer Maude. New York: MacMillan Publishing Company, 1960.

3 Hannah Arendt (1906–75) adheres to this tripartition in *The Human Condition*. Chicago, IL: University of Chicago Press, 1958.

4 John Dewey, *Art as Experience* (1934). New York: The Berkeley Publishing Group, 2005.

5 Ernst Bloch, *The Principle of Hope*, Vols. I–III, trans. Neville Plaice, Stephen Plaice and Paul Knight. Cambridge, MA: MIT Press, 1995. Henceforth cited as *PH*.

6 Ernst Bloch, 'Das Faust-Motiv', *A Philosophy of the Future,* trans. John Cumming. New York: Herder and Herder, 1970.

7 Ernst Bloch, *The Spirit of Utopia*, trans. Anthony Nassar. Stanford, CA: Stanford University Press, 2000.

8 O. Revault d'Allonnes, *Musiques. Variations sur la pensée juive.* Paris, 1979. See also E. Namenyi, *L'esprit de l'art juif.* Paris, 1957, and G. Sed-Rajna, *L'art juif.* Paris, 1985.

9 Antonio Gramsci, *Prison Notebooks*, ed. Joseph A. Buttigieg, trans. Joseph A. Buttigieg. New York: Columbia University Press, 2011, N I and N XIV. Henceforth cited as *PN*.

10 Georg Lukács, *Aesthetik I. Die Eigenart des Aesthetischen*. Neuwied: Luchterhand, 1963.

11 Georg Lukács, *Wider den missverstandenen Realismus*. Hamburg: Claassen, 1958.

12 Georg Lukács, *Über die Besonderheit als Kategorie der Ästhetik* [1954/6]. Neuwied, Berlin: Luchterhand, 1967.

13 Lukács, *Aesthetik I. Die Eigenart des Aesthetischen*, I, IV, 2. Henceforth cited as *A I*.

14 Jan Mukařovský, *Studie z estetiki*. Praha: Odeon, 1966; and *Cestami poetiky a estetiki*. Praha: Ceskoslovenský spisovatel, 1971.
15 M. M. Bakhtin, *Art and Answerability*, ed. Michael Holquist and Vadim Liapunov, trans. Vadim Liapunov and Kenneth Brostrom. Austin, TX: University of Texas Press, 1990.
16 Jean-Paul Sartre, *The Imagination: A Pyschological Critique*, trans. Forrest Williams. Ann Arbor, MI: University of Michigan Press, 1962.
17 Jean-Paul Sartre, *The Imaginary: A Phenomenological Psychology of the Imagination*, trans. Jonathan Webber. New York: Routledge, 2004.
18 Jean-Paul Sartre, *What is Literature?* trans. Bernard Frechtman. New York: Routledge, 2005.
19 Andre Malraux, *The Voices of Silence*, trans. Stuart Gilbert. Cambridge: Princeton University Press, 1978.
20 Shuzo Kuki, *Reflections on Japanese Taste: The Structure of Iki*, trans. John Clark. Sydney: Power Publications, 2011.
21 Jean Baudrillard, *Seduction*. London: Macmillan, 1990.
22 Karl-Otto Apel, *Towards a Transformation of Philosophy*, trans. Glyn Adey and David Frisby. Boston: Routledge & Kegan Paul, 1980.
23 Karl-Otto Apel, *Diskursethik und Diskursanthropologie: Aachner Vorlesungen*. Freiburg: Surhkamp, 2002.
24 Jürgen Habermas, *The Theory of Communicative Action*, 2 vols, trans. Thomas McCarthy. Cambridge: Polity, 1984–7.
25 Richard Rorty, *Contingency, Irony and Solidarity*. Cambridge: Cambridge University Press, 1989.
26 Hugh Silverman, *Textualities, Between Hermeneutics and Deconstruction*. New York: Routledge, 1994. 238.
27 Harold Bloom, *The Anxiety of Influence*. Oxford: Oxford University Press, 1973.
28 Harold Bloom, *Agon. Towards a Theory of Revisionism*. Oxford: Oxford University Press, 1985.
29 The thesis of the American philosopher of aesthetics Noël Carroll (b. 1947) has some affinity with Bloom's point of view. According to his narrative theory, objects are identified as art on the basis of their connection with the past. His thesis is well argued in the essay, 'Historical Narratives and the Philosophy of Art', in *The Journal of Aesthetics and Art Criticism*, 3 (1993): 313–26.
30 Erving Goffman, *The Presentation of Self in Everyday Life*. New York: Overlook Press, 1959.
31 Erving Goffman, *Interaction Ritual: Essays in face-to-face behaviour*. Garden City: Aldine Transaction, 1971.
32 Richard Wollheim, *The Sheep and the Ceremony*. Cambridge: Cambridge University Press, 1979.

Chapter 5

1 The word 'aesthetics' comes from the Greek word *aísthēsis* which means 'sensation', 'feeling'.

2 Just as we speak of a 'politic' distinguished from politics, an 'economic' distinguished from economy, so even here we feel the need to distinguish the 'aesthetic' from aesthetics, to grasp the essence of the phenomenon, independently of the existence of a *corpus* of homogeneous texts to which to refer. See Mario Perniola, 'Dall'estetico al superestetico,' *Rivista di Estetica*, 14–15 (1983): 60–72. 15 (reprinted in *Presa diretta: Estetica e politica*. Venezia: Cluva, 1986).

3 Friedrich Nietzsche. *Basic Writings of Nietzsche*, Translated and edited, with commentaries by Walter Kaufmann, New York: Modern library, 1968.

4 For instance, the English psychologist Edward Bullough (1880–1934) in his essay '"Psychical Distance" as a Factor in Art and an Aesthetics Principle' (1912), in *Aesthetics: Lectures and Essays*, ed. Elizabeth M. Wilkinson. Stanford, CA: Stanford University Press, 1957, claims that feeling aesthetically means to possess the experience of a psychic distance with respect to the practical 'I' involved in his needs and projects. The emotions are not erased but are kept suspended. Similarly, the German aesthetologist Max Dessoir (1867–1947) in his *Aesthetics and Theory of Art*, trans. Stephen A. Emery. Detroit: Wayne State University Press, 1970, states that the characteristics of aesthetic judgement are, on the one hand, the detachment from constant relations to personal experiences and the exclusion of desire and, on the other, a wealth of uninhibited psychological activity and the fusion with the empirical unity of the object. Therefore, something of the totality of life is missing, but this something is such that we notice its lack as a quality.

5 Sigmund Freud, *Jokes and their Relation to the Unconscious* (1905), *The Standard Edition of the Complete Psychological Works of Sigmund Freud*, Vol. VIII, trans. and ed. James Strachey, Anna Freud, Alix Strachey and Alan Tyson, 24 vols. London: Hogarth Press, 1956–74. Hereafter referred to as *SE*.

6 Sigmund Freud, *Humour* (1927), *SE*, vol. XXI.

7 Sigmund Freud, *An Autobiographical Study* (1925), *SE*, vol. XX.

8 Sigmund Freud, *Creative Writers and Day-Dreaming* (1907), *SE*, vol. IX.

9 Sigmund Freud, *The Uncanny* (1919), *SE*, vol. XVII.

10 Martin Heidegger, 'The Will to Power as Art', *Nietzsche: Volume I*, trans. David Ferrell Krell. New York: Harper & Row Pub., 1979.

11 Martin Heidegger, *Hölderlins Hymnen 'Germanien' und 'Der Rhein'* (1934–5), ed. Susanne Ziegler. Frankfurt am Main: Klostermann, 1980.

12 Martin Heidegger, 'Letter on Humanism' (1946), *Pathmarks*, ed. William McNeill, trans. Frank A Capuzzi and J. Glenn Gray. Cambridge, UK: Cambridge University Press, 1999.

13 Martin Heidegger, 'The Origin of the Work of Art' (1936), *Basic Writings*, ed. David Farrell Krell, trans. Albert Hofstadter. New York: Harper Collins, 1999.

14 Martin Heidegger, *Discourse on Thinking*, trans. John M. Anderson and E. H. Freund. New York: Harper, 1966.
15 Martin Heidegger, 'Poetically Man Dwells', *Poetry Language, Thought,* trans. Albert Hofstadter. New York: Harper Collins, 1971.
16 Martin Heidegger, *On the Way to Language*, trans. Peter D. Hertz. New York: Harper and Row, 1982.
17 Ludwig Wittgenstein, 'Lectures on Aestethics' (1938), *Lectures and Conversations on Aesthetics, Psychology and Religious Belief*, ed. Cyril Barrett. Oxford: Basil Blackwell, 1966.
18 Ludwig Wittgenstein, *Philosophical Investigations*, trans. G. E. M. Anscombe. Oxford: Basil Blackwell, 1953.
19 Ibid., Ivi, §284.
20 Ibid., Ivi, §420.
21 Ludwig Wittgenstein, *Remarks on the Foundations of Psychology,* 2 vols., ed. G. H. von Wright and Heikki Nyman. Oxford: Basil Blackwell, 1980; I §257.
22 Ibid., ivi, II §88.
23 Ibid., ivi, §507.
24 Ibid., *Philosophical Investigations*, 1953, II, XI.
25 An interesting development of this problematic can be found in the work of the American philosopher Kendall Walton (b. 1939), especially in the volume *Mimesis as Make Believe: On the Foundations of the Representational Arts* (Cambridge, MA: Harvard University Press, 1990). According to Walton, the work of art is 'a prop in games of make-believe'.
26 Walter Benjamin, *The Arcades Project*, ed. Rolf Tiedemann, trans. Howard Eiland and Kevin McLaughlin. New York: Belknap Press, 2002.
27 Ibid., Ivi, B 9, 2.
28 Walter Benjamin, *The Origin of German Tragic Drama*. New York: Verso, 1988.
29 Walter Benjamin, *The Work of Art in the Age of Mechanical Reproduction*, trans. J. A. Underwood. London: Penguin, 2008.
30 Carlo Michelstaedter, *Persuasion and Rhetoric,* trans. Giuseppe Stellardi and W. Snyman. Scottsville, South Africa: University of KwaZulu-Natal Press, 2007.
31 Victor Shklovsky, *Theory of Prose*, trans. Benjamin Sher. Elmwood Park, IL: Dalkey Archive Press, 1990.
32 In German, *Verfremdung*. Bertolt Brecht made it the foundation of his theatrical poetics. Cfr. Stanley Mitchell, 'From Shklovskii to Brecht', *Screen,* 15, 2 (1974): 74–80.
33 Victor Shklovsky, *Knight's Move,* trans. Richard Sheldon. Normal: Dalkey Archive Press, 2005.
34 Georges Bataille, *Literature and Evil,* trans. Alastair Hamilton. London: Calder & Boyars Ltd., 1973.
35 Georges Bataille, *Eroticism: Death and Sensuality*, trans. Mary Dalwood. San Francisco, CA: City Lights Books, 1986.
36 Maurice Blanchot, *The Space of Literature*, trans. Anna Smock. Lincoln: University of Nebraska Press, 1989.

37 Maurice Blanchot, *The Infinite Conversation*, trans. Susan Hanson. Minneapolis, MN: University of Minnesota, 2003.
38 Pierre Klossowski, *Such a Deathly Desire*, trans. Russell Ford. Albany, NY: State University of New York Press, 2007.
39 Pierre Klossowski, *Nietzsche and the Vicious Circle*, trans. Daniel W. Smith. Chicago, IL: University of Chicago Press, 1997.
40 Pierre Klossowski, *La monnaie vivante*. Paris: Editions Erie Losfeld, 1970.
41 Luigi Pareyson, *Estetica.Teoria della formatività*. Bologna: Zanichelli, 1960.
42 Luigi Pareyson, *Ontologia della libertà. Il male e la sofferenza*. Torino: Einaudi 1995.
43 Jacques Lacan, *The Seminar XX, Encore: On Feminine Sexuality, the Limits of Love and Knowledge*, ed. Jacques-Alain Miller, trans. Bruce Fink. New York: W. W. Norton & Co., 1998.
44 Jacques Lacan, *The Seminar, Book VII. The Ethics of Psychoanalysis, 1959–1960*, ed. Jacques-Alain Miller, trans. Dennis Porter. New York: W. W. Norton & Co., 1992.
45 Luce Irigaray, *Speculum of the Other Woman*, trans. Gillian C. Gill. Ithaca, NY: Cornell University Press, 1985 and *This Sex Which Is Not One*, trans. Catherine Porter. Ithaca, NY: Cornell University Press, 1985.
46 Luce Irigaray, *An Ethics of Sexual Difference*, trans. Carolyn Burke and Gillian C. Gill. Ithaca, NY: Cornell University Press, 1993.
47 Roland Barthes, *The Pleasure of the Text*, trans. Richard Miller. New York: Hill and Wang, 1975.
48 Jacques Derrida, *Of Grammatology*, trans. Gayatri Chakravorty Spivak. Baltimore, MD: Johns Hopkins University Press, 1976.
49 Jacques Derrida, 'Economimesis', trans. R. Klein. *Diacritics*, 11 (1981): 3–25.
50 Immanuel Kant, *Anthropology from a Pragmatic Point of View*, trans. and ed. Robert B. Louden. Cambridge: Cambridge University Press, 2006. Beside the disgusting there is abjection. The French critic of Bulgarian origins Julia Kristeva (b. 1941) takes this step in *Powers of Horror: An Essay on Abjection*, trans. Léon Roudiez. New York: Columbia University Press, 1982. See also the German philosopher Peter Sloterdijk (b. 1947) who in *Rage and Time*, trans. Mario Wenning. New York: Columbia University Press, 2010, re-evaluates wrath as a key to understanding the present psycho-political situation of the world.
51 Gilles Deleuze and Félix Guattari, *Anti-Oedipus: Capitalism and Schizophrenia*, trans. Robert Hurley, Mark Seem and Helen R. Lane. New York: Penguin, 2009.
52 Gilles Deleuze and Félix Guattari, *A Thousand Plateaus: Capitalism and Schizophrenia*, trans. Brian Massumi. Minneapolis, MN: University of Minnesota Press, 1987.
53 Gilles Deleuze and Félix Guattari, *What is Philosophy?* trans. Hugh Tomlinson and Graham Burchell. New York: Columbia University Press, 1994.

Chapter 6

1 Friedrich Schiller, *On the Aesthetic Education of Man*. Hoboken, NJ: BiblioBytes, 1999.
2 Jacob Burckhardt, *Reflections on History*, 2nd rev. edn. Indianapolis: Liberty Fund, 1979.
3 Jacob Burckhardt, *The Greeks and Greek Civilization*, ed. Oswyn Murray, trans. Sheila Stern. London: Fontana Press, 1998.
4 Jacob Burckhardt, *The Civilization of the Renaissance in Italy*, trans. S. G. C. Middlemore. Old Saybrook, CT: Konecky & Konecky, 2000.
5 Masao Maruyama, *Thought and Behaviour in Modern Japanese Politics*. London: Oxford University Press, 1963.
6 Edward W. Said. *Orientalism*. New York: Pantheon Books, 1978.
7 Alain-Marc Rieu, *Savoir et pouvoir dans la modernization du Japon*. Paris: PUF, 2001.
8 Ivan Morris, *The World of the Shining Prince: Court Life in Ancient Japan*. New York: Knopf, 1964.
9 Michael F. Marra, ed., *Modern Japanese Aesthetics*. Honolulu: University of Hawaii Press, 1999.
10 Kakuzō Okakura, *The Book of Tea*. New York: Putnams, 1906.
11 Arata Isozaki, *Japan-ness in Architecture*, ed. David Butler Stewart, trans. Sabu Kohso. London: MIT Press, 2006.
12 Katô Shuichi, *Riflessioni sulla cerimonia del tè*. Torino, 1995.
13 Kôjin Karatani, 'Japan as Art Museum: Okakura Tenshin and Fenollosa', *A History of Modern Japanese Aesthetics*, ed. M. Marra. Honolulu: University of Hawaii Press, 2001.
14 Mario Perniola, 'The Japanese Juxtaposition', *European Review*, 14, 1 (2006): 129–34.
15 Christophe Marquet, 'Le Japon moderne face à son patrimoine artistique', *Cipango. Cahiers d'ètudes japonaises de l'Inalco*, n. hors-série (Printemps, 2002): 243–304.
16 Yanagi Sōetsu, *The Unknown Craftsman. A Japanese Insight into Beauty*. Tokyo: Kodansha, 1989. See also Sarah F. Maclaren, 'Che cosa sono gli Studio Crafts?' *Agalma*, 13 (March 2007): 48–56.
17 Liang Shuming, *Les cultures de l'Orient et de l'Occident et leur philosophies*. Paris: PUF, 2000.
18 Sarah F. Maclaren, *La magnificenza e il suo doppio, Il pensiero estetico di Giovanni Battista Piranesi*. Milano: Mimesis, 2005.
19 Anne Cheng, *Histoire de la pensée chinoise*, vol. 1, XI. Paris: Seuil, 1997.
20 Heraclitus, *Fragments: The Collected Wisdom of Heraclitus*, trans. Brooks Haxton. New York: Viking, 2001.
21 *Xunzi: A Translation and Study of the Complete Works,* 3 vols, ed. J. Knoblock. Stanford, CA: Stanford University Press, 1988–94.

22 Muhammad Iqbal, *The Reconstruction of Religious Thought in Islam* (1934). New Delhi: Kitab Bhavan, 2000.
23 Muhammad Iqbal, *Javid-Nama (Book of Eternity)*, ed. A. J. Arburry. London: George Allen & Unwin, 1966.
24 Gilberto Freyre, *The Masters and the Slaves: A Study in the Development of Brazilian Civilization*, trans. Samuel Putnam. New York: Knopf, 1964.
25 Gilberto Freyre, *New World in the Tropics: The Culture of Modern Brazil*. New York: Alfred A. Knopf, 1959.
26 S. Buarque de Holanda, *Racines du Brésil* (1936). Paris: Gallimard, 1998.
27 Max Weber, *The Protestant Ethic and the Spirit of Capitalism*, trans. Talcott Parsons. New York: Scribner, 1958.
28 Ivan Lins, *Historia do positivism no Brazil*. São Paulo: Companhia Editôra Nacional, 1964.
29 Gilles Deleuze and Félix Guattari, *What is Philosophy?* trans. Hugh Tomlinson and Graham Burchell. New York: Columbia University Press, 1994.
30 Carlos Drummond de Andrade, *Sentimento do Mundo*. Rio de Janeiro: Pongetti, 1940.
31 Clarice Lispector, *The Passion According to G.H.* Minneapolis, MN: Minnesota University Press, 2000.
32 Roger Bastide, *Les Religions Africaines au Brésil: Vers une Sociologie des Interpretations de Civilisations*. Paris: PUF, 1960. Also important is the work of Roberto Motta, ed., *saudade e literature*, 2005 and of the American Robert Farris Thompson, *Flash of the Spirit: African & Afro-American Art and Philosophy*. New York: Vintage, 1984.
33 Jahnheinz Jahn, *Muntu: African Culture and the Western World*. New York: Grove Press, 1961.
34 Martin Bernal, *Black Athena: The Afroasiatic Roots of Classical Civilization*, I–II–III. New Brunswick, NJ: Rutgers University Press, 1987–2006.
35 Tetsurō Watsuji, *Climate and Culture: A Philosophical Study*. Westport, CT: Greenwood Press, 1961.
36 Tetsurō Watsuji, *Rinrigaku (Ethics in Japan)*, trans. Yamamoto Seisaku and Robert E. Carter. Albany, NY: State University of New York Press, 1996.
37 For a comparative analysis of the notion of aesthetic detachment in Western and Japanese thought, see Steve Odin, *Artistic Detachment in Japan and in the West*. Honolulu: University of Hawaii Press, 2001.
38 Mario Perniola, 'Pensare il Between. Sul pensiero di Hugh J. Silverman', *Agalma*, 13 (March 2007): 80–90.
39 Robert Carter, 'Interpretative Essay: Strands of Influence', in Tetsurō Watsuji, *Rinrigaku (Ethics in Japan)*, trans. Yamamoto Seisaku and Robert E. Carter. Albany, NY: State University of New York Press, 1996. 326–65.
40 Augustine Berque, *Du geste à la cite: Formes urbaines et lien social au Japon*. Paris, 1993; *Être humains sur la terre. Principes d'éthique de l'écoumène*. Paris, 1996; *Écoumène. Introduction à l'étude des milieu humains*. Paris: Belin, 2001.

41 The other fundamental types of *fūdo* are the European one characterized by pasture and the African, Arabic and Mongolian ones characterized by the desert.
42 David Chou-Shulin, 'Introduction to the Aesthetics of Southeast Asia', *Asian Aesthetics*, ed. Ken-ichi Sasaki. Kyoto: Kyoto University Press, 2010.
43 A very interesting case of aesthetic modernization independent of the Western one is represented by Singapore where the philosopher Sor-hoon Tan (b. 1965) has shown with great refinement and linguistic competence the affinities between the aesthetic-political thought of Confucius and that of John Dewey in *Confucian Democracy. A Deweyan Reconstruction*. New York: Albany State University Press, 2003. Singapore has an autonomous culture called *Peranakan* whose origins go back to the fifteenth century: this is the theme of a museum but is devoid of any aesthetic conceptualization that connects it to the present.
44 Ken-ichi Sasaki, ed., 'Introduction to Japanese Aesthetics', *Asian Aesthetics*. Kyoto: Kyoto University Press, 2010.
45 Li Zehou, *A Path of Beauty. A Study of Chinese Aesthetics*. Hong Kong: Oxford University Press, 1994.
46 Anne Cheng, *Histoire de la pensée chinoise*, Paris: Seuil, 1997.
47 Ibid.
48 Reinhart Koselleck, *Critique and Crisis: Enlightenment and the Pathogenesis of Modern Society*. Cambridge, MA: MIT Press, 1998.
49 T. S. Eliot, *Notes towards the Definition of Culture*. London: Harcourt, 1948.
50 W. Tatarkiewicz, *History of Aesthetics,* 3 vols. London: Continuum, 2005.
51 W. Tatarkiewicz, *History of Six Ideas,* trans. Christopher Kasparek. Boston: Kluwer Boston, 1980.
52 Raymond Williams, *Culture and Society 1780–1950*. New York: Columbia University Press, 1983.
53 Daniel Bell, *The End of Ideology: On the Exhaustion of Political Ideas in the Fifties, with 'The Resumption of History in the New Century.'* Cambridge, MA: Harvard University Press, 2000.
54 Roy Olivier, *Holy Ignorance: When Culture and Religion Part Ways*, trans. Ros Schwartz. New York: Columbia University Press, 2010.
55 Arthur Danto, 'The Artworld', *Journal of Philosophy*, 61, 19 (1964): 571–84.
56 George Dickie, *Aesthetics: An Introduction*. Indianapolis: Bobbs-Merrill, 1971.
57 A. C. Danto, *The Philosophical Disenfranchisement of Art*. New York: Columbia University Press, 1986.
58 Pierre Bourdieu, *Practical Reason: On the Theory of Action*. Stanford, CA: Stanford University Press, 1998; *Pascalian Meditations*. Stanford, CA: Stanford University Press, 2000.

Index